T0305330

Reforming Economic Systems in Asia

ISPI
(ISTITUTO PER GLI STUDI DI POLITICA INTERNAZIONALE)

Founded in 1933 by Alberto Pirelli, ISPI is one of Italy's oldest and most prestigious Institutes specialising in activities of international nature. It was created as a private association and became a non-profit organisation in 1972, operating under the supervision of the Ministry for Foreign Affairs.

ISPI's principal fields of interest are international politics and economics, in addition to the analysing of international relations and strategic problems. The Institute's goals are to promote the study and analysis of international issues, to provide a forum for debates gathering representatives of the political, academic and business world, and to prepare individual experts for work in international environments.

ISPI is at the same time a research centre, an information centre, and a training centre. ISPI is also a documentation centre open to the public and publishes a quarterly review, as well as books and working papers related to the research projects.

This book is the result of a project organised by ISPI, whose research activities are framed into sections corresponding to political and economic regions of the global world. Asia occupies a peculiarly important place in this framework. This research has been preceded and will be followed by other projects, monitoring the developments of an area that is considered strategically crucial for our understanding of international relations. Each of ISPI's project is under the responsibility of a co-ordinator and it involves a network of contributors located in Italy and abroad, assisted by a group of young research fellows at the Institute. Maria Weber is Senior Research Fellow for Asia.

Reforming Economic Systems in Asia

A Comparative Analysis of China, Japan, South Korea, Malaysia and Thailand

Edited by

Maria Weber

Associate Professor of International Relations and Comparative Politics, Bocconi University, Milan, Italy

Edward Elgar
Cheltenham, UK • Northampton, MA, USA

In association with

Published by
Edward Elgar Publishing Limited
Glensanda House
Montpellier Parade
Cheltenham
Glos GL50 1UA
UK

Edward Elgar Publishing, Inc.
136 West Street
Suite 202
Northampton
Massachusetts 01060
USA

A catalogue record for this book
is available from the British Library

ISBN 1 84064 845 7

Printed and bound in Great Britain by MPG Books Ltd, Bodmin, Cornwall

Contents

List of Tables   *vii*
List of Figures   *ix*
List of Abbreviations   *xi*
List of Contributors   *xv*
Editor's Introduction   *xvii*

1. China: Old and New Challenges   1
    Maria Weber and Stefania Paladini
2. Structural Reforms in Japan: the Attempt to Transform the
    Country's Economic System   43
    Corrado Molteni
3. Something New, Something Old: the South Korean Economy
    after the Financial Crisis   61
    Vasco Molini and Roberta Rabellotti
4. Economic and Policy Convergence in ASEAN: Malaysia and
    Thailand Compared   95
    Michael G. Plummer and Benedetta Trivellato
5. New Impulses Towards Economic Integration in East Asia:
    Prospects and Issues   127
    Robert Scollay
6. APEC and Trade Liberalisation after Seattle: Transregionalism
    without a Cause?   149
    Vinod Aggarwal
7. Shifts in East Asia Regional Security: Old Issues and New
    Events Amidst Multilateral-Bilateral Tensions   179
    Maria Julia Trombetta and Maria Weber
8. Conclusions   205
    Maria Weber

Index   213

List of Tables

1.1	Total amount of employees and unemployment index (1995–1999)	3
1.2	Foreign direct investments in China in 1998–1999	4
1.3	Foreign direct investment from Asian countries, European Union and US in 1998	5
1.4	China: annual indicators	6
1.5	Non-performing loans and different estimates on the bank restructuring (%)	14
1.6	Number of listed companies	19
1.7	Shares markets from 1987 to 1998	19
2.1	Total bad loans and disposed bad loans of 16 major banks (as of end of March, 2000)	50
2.2	Long-term debt	56
3.1	Macroeconomic indicators: 1990–2000 (%)	63
3.2	Main products on total manufacturing export: 1992–1998 (%)	63
3.3	Korean selected exports rate of growth: 1992–1998 (%)	64
3.4	Korean selected exports on total manufacturing exports: 1992–1998 (%)	64
3.5	Concordance for macro-sectors	65
3.6	RCAs: manufacturing sectors	65
3.7	Korean selected imports rate of growth: 1992–1998 (%)	66
3.8	Korean selected imports on total manufacturing imports: 1992–1998 (%)	66
3.9	The structure of foreign debt (US$ million)	68
3.10	Financial conditions of top Korean chaebol at the end of 1996 (hundred million won and %)	69
3.11	The 'Big Deal'	79
3.12	Number of out-of-business financial institutions as a result of financial sector restructuring (at the end of July 1999)	82
3.13	Research and development expenditures: 1970–1998 (billion of won)	89
4.1	ASEAN countries growth rate of GDP (per cent per year)	100
4.2a	Trade bias calculations for ASEAN and selected countries (1980)	101
4.2b	Trade bias calculations for ASEAN and selected countries (1986)	101

4.2c Trade bias calculations for ASEAN and selected countries (1994)   101
4.3 ASEAN sectoral share of GDP (per cent)   102
4.4 Overall budget surplus or deficit of central government (percentage of GDP)   103
4.5 Foreign direct investment ($million)   103
4.6 Exchange rate to the Dollar (local currency/US$, average of period)   105
4.7 Balance of payments on current account (percentage of GDP)   105
4.8 Summary of measures directed at financial sector restructuring   119
4.9 Fiscal costs of re-capitalisation (mid-October 1999) (per cent of 1998 GDP)   121
5.1 Comparative GNP data for selected economic groupings   130
5.2 Shares in East Asian GNP and population   131
5.3 Shares of East Asian/APEC economies in trade of Northeast Asian economies (%)   132
5.4 Shares of East Asian/APEC economies in trade of principal Southeast Asian economies (%)   134
6.1 Trading arrangements   151

List of Figures

1.1 China's top web sites (31 December, 1999)   29
3.1 Manufacturing exports and machinery and transport
     equipment import rate of growth: 1993–1998 (%)   67
3.2 Consumption, investment and GDP rate of growth:
     1997–1999 (%)   73
3.3 Import and export values: 1996–2000 2nd Q (million US$)   73
3.4 Foreign direct investment: 1996–2000 (million US$)   74

List of Abbreviations

ABAC	APEC Business Advisory Council
ADR	American Depositary Receipt
AFG	APEC Financiers Group
AFTA	ASEAN Free Trade Agreement
AIG	American International Group
AMC	Asset management company
AMF	Asian Monetary Fund
ANZUS	Australia-New Zealand-United States
APEC	Asia-Pacific Economic Co-operation
APIAN	APEC International Assessment Network
APL	Administrative Procedure Law
ARF	ASEAN Regional Forum
ASEAN	Association of South East Asian Nations
ASEM	Asia-Europe Meeting
BLAR	Basic Law Administrative Reform
BNM	Bank Negara Malaysia
BOK	Bank of Korea
BOT	Bank of Thailand
CAP	Common Agricultural Policy
CB	Central bank
CBM	Confidence-building measure
CCP	China Communist Party
CDRC	Corporate Debt Restructuring Committee
CER	Closer Economic Relations
CGE	Computable general equilibrium
CIS	Commonwealth of Independent States
CPPCC	Chinese People's Political Consultative Conference
CRA	Corporate Restructuring Agreement
CRCC	Corporate Restructuring Co-ordination Commitee
CSCAP	Council for Security Cooperation in the Asia Pacific
CSCE	Conference on Security and Co-operation in Europe
CSIP	Capital Structure Improvement Plan
CSRC	China Securities Regulatory Committee
DAEs	Dynamic Asian Economies
DMZ	Demilitarised Zone

DPP	Democratic Progressive Party
EAEC	East Asian Economic Caucus
EAEG	East Asian Economic Group
EALAF	East Asia Latin America Forum (EALAF)
EMS	European Monetary System
EOI	Export-oriented industrialisation
EU	European Union
EVSL	Early Voluntary Sectoral Liberalisation
FDI	Foreign Direct Investment
FIDF	Financial Institutions Development Fund
FIL	Freedom of Information Law
FRA	Financial Restructuring Agency
FRC	Financial Reconstruction Commission
FSA	Financial Supervisory Agency
FSAP	Financial Sector Assessment Program
FSC	Financial Supervisory Commission
FTA	Free Trade Agreement
FTAA	Free Trade Area of the Americas
GATT	General Agreement on Tariffs and Trade
GDP	Gross domestic product
GMD	Guomindang
GNP	Gross national product
GSP	General System of Preferencies
IAC	Independent Administrative Corporations
IAEA	International Atomic Energy Agency
IAP	Individual Action Plan
ICBC	Industrial and Commercial Bank of China
IDE	Institute of Developing Economies
ILO	International Labour Organisation
IMF	International Monetary Fund
ISIS	Institute for Strategic and International Studies
KAMCO	Korean Asset Manager Corporation
KEDO	Korean Peninsula Energy Development Organization
LDC	Less Developed Countries
LTCB	Long Term Credit Bank of Japan
M&A	Merger and acquisition
METI	Ministry of Economy, Trade and Industry
MFN	Most Favoured Nation
MITI	Ministry of International Trade and Industry
MNC	Multi-national corporation
MOF	Ministry of Finance
NCB	Nippon Credit Bank
NAFTA	North American Free Trade Agreement

NEACD	Northeast Asia Cooperation Dialogue
NGO	Non-governmental organisation
NPC	National People's Congress
NPL	Non-performing loans
PECC	Pacific Economic Co-operation Council
PD	Preventive diplomacy
PDP	Progressive-Democratic Party
PNTR	Permanent Normal Trade Relations
PRC	People's Republic of China
RCA	Revealed Comparative Advantage
R&D	Research and Development
RMB	Renminbi
ROK	Republic of Korea
ROSC	Reports on Observance of Standards and Codes
SDB	Shenzhen Development Bank
SEATO	South East Asia Treaty Organization
SIE	Single investor enterprise
SOE	State-owned enterprise
SOM	Senior Official Meeting
SME	Small-medium enterprise
SPDB	Shanghai Pudong Development Bank
SSE	Shanghai Stock Exchange
SZSE	Shenzhen Stock Exchange
TVE	Town and Village Enterprise
UN	United Nations
UNCLOS	United Nations Convention on the Law of the Sea
UNTAET	United Nations Transitional Administration in East Timor
US (USA)	United States of America
WEO	World Economic Outlook
WHO	World Health Organisation
WTO	World Trade Organisation
WW	World War

List of Contributors

Vinod K. Aggarwal is Professor of Political Science, affiliated Professor at the Haas School of Business and Director of the Berkeley APEC Study Centre at the University of California at Berkeley. He is also Editor-in-Chief of the journal *Business and Politics*.

Vasco Molini graduated in Political Economics at Bocconi University. He is currently a researcher on East Asia at the Institute of Economic and Social Studies for East Asia (ISESAO) – Bocconi University. His research interests include the Korean economy from the development to the post-crisis period and the economic development of the East Asian region.

Corrado Molteni is associate Professor of Japanese studies at the State University of Milan and affiliated Professor of Comparative Economic Systems at Bocconi University. He was awarded a Ph.D. in Social Studies from Hitotsubashi University in Japan.

Stefania Paladini graduated both in Humanities (Modern History) and in Economics and obtained a Master Degree in International Taxation. She lives in Hong Kong, where she works as Deputy Trade Commissioner for the Italian Trade Commission and she is working on her Ph.D. in International Relations.

Michael Plummer, associate Professor of Economics at Brandeis University and visiting Professorial Lecturer at Johns Hopkins University SAIS-Bologna. His main field of interest is international economic integration with a focus on Asia in general and ASEAN in particular.

Roberta Rabellotti is associate Professor of Economics in the Department of Economics and Quantitative Methods at Università del Piemonte Orientale. She is a consultant for several international organisations in the field of industrial development.

Robert Scollay is Director of the APEC Study Centre and a member of the Economics department at Auckland University, New Zealand, a convenor for the Trade Policy Forum of the Pacific Economic Cooperation Council (PECC) and executive member of the Asia-Pacific International Assessment Network

(APIAN). His research interests are primarily in international trade policy issues, including economic integration through regional trade agreements, in the Asia-Pacific.

Benedetta Trivellato graduated in Economics from Bocconi University and is currently a postgraduate student in Development Economics at St Antony's College in Oxford. She was formerly a Research Assistant on East Asia at ISPI and Visiting Research Fellow in Singapore, Malaysia and Thailand on a Junior ASEAN – EU Research Grant by the European Studies Programme (ESP), EU Project at Chulalongkorn University, Bangkok. Her interests include international trade and regional co-operation issues.

Maria Julia Trombetta holds a degree in Discipline Economiche e Sociali from Bocconi University and a master in Environmental Management. She is currently pursuing doctoral research on environmental security in the Department of International Politics, University of Wales, Aberystwyth.

Maria Weber is associate Professor of International Relations and Comparative Politics at Bocconi University in Milan and Senior Research Fellow on Asia at ISPI. She is the author of many publications on China and East Asia. Her book *Vele verso la Cina* (Sails toward China, Edizioni Olivares, 1996) won the Booz-Allen & Hamilton – Financial Times Awards 1996. Her latest books are *After the Asian Crises,* published by MacMillan in 2000 and *Il miracolo cinese* (The Chinese Miracle) published by Il Mulino in 2001.

Editor's Introduction

Maria Weber

With the 1989 end of the Cold War, many proclaimed the triumph of global capitalism. Globalisation and rapid technological change cover a broad sweep of economic developments, even if some authors demonstrate the fragility of a global and integrated economy.[1] One of the most valuable issues in the debate concerning globalisation is the 20th century diffusion of capitalism, particularly in its Anglo-American version. The successful exportation of such a capitalistic model in many non-Western countries gave birth, among others, to the concept of global capitalism, which seems, in a sense, to demonstrate the theoretical consistency of the so-called 'convergence theory'. According to this theory the globalisation processes lead more or less naturally to a progressive homogenisation of the various cultures around a universally shared value-system, and institutional and economic models. Thus, a deeper analysis of the forms capitalism assumes in Asian countries, interacting with the indigenous character settings, could offer some theoretical tools really useful in the particular studies that globalisation seems to need. Will socialist economies make a successful transition to market type economies?

After the Asian crisis, almost all the Asian countries have started a serious process of reform in the state sector, in banking and financial systems, which has generally consisted in ending easy loans, deregulation of interest rates, improving accounting practices, writing off bad debts of the state banks and allowing new banks into the business. We have also considered that the relentless process of globalisation that characterises the world economy makes national economies increasingly interdependent. The chain effects of the Asian crisis are not confined only to a regional economic context. Besides leading to shifting competitive positions in a number of countries, the Asian crisis seems to be strong enough to put into question geopolitical and strategic equilibrium after the end of the Cold War. In its recent history, Asia has not produced security strategies of its own, having been dominated by colonial powers, and then by the juxtaposition of the superpowers. It is difficult to predict medium-term scenarios for the evolution of Asia with any certainty, as the end of the bipolar system has changed the global geopolitical equilibrium, and created a particularly fluid and dynamic situation in Asia as well.

The first part of this book includes area studies of the main Asian countries after the crisis, beginning with China, Japan, South Korea, Malaysia and Thailand. The second part focuses on international variables, including the role of the Asia-Pacific Economic Co-operation (APEC) forum in the process of the trade liberalisation after Seattle and the shifts in East Asia regional security: old issues (the two Koreas) and new events (new dialogue between China and Taiwan).

In the first chapter on 'China: Old and New Challenges', Maria Weber and Stefania Paladini investigate the main issues of the Chinese reform process, focusing on the most important ones. The state owned enterprises (SOEs) reform, first of all, is a key issue of the transition to a market economy. Most SOEs tend to lose money through the transfer of profits to loss-making departments and divisions and they are often overstaffed. The eventual success of economic reforms under way in China will depend mainly on revitalising these 'socialist relics'. The chapter provides the guidelines adopted for SOE reform, as selling, merging, listing in stock exchanges, and analyses some interesting results obtained. The reform of the financial system is another big challenge China has to face. Chinese banks are among the largest banks in the world in terms of assets, but despite its size, China's banking system remains one of the most backward in Asia. Most banks are government-owned, lending is under government control, and the main ones are unprofitable. By the year 2002, Zhu Rongji intends to complete the reform of the financial sector, which he himself initiated when he was governor of the Central Bank (CB). The re-organisation of the CB should proceed on a regional basis, thus reducing political interference and increasing the decision-making autonomy. Important reforms have been carried out in the tax system too, with the establishment of the new interest tax. And, last but not least, the standards of the security markets are now more similar to western ones.

Joining the WTO is nowadays the central topic in China's external and internal political debates. After the favourable vote of US House of Representatives about PNTR, and the granting of MFN status to China, the way to China's entrance in the WTO is fully paved. And China has already signed two important bilateral agreements, with US (November 1999) and European Union (May 2000). The re-entry of China in the WTO brings great prospects to the opening up and transformation of the Chinese economy but also, in the short term, considerable risks for employment and new challenges to the local enterprises and financial institutions. The chapter aims at assessing the effects of China's complete involvement in the multilateral trade system on the domestic economy, on East Asia and on the world.

In the second chapter on 'Structural Reforms in Japan', Corrado Molteni analyses the attempt to transform the economic system. The Japanese market economy differs from the so-called Anglo-Saxon model in four respects: the employees-centred system of corporate governance; the underdeveloped labour and capital markets; the tight regulation and control of financial markets; and the strong role of government in guiding, controlling and regulating economic activities. This system has worked very effectively in the past, but today it is under pressure to change.

The major sources of change are the structural changes in the economy, the financial crisis and the long stagnation that followed the burst of the bubble in the early nineties, and the renewed authority of the American model and its cultural underpinnings. As a result, in the last decade major reforms have been initiated and implemented. These reforms are apparently moving the Japanese economic system towards the Anglo-Saxon type of market economy. In the case of corporate governance, there is a shift from a system based on 'employees sovereignty' towards a system favouring shareholders and their interests. The traditional lifetime employment system is also openly questioned, while labour mobility is increasing. At the same time, the process of deregulation and liberalisation of financial markets has introduced structural changes in Japan's financial industries and the regulatory system. Finally, administrative reforms have set the stage for a possible shift in power from the bureaucracy to the political parties.

Of course, there is a strong resistance against change and even the possibility of a reversal of this trend. The aim of this chapter, therefore, is to understand whether the process of reforms can be sustained and successfully implemented, and what will be its impact on Japan's economic and social structures. Are Japanese firms really going to be managed as American corporations? Is the Japanese bureaucracy ready to abide to the rules of a free-market economy or will it continue to monitor and guide the activities of private companies? Will the bureaucracy decide the policy goals and instruments or will they leave this task to elected representatives of the people? These are some of the questions that are addressed and discussed in Molteni's chapter, focusing on three main points: the reform of corporate governance, the changes in the financial system and the reform of public administration.

In the third chapter on the South Korean economy after the financial crisis, Vasco Molini and Roberta Rabellotti analyse how far has the implementation of reforms gone in South Korea, attempting to understand if the expected renewal is really starting to take place. The structural reform plan is based on two fundamental principles: exposing the economy more fully to world competition and introducing more effective governance structures into financial institutions and the corporate sector. Its implementation is therefore aimed at substituting the interventionist role of the government of the past with a market-based paradigm. Establishing such a paradigm requires first a rehabilitation of the corporate and the financial sectors, a reform of the public sector as well as an increased liberalisation in goods and capital markets and in the labour market regulations. In the first section the authors analyse the main causes behind the 1997 crisis and the explosion of the financial turmoil. Just before the slowdown of 1997 the Korean macroeconomic performance was not showing many signals of adversity and it is therefore unsurprising why such a deep crisis was not forecasted. Nevertheless, although the situation of the main macroeconomic indicators was good, in the backstage of a generally fine performance, some unsolved issues remained, both at the macro and at the structural level.

At the beginning of 1997, Korea disclosed the first evident signals of economic distress during the strong struggle between workers and government on the new labour bill. Moreover, on January 1997 the 14th largest *chaebol*, Hanbo, went bankrupt, opening a period of several breakdowns of other important groups like Sammi, Jinro, Daiong and Ssangyong Motor. Immediately, the crisis extended to the financial sector as well, due to the increase in non-performing loans.

In early December, the crisis rapid degeneration led the Korean government to sign a 60b US$ IMF-led rescue package, the biggest in the history of stand-by-credits.

Then, after considering the first impact of the IMF bailout, the chapter focuses on the implementation and the first results of reforms in the corporate sector, the financial system, the public sector, the goods, capital and labour markets. Special consideration is given to the reform of the *chaebol*, the large conglomerates constituting Korea's industrial base. Finally, the boom in the new economy is considered to be one of the most interesting novelties in the Korean economic system.

In the fourth chapter on Malaysia and Thailand, Michael Plummer and Benedetta Trivellato analyse the economic and policy convergence in ASEAN, focusing on the cases of Malaysia and Thailand. Prior to the Asian crisis, there existed a perceived process of economic and policy convergence in Asia generally and in ASEAN particularly. In the post-crisis era, some have argued that this convergence is breaking down. The authors test this latter hypothesis, using a comparison of Malaysia and Thailand as a case study. The chapter focuses on questions surrounding policy convergence (that is, common policy stances embraced by governments) and real convergence between Malaysia and Thailand in the context of economic interdependence and co-operation. In order to do this, the authors begin by defining what is meant by convergence, proposing various indicators. As the questions surrounding convergence between Malaysia and Thailand tend to be more on the policy side, they focus much of the paper on this area. Corporate, financial and banking sector reforms in both countries are analysed in detail.

Malaysia and Thailand are excellent candidates for such a comparison, in that each appeared to share a common policy stance prior to the crisis and experienced common results: rapid growth, strong macroeconomic fundamentals, reduction in poverty: in brief, economic development. On the other hand, during the crisis and so far in the post-crisis era, there is a common perception that policy and economic convergence may be going in opposite directions: Malaysia declined an IMF rescue plan, opting for capital controls, and closed no financial institutions; Thailand, on the other hand, turned to the IMF for financial support, closed virtually all its finance companies, and subsequently adopted a more gradual, market-based approach to restructuring, with banks allowed to raise equity capital over a long period. However, even if the details have varied among crisis countries, the broad principles of financial and corporate restructuring are largely similar.

The second part of this volume focuses on international variables, including the analysis of the progressive economic integration in East Asia, the role of APEC in the trade liberalisation after Seattle and the shifts in East Asia regional security. In chapter five, Robert Scollay considers the fact that, in the aftermath of the East Asian economic crisis, the East Asian economies are facing crucial choices not only in relation to internal economic reforms but also in relation to the future configuration of their international economic relations. While East Asia has long been recognised as one of the three major centres of global economic activity, it has not hitherto sought to establish itself as a formal economic bloc. Establishment of an East Asian economic bloc would bring to fruition a concept first floated at the beginning of the 1990s by Malaysian Prime Minister Dr Mahathir Mohammed, with his stillborn proposal for establishment of an East Asian Economic Group (EAEG). An East Asian bloc would also signal the emergence of a tripartite, or 'three-bloc' world. The first of the three blocs, based on the European Union, already exists. NAFTA forms a substantial bloc in North America, which will be expanded into a Western Hemisphere bloc if the countries of the Western Hemisphere follow through on their 1998 decision to establish the Free Trade Area of the Americas (FTAA) by 2005. An East Asian bloc would thus be the final step in the development of a 'three-bloc' global economic architecture. Scollay's chapter endeavours to provide a preliminary comparative analysis of this nature. The discussion focuses first on trade integration, and then widens to consider the financial and monetary aspects of economic integration.

In chapter six on APEC and Trade Liberalisation After Seattle, Vinod Aggarwal begins his analysis from the eruption of protests in the streets of Seattle in November 1999 against the Millennium Round of the WTO, which marked the peak of anti-globalisation issue. Protesters claimed the WTO is insensitive to the negative externalities produced by free trade on the environment and U.S. labour, and criticised its lack of lack of transparency. While there is considerable debate about the root of the WTO's problems in Seattle, there is no doubt that the multilateral trading system faces severe challenges. Meanwhile, across the globe in Asia, the APEC was still picking up the pieces left from the Asian crisis of 1997–8. Because APEC and the

WTO both pursue similar goals of free trade (among other goals) and are seen by their members to be inextricably and purposefully linked, some of the criticisms levelled at the WTO should resound in APEC. Yet in 1993, APEC proved to be the beneficiary of the impasse in the GATT Uruguay Round, and was invigorated with the creation of an annual leaders' meeting. How has APEC responded to the pressures felt in Seattle? What progress, if any, has it made toward its trade goals in the wake of the Asian crisis, the Seattle debacle, and anti-globalisation sentiments? Has APEC benefited from the WTO problems or has it been unable to step into the vacuum of trade liberalisation at the multilateral level? Finally, has APEC continued to prove its usefulness as a trans-regional trade organisation, or is it being institutionally squeezed, both from above and below?

In chapter seven, Maria Julia Trombetta and Maria Weber analyse the main shifts in East Asia regional security. The geo-political and security scenario in East Asia has changed deeply during the last months, largely as a result of two landmark events. On the one hand, the election in Taiwan of Chen Shui-bian, the first non Guomindang leader, outlines a fundamental change in the cross strait relations. On the other hand, the historical summit between South Korean President Kim Dae-jung and North Korean leader Kim Jong-il necessitates a rethinking of what is or is not possible in the peninsula. These events, which will have a profound impact on stability and security strategies in East Asia, obscured the recent outcomes in a slow process of multilateral security co-operation, encompassing the Asia Pacific region, which progressively emerged in the last decade.

The recent ASEAN Regional Forum (ARF) meeting in Bangkok (in July 2000) opened the door for North Korea's membership in the Forum and the gathering of all key Northeast Asian players in the ARF could provide the opportunity for multilateral discussions on regional security, analogously the G8 summit in Okinawa created the opportunity to discuss the US military presence in a multilateral context. These events, anyway, have been veiled. Bilateral relations, which have long been important to regional peace and stability, are still critical and more relevant. In the post-Cold War environment, these relations have taken on new forms, since the states are involved in multiple ties and the strategic environment is more fluid and complex. In the aftermath of the Cold War, there was an enthusiastic attempt to create regional security institutions, but they are still embryonic and they proved themselves unable to cope with crises, as the Timor East tragedy clearly demonstrates. This situation has determined a legitimisation of the existing institutions and has renewed the debate on regional security – its subject, content and meaning. The concept of comprehensive security has emerged in the debate. The basic question is how to define security strategies for a region that, in its recent history, has not produced security strategies of its own. In this perspective Trombetta and Weber try to give an account of the paradox of the co-existence of an emerging regional security narrative, which considers new threats and multilateral security institutions, and the still dominant realistic strategies based on bilateral accords and balance of power among the main players of the region.

This book is a result of a project organised by Milan's Institute for International Political Studies (ISPI) on the structural reforms after the Asian crisis in China, Japan, South Korea, Malaysia and Thailand. I would like to thank my friends and colleagues who accepted to contribute at this project. Thanks to Silvia Zanazzi for her assistance in the long editing process of this volume and also to Franco Bruni, Director of ISPI Scientific Committee, who strongly supported me in this research.

Milan, 28th of February 2001

NOTE

1. R. Gilpin, *The Challenge of Global Capitalism. The World Economy in the 21st Century*, Princeton: Princeton University press, 2000.

1. China: Old and New Challenges*

Maria Weber and Stefania Paladini

---

1. THE MAIN EFFECTS OF ASIAN CRISIS ON CHINA

1.1 Deflation and unemployment

The Asian crisis has not involved China directly, but it is having a direct impact on its economy, partly because of the declining competitiveness of Chinese products in an area of the world in which most countries have been compelled to devaluate. Furthermore, China is very vulnerable because it suffers from the same structural problems as South Korea, Thailand and Indonesia. The banking system suffers from many bad debts, or potentially so. This was mainly the result of lending to the loss-making state owned enterprises (SOEs) sector. Many SOEs are insolvent and the banking system does not have the means to recover its debts. A further indicator of China's weakness is the residential property speculation, also financed in excess by the banking system.

China has been forced to face some important consequences of the crisis. Most of all: the decline of demand from Asian countries, relevant because Japan, Korea and the Southeast Asian countries absorb more than 50 per cent of the Chinese exports. At the end of 1997 Chinese exports had grown by 18 per cent compared to the preceding year and foreign currency reserves were still sufficient to finance a whole year of imports. However, in 1998 the figure had decreased to 8 per cent. This partly depends on the fact that one third of Chinese exports are traditionally directed towards neighbouring countries – 15 per cent to Japan, 11 per cent to Taiwan, 7 per cent to the ASEAN countries and 5 per cent to Korea. As a consequence of the reduction in exports, the Chinese government has sought to diversify its export markets' and foreign investments' strategy, no longer concentrating on the Asian markets, but on European and North American partners. In addition to the contraction of the regional market for Chinese exports, China has also felt the rise of competitiveness of the products exported by the countries more stricken by the crisis.

Following the devaluation, the prices of products exported from Thailand, South Korea, Indonesia, Malaysia and the Philippines have been reduced by

10 per cent to 40 per cent and even though the cost of production in China has always been relatively low, the competition on international markets has become more fierce.

China has therefore not been able to avoid all the effects of the crisis, but these effects are significantly different from those experienced by the other East Asia countries. The renminbi (RMB), in fact, did not follow the other currencies of the region in their devaluation: the exchange rate compared to the US dollar remained close to 8.27 RMB to a dollar, and because the currency is not freely convertible, the country did not experience capital flee which has caused devastating effects on the nearby countries. Furthermore, the financial crisis influenced the timing and manner of the implementation of reforms in China.

Growth slackening off makes it more difficult to create supplementary jobs, however necessary for carrying out the restructuring of the state owned companies. Moreover the processes of speculation and devaluation verified in the rest of the region underline the importance of prudence in the deregulation of the financial market and in the realisation of the necessary reforms (in order to enhance the convertibility of the currency). Commercial surplus and reserves, which exceeded by far the foreign debt, have not prevented the growth of unemployment and the slowing down of the economic growth.

The enormous population of China is both a great resource and a big challenge for the country. The population has grown at the medium rate of 1.1 per cent per year between 1997 and 1993, reaching the number of one billion three hundred million people in 1999. The one-child policy has slowed the growth down, but at the same time it has unbalanced the age structure of the population, which today has a growing number of elderly people to maintain. According to official data, in 1999 there were 705.9 million employees and the unemployment rate in the urban areas was around 3.1 per cent (Table 1.1). It is however reasonable to maintain that this data underestimates the real amount of unemployment, which in some areas easily reaches 20 per cent. To this has to be added the number of under-employed and the thirty million young people who enter the labour market every year. The reform of the state enterprises has a significant effect on the growth of unemployment. In 1999, 6.1 million workers have been laid off from the SOEs, but the Ministry of Labour and Social Security foresees that another 12 million will lose their occupation during the year 2000. The deterioration of the situation in labour markets in the public sector should be balanced by the effects of the politics enacted to favour the activity of the private sector, and also by foreign investments.

Unemployment means poverty because the absorbers present in Europe do not exist. In the past, there have been some attempts to create minimum subsidies for the unemployed. The first attempt took place in 1986 when the state introduced an insurance scheme for unemployment, but only those who

Table 1.1 Total amount of employees and unemployment index (1995–1999)

	1995	1996	1997	1998	1999
Total amount of employed people (in million)	679.5	688.5	696.0	699.9	705.9
Unemployment Index in urban area (%)	2.9	3.0	3.1	3.0	3.1

Source: Italian Embassy in China; EIU Country Profile 2000.

were left unemployed due to bankruptcy or restructuring of the company, expiry of contract, or discharge due to lack of regulations observation were entitled. Presently this form of insurance covers 70 million unemployed workers laid off from the SOEs that have been declared bankrupt and, only in some regions, it also covers workers coming from collective enterprises, joint-ventures and private enterprises. During the 1990s, the government approved an Insurance Rule for unemployment, to bring under the insurance program also the labour force abounding in the SOEs (which according to some estimates amounts to 20 million workers of the total of the 104 employed). The stagnant domestic demand and the tendencies of deflation have driven the authorities to rise the unemployment subsidies of the 9 million workers laid off because of the restructuring of the SOEs, and to grant rises to a vast category of state functionaries.

1.2 The policies to revitalise the economy

In face of the negative effect of Asian financial crisis, the government lead by Premier Zhu Rongji has taken a series of measures for revitalising the economic development. First and foremost, China pushed forward reforms in the areas of state owned enterprises, financial systems, government institutions, grain circulation systems, housing systems, social and medical security systems. Second, greatly increased investment in infrastructure development to stimulate domestic demand. China's economy was affected to a certain degree, as reflected by slowdown of the growth rate and insufficient domestic demands. The impossibility of promoting has an export led growth therefore forced the authorities to stimulate domestic demand by raising the costs of the infrastructure, particularly in the energy and the real estate sectors. In August 1998 the authorities introduced 12 billion dollars worth of increases in taxation, equal to 1.4 per cent of the GDP, which were to be financed mainly by issuing bonds of state owned financial banks. The package allowed GDP to grow by 7.8 per cent in 1998, but the reduction of growth of fixed investments in the first months of 1999 has forced the Chinese authorities to predispose new interventions. In August 1999 the government in fact did announce its new issue of state bonds, this time to finance the infrastructure and the technological upgrading of some key sectors.

Third, great efforts have been made to expand exports, utilise foreign investment, develop foreign trade and conduct international technical and economic cooperation. The relevant data showing the approved investments in China in 1998 and 1999 reveal a decline in the inflow of investments (Table 1.2). And this fact has contributed, among others, to the slowing down of the economic growth. To further optimise the industrial structure of foreign investment, China promulgated the Regulations on Guiding Foreign Investment Directions and the Industrial Catalogue for Foreign Investment, according to which, foreign investment industries and projects are classified into four categories: encouraged, permitted, restricted and prohibited. The government encouraged foreign investment in agriculture, high-tech industry, basic industry, infrastructure, environmental protection industry and export-oriented industry. For infrastructure projects, the state gives special encouragement to investment in development of agriculture, water conservation and ecological environment, in the construction of railways, highways and some key airports, and in expanding the scale of urban environmental protection and urban infrastructure development.

The government decided, too, preferential tax policies for foreign-invested enterprises. Corporate income tax rate is 15 per cent in the special economic zones, high/new technology development zones, and economic and technical development zones. For the coastal open belt and all provincial capitals the

Table 1.2 Foreign direct investments in China in 1998–1999

Forms of FDI	1998		1999	
	Actually Utilised FDI (bn $)	Growth rate over 1997	Actually Utilised FDI (bn $)	Growth rate over Jan-Sept 98
TOTAL	45.6	0.67%	29.2	–6.77%
Equity joint venture	18.8	–3.79%	11.8	–6.33%
Co-operative joint venture	9.3	4.7%	5.6	–18.17%
Wholly foreign owned Enterprises	16.1	2.26%	11.3	–0.49%
Stock Enterprises with Foreign Investment	0.6	109.38%	0.14	–46.99%
Co-operative Development	0.3	–15.84%	0.3	63.54%

Source: MOFTEC.

Table 1.3 Foreign direct investment from Asian countries, European Union and US in 1998

	Contractual volume of FDI		Realised volume of FDI	
	Growth rate over 1997	Change of Share in China's FDI: %	Growth over 1997	Change of Share in China's FDI: %
Asian countries/ Regions	−13.40%	−9.74	−9.27%	−7.46
European Union	39.79%	3.05	3.06%	0.22
U.S.	25.84%	2.24	20.79%	1.43

Source: MOFTEC.

corporate income tax rate is 24 per cent, while for the rest of China, the income tax rate is 33 per cent. Foreign-invested enterprises are entitled to the treatment of two-year tax exemption and three-year tax reduction by half from the profitable year. For technologically advanced enterprises, the period of half tax payment is extended to six years. For export-oriented enterprises, in addition to the above mentioned two-year tax exemption and three-year half tax incentives, they are entitled to half corporate income tax as long as their annual exports account for 70 per cent or above their total sales. Foreign investors who reinvest their profits made from their investments in China can get 40 per cent refund of the corporate income tax paid.

1.3   An outlook on China in 2000

The year 2000 has been a good year for China, better than the two past years. The official figures show that the GDP in the first quarter of the year grew by 8.1 per cent since the same period in 1999, and exports (a constant worry for China after the other Asian currencies devaluation) increased by 39 per cent for the same period, which makes it the best performance of the 1990s. In fact, this accelerated GDP growth in 2000 is largely due to increasing quote of foreign trade with US becoming China's largest export destination. Total profits had reached a high record last year, exports were up and the textile sector, a test for the reforms, had returned to profitability. Exports soared 33.1 per cent during the first three quarters of 2000 and imports rose 38.7 per cent thanks to a more active domestic economy. 'Deflation is now over' said Zhang Xueying, chief of the State Information Centre.[1] China has succeeded in its fight against deflation: the consumer price index rose 0.2 per cent year on year during the first nine months. Retail sales, the main indicator of consumption, rose 9.9 per cent from January to September to US$293.2 billion. The government's policies to stimulate consumer spending would also continue and the Central Bank has cut the interest rates seven times over the past three years. According to a report recently completed by the State Information Centre, 'China is expected to have an 8.5 per cent GDP growth in 2001 with an improved macroeconomic performance and low inflation' (*China Daily*, November 4th 2000).

The year 2000 will be the last of the five-year plan started in 1997, with great emphasis over reforms.[2] This year, moreover, was also the beginning of the third year of Zhu's government.[3] He is half-way through his term. There are no doubts about his priorities for the next two years. The government work report, presented at the 9th National People's Congress (NPC), in March, warned state industry to 'lose no time' in preparing for entry to the WTO. For 2002, he promised also to privatise housing and turn it into a major industry, while little progress was shown in reaching his ambitious goals of creating a new urban welfare system to replace the social security system operated by the enterprises.[4]

Another proposed measure for development concerns the Western Region of China, which has been left behind in the 'economic miracle' that has transformed much of the country's coastal regions. There are plans to invest there more state money, and to set up mainly infrastructure, such as new

Table 1.4 China: annual indicators

	1997	1998	1999	2000*	2001°
Population (m)	1230.08	1242.38	1254.6	–	–
GDP at market prices (US$ bn)	898 222	946 1957	991 0667	1070 724	1162 673
Per-capita GDP (US$)	730 2216	762 1804	791 3046	847 7325	913 1714
Real GDP growth (%)	8.8	7.8	7.1	7.5	7.3
Consumer price inflation (av; %)	2.8	–0.8	–1.4	0.5	1.2
Official unemployment rate (%)	3.1	3.0	3.1	3.9	–
Exports fob (US$ bn)	182.7	183.5	194.7	226.6	258.3
Imports fob (US$ bn)	136.4	136.9	159.0	192.7	224.6
Current account balance (US$ bn)	29.7	31.5	15.7	9.4	7.7
Total external debt (US$ bn)	159.2	167.8	164.8	162.1	165.3
Reserves excl gold (year-end; US$ bn)	142.8	149.2	157.7	160.1(a)	–
Exchange rate (av; RMB:US$)	8.290	8.279	8.278	8.28	8.30

* *provisional data;* ° *forecasts; (a) November 2000.*

Source: IMF WEO Database; EIU; Yahoo Finance.

airports. But western deputies are warned not to count only on state aid and to use more free-market initiatives to attract domestic and foreign investments. There is a proposal, for example, to transform the Shenzhen Stock Exchange into a high-tech exchange Nasdaq-like, and move the traditional exchange to Chongqing, in Sichuan. In these efforts, in April 2000, the State Council has approved the transformation of the Xinjiang Shihezi Economic and Technological Development Zone to state economic and technological development zone from provincial one. This is important, because these are the most attractive territories for foreign investments. China has at present 40 state-level economic and technological development zones, but most of them are located in the eastern region.

The government heavily used state resources to stimulate China's economy in a period of slow internal demand. The growth registered in 1999 (+7.1 per cent) depended mostly on these expenses. During the year 2000, Zhu Rongji promised that the government would pour at least another $12 billion into the state sector and on infrastructure projects in order to maintain annual economic growth at 7 per cent. That means incurring a budget deficit of $18 billion, about the same as in 1999. With an ambitious ten-year plan (2000–2010), China will invest 180 billion yuan (US$21.7 billion) in building nation wide highways, inter-provincial highways and roads in rural areas. According to this plan, by the end of 2010, eight highways will run from the east to the west, and 195 000 km of inter-provincial highways and 150 000 km of roads in rural areas will be constructed.

On the other hand, a number of Chinese enterprises have begun multinational operations in the last years of the century, a sign that the flows of international capital are no more only towards China, but also from China outwards.

The first to enter this field were the household electrical appliance manufacturers, who were also among the earliest to import foreign technology. What had pushed them to explore new markets and set up factories overseas was the stagnant domestic markets for these goods, while the corporations were expanding dramatically their productivity. Two names for example are Shenzhen Konka Electronic Group Co. Ltd., that is establishing a colour television assembly factory in India made with components from China and Changhong Electronics Group Corporation who is doing the same with Russian Companies, aiming at the Russian and Eastern European markets.

All the Chinese plans for investment abroad have to be previously approved by the authorities.

In 1999 the Chinese government gave approval to 50 competitive domestic enterprises to invest in overseas markets. These businesses account for a combined investment of US$40 million in the areas of household electrical appliances, light industry, pharmaceuticals, electro-mechanical products, and clothing. Their main target areas include Asian countries, CIS, and Eastern Europe.

Three years after the outbreak of the crisis, it is possible to conclude that the Chinese authorities have been able to avoid the risk of contamination and to prepare the instruments necessary to limit the effects on the growth of the economy. In the short/medium and long term, the complex impact of the Asian crisis on the Chinese economy will manifest itself in terms of effectiveness and efficiency of the processes of reformation and restructuring, in particular in what regards the financial sector and the state owned enterprises.

2.   THE REMAINING CHALLENGES

2.1   The reform of the state owned enterprises

The primary objective of the government is to complete the SOE reform. It is expected to be completed relatively smoothly by the year 2002. SOEs tend to be overstaffed and to lose money through the transfer of profits to loss-making departments and divisions. Party cadres in charge of such enterprises and employees with lifetime tenures all have vested interests in perpetuating the state sector. The eventual success of economic reforms under way in China will depend mainly on revitalising these 'socialist relics'. In fact, although state enterprises' share of industrial output has shrunk since reforms began (27 per cent today, nearly 80 per cent in the late 1970s) and – according to government statistics – one third of them were loss-making at the end of 1995, these firms still constitute the single most important sector in the national economy and claim the lion's share of investment resources. We need only to consider that 484 of China's 500 biggest companies are SOEs.

The majority of the SOEs operate at a loss and on a level of competitiveness, which is a lot lower compared to the private enterprises and to those that receive foreign investments. The problem becomes even more serious if you take into account the fact that the state enterprises absorb more than two thirds of the Chinese labour force, but generate less that one third of the total product. State owned enterprises employ 108 million people, which represent a substantial proportion of the urban industrial work force (79 per cent of the workers in the industrial sector). Presently the state enterprises contribute only to 27 per cent of the national industrial product while they employ 70 per cent of the workers in the industrial sector. The Chinese government estimates that at least a third of the work force in the state enterprises is in excess. The incapability of the SOEs to operate on a level of efficiency high enough to compete with the growing competition from the private sector has thrown the public sector in a whirl of debts and has weighed heavily both on the balance of the nation and on the effectiveness of the banks. These were constrained by political ties and triangular links of debt (for example: agency A has a debt with agency B which has a debt with agency C etc.) to guarantee credits without security to enterprises.

Obsolete equipment, production of goods not in line with new technology or market standards, and generally poor quality of management, where posts of responsibility are granted for political merit rather than for proven competence, weigh on the profitability of the SOEs. A considerable part of the state enterprises, due to historical ties, to close relations with a corrupted and inefficient administration and the presently unsustainable social function they have been put in charge of, are now unable to keep up with their debts. In a free market economy such firms would already have been declared bankrupt and dissolved, mobilising the workers in the labour market. In China, though, neither an effective labour market nor a social security net exists: the worker has always been trusted in the care of the company, which has traditionally provided health care, pensions and housing for 'political' prices. Once deprived of 'the cradle' of the mother-company, the Chinese workers would therefore find themselves literally thrown out in the streets.

Considering the number of state enterprises presently irrecoverably in the red, and the relevant dimension of these companies in terms of labour force, a complete restructuring program would require that millions of workers be abandoned on their own. It was clear from the start for the Chinese government that the way of lay-off, for the majority of the SOEs, was not possible. Therefore, the political leaders have decided to proceed on a gradual reforms pathway, slowing down all the processes of restructuring of the ownership of the enterprises, and concentrating instead with dedication, by means of cautious experiments and interesting alternative attempts, on the creation of a macroeconomic environment in which the enterprises could prosper 'as if' in a market economy.

The Chinese industrial structure is historically surprisingly parcelled with an infinite number of small companies, unable to collaborate and to exploit an economy of scale. The intention of the authorities would be to aggregate them according to sectors of production through a series of fusion and acquisition of crossed holdings as in the Japanese keiretsu. This should allow the joining of companies in the red to a series of companies whose activities would permit the former to recover slowly without the need of fast cuts in employment, and would also prevent them being declared bankrupt. The idea was to interpose holding companies and other organs of administration between ownership and management to realise the hoped for separation between ownership and management without having to turn to the undesired privatisation.

Efforts in reforming have been made since 1995, but they were mostly exploratory, and the lack of theoretical experience has led to a slow, tortuous way. At the time there were 305 000 SOEs which gave work to 60 per cent of the entire urban work force and to 70 per cent of the industrial work force. Of the 76 million employees, 15 million were officially considered in excess. In addition to the excess employees, the 20 million retired employees, still under responsibility of the SOEs, also weighed on the balance of the state owned enterprises. The majority of the state enterprises, in fact, paid between 18 and 20 per cent of the value of the salaries to maintain retired ex-employees (Lardy 1998). Furthermore the SOEs gave work to one third of the national medical staff and to 600 000 teachers and administrators. The benefits were seen as a right of the employees and the problem of giving them new dimensions, in fact consisted in creating a new social system around the state industries. Almost all of the SOEs had a negative balance. From the mid 1980s to the mid 1990s the losses produced by the SOEs grew from 55 billion yen in 1985 to 541 billion in 1995. At the same time their contribution to the industrial output more than halved, falling from 70 per cent in 1985 to 35 per cent in 1995 (Lardy 1998).

The great inefficiency of the state enterprises has substantially contributed to the public deficit since the SOEs financed themselves with credits granted by the banks. The subsidies and loans from the banks to keep alive the complex machine of state enterprises created a strong growth of inflation in the two-year period from 1993 to 1994. In 1994, to block the inflation, it was decided to fix a limit to the subsidies, to reduce loans from the central bank, to reduce investments in enterprises that were heavily indebted and to collect funds by releasing state obligations.

The Chinese leaders nominated 1995 the year of the reform of the state enterprises. The reason behind the reform project was the fact that only 500 of the SOEs had a relevant impact on the government revenue and that only 50 of these same enterprises were at heavy loss. The revitalisation of these companies was supposed to be completed by the end of 1998. All the other SOEs were supposed to be semi-privatised through collective shareholding by the employees, or to be declared bankrupt. The small state enterprises were to be bought by bigger ones, or to be transferred to private owners. The government decided to launch a pilot project of reform: experiment on a new model of enterprise on a big scale with all the characteristics of a capitalist style company. A hundred medium-large SOEs were chosen for the experiment: the same project was repeated on a local scale, with 2500 medium-small companies transformed into a limited company.

At the beginning of 1996, the state allocated 50 billion renminbi as a reserve fund to the banks that had financed the SOEs, a fund that was used to carry out mergers and to declare the bankruptcy of some heavily indebted SOEs. At the same time was launched the creation of a welfare system, which is now run by the state and no longer by the SOEs. At the end of 1996, the results of the experiments conducted in 58 cities were the following: 1099 companies had been liquidated, 1192 had been absorbed by other companies, 5908 non commercial organisations had been separated from the enterprises and 1.25 million excess employees had been employed elsewhere. The project approved by the 15th Congress of the Party in September 1997, with the consecration of the principle of socialist free market economy. The definition of a strategy for the SOEs was very clear in its fundamental lines: restructure the whole sector, leave out the small companies in order to concentrate on the medium-large ones, make real conglomerates out of the approximate 1000 big SOEs, sell, close and enact mergers and acquisitions for the majority of the small and medium sized companies, which were those most afflicted by balance problems.

For 512 medium sized and big SOEs the government had foreseen a bank of supervision with the task of supervising the financial management of the company and guiding the transition. Preferential treatment for the emission of vouchers to be distributed to the employees was also foreseen. The 512 enterprises were not chosen casually: they were only about 0.44 per cent of the industrial SOEs, but they represented 43.7 per cent of the sales of the state owned industrial sector, and 65.8 per cent of the profits. The sectors of production that remained entirely covered by the state would be the sensible ones, such as the national security sector, the sectors in some way connected to it through dual-use technologies (electronic industry, high-tech and aeronautics) and the infrastructure, together with everything that has relevance on the social level.

At the 4th Plenum of the 15th People's Congress Central Committee (19–22 September 1997), a new resolution[5] was adopted summarising the lessons of SOE reform to date, while setting goals and guidelines for a step-by-step reform through 2010. And the designation of Zhu Rongji as premier, in 1998, gave a great acceleration, as he proposed SOE reform among his first goals. But some important issues remain unsolved. Over 40 per cent of all SOEs operated in the red in 1998. Production was hampered by obsolete skills and equipment. Idle excess-capacity existed for some 50 per cent of industrial producers. The last official guideline for SOE reform was released by the central government on 22 September 1999, on the occasion of the 4th Plenum of the 15th Cpc Central Committee, and is known as 'The decision of the Central Committee of the Communist Party of China on major issues concerning the reform and development of State Owned Enterprises'.[6]

These are, in synthesis, the guidelines adopted for SOE reform:

– first of all, the strategy known as zhua da fang xiao (manage the large and let the small go), that aims to let the state control only over the biggest 1000 SOEs, and let the other 117 000 'sink or swim'. According to this, the biggest 1000 will be reformed on the Asian model of conglomerates (as chaebol), while the medium or small SOEs will be sold (to foreigners as well as to domestic companies), merged or forced to declare bankruptcy;
– make strong efforts to restructure even profitable SOEs, by reducing the corporate debt/equity balance (too high for occidental financial standard),

the exposure of banking sector to the property sector (that caused the Japanese financial bubble and the hardest recession of its recent history), and the ratio of non-performing loans in public bank (mainly the Big Four);

- at corporate governance level, realise an actual and sharp division between management and bureaucracy, still very powerful in Chinese apparatus, most of all on a provincial level;
- whenever possible, transform the firms in joint stock, limited liability or partnership companies, and push the new corporations to go public to raise fresh money from markets (internal as well as the overseas ones). To persuade people to invest in stock exchange, authorities lowered interest rates in 1999 (reducing the benchmark's one-year deposit rate from 3.78 to 2.25) and introducing for the first time in history of China an interest tax on these deposits;
- sustain the reform by improving and developing a legal, financial and regulatory framework essential for a sound market economy;
- in addition to this, considering the social role of the SOEs, which contributed in previous socialist economy to create a 'cradle-to-death' security system, the provision of an unemployment insurance scheme (paid mainly by state revenue and with a contribution of workers for 1 per cent).[7]

It is rather obvious that the success or the failure of the SOE reform is strictly related to the take-off of the market economy, with an increasing number of high-profitable private companies. The collapse of some East-European states happened because of lack of a strong private economy able to sustain transition. It is the reason why there are no successful strategies to reform a socialist system that could avoid depending on market. It is a huge task for the state alone as Russia or Romania well demonstrated. So, Chinese leaders both strongly support SOE reform with state aid and provide incentives for the development of a private economy by removing all legal constraint to set up a private company. In March 1999, a constitutional amendment officially recognised the private sector's role in the national economy and government hoped this would improve private sector's contribution to state company restructuring.[8]

In August, 1999, the Standing Committee of the National People's Congress (China's permanent legislative body), adopted a new law on private enterprise, known as SIEs Law (Law on Single-Investor Enterprises). It is perhaps the most important law in paving the way to capitalistic economy, join to the Company Law of 1993 and the Law on Partnerships of 1997. According to this new disposition, a person can register his or her own business and be legally 'qualified' to set up a joint venture with foreign partners, even if the enterprise is a one-person business. The aim of this law is to encourage Chinese people to start their own businesses (if a foreign investor wants to set up a SIE in China, the law applicable will be the Law on Wholly Foreign-Invested Enterprises). It sets virtually no requirement on minimum start-up capital or registered capital. There is also no requirement on the minimum number of employees (while the companies or partnerships are normally composed by a minimum of two). One of the most important changes may be the possibility of a private person entering into joint ventures with foreign investment partners. The existing Chinese laws on sino-foreign joint ventures, whether equity or contractual, preclude individuals from establishing joint ventures with foreign partners. But an important and negative point is that, unlike companies, SIEs are subject to unlimited liability for the debts of the enterprise. And this, in China more than in other places, would mean excessive risks.

2.2 Banking reform

Chinese banks are among the largest banks in the world in terms of assets, but despite its size, China's banking system remains one of the most backward in Asia. Most banks are government-owned, lending is under government control, and the main ones are unprofitable. The four largest banks[9] in China, which account for 78 per cent of the sector's assets, are government-owned, bureaucratic, with very low capitalisation, and were burdened by years of policy lending to SOEs (some 30 per cent of loans are non-performing). Their reform is strictly tied to reform of SOEs, and often the provisions to reshape them are common and related. Interest rates are still regulated, financial disclosure is minimal, and managerial accountability is questionable. At present, when a SOE wants a loan, the bank will probably grant the loan even though the SOE has been running up losses and the bank knows that it will never recover the loan. For loans provided to SOEs, even if nine out of ten go down the drain, the bank is still contributing to the revitalisation of the SOEs. For loans provided to private enterprises, however, even if only one out of 10 goes wrong, the bank will be accused of 'draining away state owned assets'.

The most obvious indicator of the weakness of the Chinese banking system is, in fact, the high proportion of non-performing loans (NLP), whose amount in the period preceding 1997, has been estimated to be around 24 per cent of the GNP and around 30 per cent in the two following years (Lardy 1998 and 1999a). The fiscal cost of cancelling the NLP is in any case high: 25 per cent according to Dornbush and Giavazzi (1999), 31 per cent according to Lardy (1999a). China has therefore to face a complete restructuring of the banking and financial system, reducing political interference and increasing the decisive autonomy of the central bank. The Chinese banking system suffers from many unsettled loans or potentially so. The reform of the banking system is closely tied to the reform of the state companies: in fact the major banks are

Table 1.5 Non-performing loans and different estimates on the bank restructuring (%)

	Year	Estimate
NPLs (% on the total amount of loans)		
Li Xinxin (1998)	1996 (year-end)	24.4
CCER (1998)	1997	24.0
Fan Gang (1999)	1997	26.1
Cost of the restructuring (% of GDP)		
Moody	1999	18.8
Dornbush and Giavazzi (1999)	1999	25.0
Nicholas Lardy (1999a)	1998	31.3

Source: Completing China's Transition, Salomon Smith Barney 2000.

of public ownership, and the majority of the loans have been granted to the SOEs. From 1978 to 1997, the overdue loans have increased from 190 billion RMB to 7.5 trillion RMB doubling as a percentage of the GNP (from 53 per cent in 1978 to 100 per cent in 1997). The growth of debt in China has hence been as fast as in South Korea or in Thailand immediately after the outbreak of the crisis. The expansion of the credit system has been caused mainly by the deterioration of the situation in the sector of the state owned enterprises, the debt of which at the end of the 1995 exceeded the balance by 500 per cent (Lardy 1999a).

Starting from the mid 1990s, the banking system has been subject to a vast restructuring program. In 1993, with the reform of the commercial banks, the role of the Central Bank was re-defined (People's Bank of China), development banks which carry out financial activity according to political directives have been created, together with numerous commercial banks which operate according to the principles of the market. Ten years after the beginning of the reform the structure of the banking system can be synthesised in the following way: in addition to the central bank, which consists of three structures (Industrial and Commercial Bank, Agricultural Bank, Bank of China and Construction Bank) there are three development banks (state development bank, Agricultural Development Bank and Export-Import Bank of China), two subsidiary banks (CITIC Industrial Bank and China Investment Bank), and two specialised banks (Yantai Housing Savings Bank and Bengbu Housing Savings Bank). Lastly there are thousands of branches of the co-operative banks, of which 48 586 are rural co-operatives and 2324 urban co-operatives (Salomon Smith Barney 2000).

Within the banking system the state owned banks dominate the financial assets, even though their power declining: in 1993 they controlled 78 per cent of the financial assets, today they control only 68 per cent, the commercial banks control 7 per cent of the assets, the urban and rural co-operatives 14 per cent and the other banking institutions 10 per cent (Salomon Smith Barney 2000). The high concentration of the financial assets increases the financial risk due to the lack of diversification and competition.

The Prime Minister Zhu Rongji has declared many times that he intends to complete the reform of the banking system, launched by him when he was governor of the Central Bank, before the end of the year 2002. The reform of the Central Bank should proceed on regional basis reducing the political interference and increasing autonomy in decision-making. The Prime Minister has strongly insisted on the necessity for higher capacity of supervision and regulation for the Central Bank, promising moreover that a stronger control will be followed by more autonomy for commercial banks. An injection of 270 billion RMB in the four big commercial banks has allowed them to double their capital and should encourage their managerial autonomy. The commercial banks should be encouraged to take commercial risks by granting flexibility in the management of interest rates.

Among the most important changes, stands the constitution of the Asset Management Companies (AMC), founded to manage bankrupt companies, in order to free the four most important banks from the enormous bulk of bad loans of the SOEs. The operation has two objectives: on the one hand, to restore the balance of the banks and to allow them to concentrate mainly on profitable operations, and on the other hand to make the financial management of the companies in the red more efficient. Between April and October 1999, the Ministry of Finance has created four investment trusts, one AMC for each of the commercial banks: Cinda (CBC), Huarong (ICBC), Orient (BOC) and Great Wall (ABC). Each bank received a fund of 10 billion renminbi cash to cover the expenses. The AMC should operate for the next ten years with three objectives: to collect, catalogue and clear bad loans, to create swap centres for the settling of the debts and to create financial agreements for the management of the restructuring of the SOEs. The supervision of the AMC has been assigned to the Central Bank, which also carries out the function of compensating for the debts. The creation of the AMC is an important step forward, even if many observers have noted that these financial trusts are owned by the state and do not have the necessary flexibility nor the necessary technical competence to operate in a field as delicate and dangerous as this (Salomon Smith Barney 2000).

The politics adopted by the government have always been oriented towards protecting the domestic banking system from international competition. Nevertheless, the attempt to favour China's entry in the WTO has made a series of changes necessary, and their realisation started in 1999. The openness towards foreign banking institutions also has grown. Until 1999, the only zones in which the foreign banks could operate were the district of Shanghai (the Pudong New Area) and the city of Shenzhen. Today, the admitted areas include the provinces of Jiangsu, Zhejiang, Guangding and Hunan and the autonomous region of Guangxi. The foreign credit institutes which have been authorised to operate in China with representative offices are more than 166, of which only six are entirely foreign property and seven are joint-ventures. The ratio between statements in renminbi and the debt in foreign currency has been brought from 35 to 50 per cent and the transfer of funds in renminbi between affiliates of the same bank has been liberalised.

By the end of the year 2002, Zhu Rongji intends to complete the reform of the financial sector, which he himself initiated when he was Governor of the Central Bank (CB). The re-organisation of the CB should proceed on a regional basis, thus reducing political interference and increasing the decision-making autonomy. The Prime Minister has very much insisted that the CB should have greater supervisory and regulatory powers, promising that more control through the People's CB will mean more independence for the trading banks. However, it is not clear how determined Zhu is to pursue obtaining full convertibility of the renminbi. In the year 2000 bank listing began, which is considered the main way to modernise the whole system. The big four are, at the moment, unable to go public, because they have to be previously converted in joint-stock companies and, moreover, they are burdened with a considerable amount of non-performing loans. But the commercial banks are preparing their listing on the stock market, especially the ten nation-wide shareholding banks. Among them, only the Shenzhen Development Bank (SDB) and Shanghai Pudong Development Bank (SPDB) have already been listed on the Shanghai or Shenzhen exchanges. The China Merchants Bank, one of the biggest shareholding banks in China with more than 180 billion yuan (US$21.7 billion) in assets, applied for listing A and H shares, and is also preparing for a Nasdaq listing for part of its on-line banking business. The Bank of Communication, the Mingsheng Bank, the Everbright Bank and CITIC Industrial Bank are all preparing their listing.[10]

Another way, as in the SOEs case, is to merge a state unit with a per-forming, private one. According to this, ICBC (Industrial and Commercial Bank of China), China's largest state owned bank, will probably acquire the China Merchants Group stakes in the Union Bank of Hong Kong Ltd., and this will be the first case of an acquisition overseas by a Chinese Bank. For the agreement, ICBC will purchase 239.98 million shares, or 53.24 per cent of Union Bank's total stake, valued at 7.52 Hong Kong dollars each, with HK$1805 billion (US$239.2 million).

An important issue regards the reform of regional banks, which are becoming a force of considerable strength in China's financial industry, especially for small business and firms in small cities and town.[11] All these regional banks resulted from mergers of thousands of urban credit co-operatives, the first of all founded in 1995, in Shenzhen, and, for the most part, are small or medium-sized. Many of them have been allowed to do business only in specific regions, and their main problem is the bad quality of assets and employees (worse than the big four's ones), even if they are not forced to lend to the SOEs. The Authorities seem more willing to support the efforts of these medium and small-sized banks that are trying to obtain more direct financing. The China Securities Regulatory Committee (CSRC) said earlier that China will increase the use of direct financing in 2000, and many people believe that China's expected WTO entry will force more banks to apply for direct financing to enlarge their capitalisation to survive cut-throat competition with foreign banks.

But the appearance of the entire system remains, at the moment, still uncomfortable and too much state-driven. Both the interest and the capital subscribed will be paid in a lump sum when the maturity is due, with 2 per cent of penalty if the investor sells the bond earlier. This discouraged the investment a lot, and this is the reason why the rates granted are so interesting.

The May 2000 issue of 60 billion yuan (US$7.25 billion) grants annual interest rate from 2.55 per cent for 2-year term of investment to 3.14 per cent for 5-year term. In contrast, the interest rates run at 2.43 and 2.88 for bank deposits of two and five years, respectively. And no fundamental reforms have been made in the interest rate system yet. The Central Bank still strongly controls the fluctuation of interest rates in the market, and the whole system remains very different from the other nations' ones.

Another issue about Chinese banks' reliability concerns money laundering. One of the most relevant problems of Chinese banks is, according to experts, that they are a haven for money laundering and tax evasion. For this reason, new banking rules launched on 1 April 2000 require depositors to show identification when opening an account, to avoid people opening bank accounts using false names. There are tens of millions of bank accounts already opened under false names.[12] It often happens that companies open a bank account in the name of their employees. According to a central bank survey (conducted between 1997 and 1998), more than 10 per cent of the deposits in the mainland banking system were from companies depositing cash in the names of individuals. The new rules will prevent the problem of bank accounts opened under false identities, but the rules will be easy to circumvent, as false identity cards circulate widely. The media have reported that bank employees will have difficulty checking the veracity of identity cards and people wishing to open a new bank account will not be required to show any further proof of identification. If the new rules are implemented, everybody should provide their real name for bank savings, even buyers of the T-bonds.

2.3   Financial system reform

The financial market is another of the key issues of China's reformation, and is strongly related with the banking system. The stock market, traditionally based on Shanghai and Shenzhen stock exchanges, is now regulated by the Securities Law approved by the Standing Committee of the National People's Congress on 29 December 1998 (and effective on 1 July 1999). This was the first Chinese law on this matter, inspired by the legislation of the Hong Kong Stock Exchange, and contains some important provisions to grant efficiency and transparent transactions.

Opened for business on 19 December 1990, Shanghai Stock Exchange (SSE) is one of the two mainland securities exchanges, and a non-profit membership institution and legal person. The 1998 data: 438 listed companies with market capitalisation of RMB 162.6 billion, equivalent to 13.3 per cent of GDP; and 528 listed securities with various types of securities including: equity shares (A and B shares), securities investment funds, government bonds, corporate bonds, and corporate convertible bonds. The SSE uses a computerised trading system and made effort to internationally cooperate with other stock exchange, to implement better the new trading technology. Concerning this matter, the SSE signed a memorandum of understanding with the London Stock Exchange in March 1995, renovated with Blair in 1998.

The other national stock exchange, Shenzhen, the first to be opened (on 1 December 1990, with a status equal to Shanghai's), by the end of 1998 counted in 413 listed companies with market capitalisation of RMB 888 billion. This is equivalent to 11.13 per cent of GDP and 483 listed securities, of which 454 were equity shares, 10 funds and 19 bonds. The SZSE has raised a total of RMB 128 billion capital for listed companies over the past eight years and played an important role in promoting the restructuring of state owned enterprises and bringing forth a socialist market economic system. Shenzhen distinguished itself over these years by its general attitude towards foreign markets, whose openness is favoured even by its geographical position (it is very close to Hong Kong). The first opening of investment to foreigners was in 1991, when the Shanghai Stock Exchange (SSE) and Shenzhen Stock Exchange (SZSE) began to offer B shares. The level of these shares has always been swinging, and, since 1994 – the year of monetary restraint decided by Zhu Rongji,[13] they have never turned back to the initial quotations.

However, the boosting economy of 2000 had made even B-share recovering and setting new records. Both the Shanghai and Shenzhen B-share indices are now at their highest levels since September 1997. And on 28 August, the Shanghai B-share index surged 6.18 per cent, or 4838 points, with a turnover amounting to a historical US$68.3 million. Shenzhen's sub-index also soared 7.8 per cent, or 68.07 points, up to 942.72, while its transaction volume was HK$318 million (US$42 million).

This astonishing improvement is also due to the above-mentioned global modernisation of the securities framework. Brokers said local securities houses were upgrading their technology to allow investors to trade B-shares through computerised systems. This kind of trading has so far been available only for domestic A-shares. Brokerages also proposed that the Shanghai stock-exchange give B-share investors transaction reports on the day of trading itself, so as to allow them to prepare for the next day, while, at present, such reports are now available only on the day after. Investors believe plans to improve B-share trading services are an indication that brokerages are preparing for a long term B-share upward trend.[14]

Here are some general figures about the Chinese stock market, which could help to understand better its peculiarities. By the end of 1998, China's listed companies had issued a total of 74.61 billion shares on the market and had raised a total of RMB 355.31 billion. The total can be divided in the three main stocking issues as follows: (1) A-share market: 34 302 billion shares and RMB

Table 1.6 Number of listed companies

Companies	1990	1991	1992	1993	1994	1995	1996	1997	1998
Issuing A Share	10	14	35	140	227	242	431	627	727
Issuing B Share	0	0	0	6	4	12	16	25	26
Issuing A and B Share	0	0	18	34	54	58	69	76	80
Issuing A and H Share	0	0	0	3	6	11	14	17	18
Total	10	14	53	183	291	323	530	745	851

Source: Data processing on China Council for the Promotion of International Trade 1999.

Table 1.7 Shares markets from 1987 to 1998

	1987	1988	1989	1990	1991	1992	1993	1994	1995	1996	1997	1998	Total
Shares Issued (100 MM)	10	25	7	4	5	21	96	91	32	86	268	102	746
A Share	10	25	7	4	5	10	43	11	5	38	106	79	343
H Share							40	70	15	32	137	13	307
B Share						11	13	10	11	16	25	10	96
Capital Raised (RMB 100 MM)	10	25	7	4		94	375	327	150	425	1294	837	3553
A Share	10	25	7	4		50	195	50	23	224	655	440	1687
H Share							61	89	31	84	360	38	763
B Share						44	38	38	33	47	81	26	307
Rights Offering of A and B Share							82	50	63	70	198	335	797

Source: Data processing on China Council for the Promotion of International Trade 1999.

168 709 billion; (2) B-Share market: 9598 billion and US$4745 billion; and
(3) H-share markets: 30 719 billion shares and US$10.02 billion. In 1998,
there were 851 companies listed in Shanghai and Shenzhen stock exchanges
with 252 677 billion shares, divided as follows: (1) A-share Companies: 825;
(2) B-share Companies: 106; (3) Companies issuing both A and B shares: 80;
and (4) Companies issuing both A and H shares: 18. Moreover, 43 enterprises
from the Chinese mainland had taken in a total of 10 billion US dollars
through listing on overseas stock markets. 31 in Hong Kong, 8 dual listed in
Hong Kong and New York, 1 in New York, 2 dual listed in Hong Kong and
London, and 1 in Singapore. The total capital raised is US$10.02 billion. By
the end of 1999, there were 949 Chinese enterprises quoted on domestic
markets, and 46 overseas. The first Chinese mainland enterprise to be listed on
an overseas exchange, the Hong Kong Stock Exchange, was the Qingdao Beer
Company Limited, in 1993. All shares are divided in two categories: un-
tradable and tradable. According to 1998 data, the first ones were 166 484
billion shares, 65.89 per cent of the total equity of the listed companies, half
(86 551 billion) owned by government, 71 617 billion owned by other legal
entities (as corporations) and the rest (8317 billion) owned by employees and
others. Tradable shares raises to 86 193 billion, 34.11 per cent of the total.

Investors have been increasing ever more since 1992. Furthermore, during
this period, the gap between Shenzhen and the more capitalised Shanghai has
been reducing, and now their contribute is somehow equivalent. In 1999, a lot
of companies were listed, 10 of them with more than 200 million negotiable
shares, and the ratio of high-tech companies increased up to 18 per cent. The
cashing SOE shares are making progress, and some companies in 1999 have
placed SOE shares to the public as an experiment (a very important item). In
1999, moreover, placing of B and H shares in US and HK dollars increased as
well (red-chips reach 42.6 billion dollars, +98 per cent over 1998).

Getting listed on overseas markets is, as said, one of the preferred methods
for reforming state firms. Hong Kong Stock Exchange has represented the first
choice, since the beginning of the reform, where the first Chinese firm was
listed abroad. Two different types of companies issue the shares traded abroad.
The first one is known as 'red chip', and consists of firms both incorporated
and listed in foreign markets (only Hong Kong, until 1999). They are a
subsidiary of Chinese parent companies, but with an independent legal status
and management. The second one is represented by companies incorporated in
China (according to the Chinese Company Law) but listed on overseas
markets, such as Hong Kong, Singapore, New York and London. Usually
these are state-run factories that have been chosen by the authorities among
the most brilliant SOEs and restructured to be sold to foreigners. Even B-
shares traded in domestic stock exchanges are from this type of corporation.

SOEs traded on the New York Stock Exchange are known in China as
N-shares.[15] They are listed by using ADRs (American Depositary Receipts)

which is a negotiable certificate, held in a US bank representing a specific number of shares of a foreign stock. ADRs make it easier for investors to invest in Chinese state owned enterprises (SOEs), because of the low reputation of these enterprises abroad. Nevertheless, the corporations included are the ones the Chinese government shows to the world as an example. They've had the best – and the most profitable – business records and the depth and regularity of their financial reporting are much better than most SOEs'.

PetroChina became a case study of a successful transforming of a SOE in a profitable company. PetroChina was spun off from its parent firm, the China National Petroleum Corp,[16] a wholly owned state oil giant, which in Asiaweek 1000 of 1999 was ranked 19th with a relevant improvement over its last year's performance (in 1998 ranked 40th). It was listed in Hong Kong and New York in April 2000, and even if the current performance on securities markets is far from what was originally expected, the listing should be regarded as an undoubted success. The listing has helped PetroChina diversify its shareholdings, to break a state monopoly in such a way as to open the way for other investors, improving even the corporate governance structure.

Intermediaries in securities are of different types, and they depend on CSRC. They include securities houses, law firms, accounting firms, investment advisory firms, and other entities in securities businesses. At present, there are 90 securities houses, 299 law firms, 103 accounting firms, and 100 securities and futures investment consulting institutions (97 for securities and 3 for futures). The Shanghai Stock Exchange (SSE) will introduce during this year an SSE Fund Index to reflect changes in China's growing securities investment fund market; for this reason, all 12 securities investment funds currently listed on the SSE will be taken as samples in the composition of the index. From 9 May onwards, the SSE Fund Index will take the day of its formal issue as the basis day, on which the index will read 1000 points. China, at present, has 24 securities investment funds listed on the Shenzhen and Shanghai stock exchanges, and the government plans to transform all the old investment funds launched in early 1990s into securities investment funds. The new index will be the first specially designed for officially recognised securities investment funds (the new ones).

For the moment, a stock issuance is subject to approval by the CSRC. Based on Article 11 of the Securities Law, 'a public stock issuance shall follow the conditions as stipulated in the Company Law and be submitted to the securities regulatory agency under the State Council for verification'. Standards of disclosure and transparency for China-listed companies remain relatively undeveloped; this is one of the most relevant problems, together with insufficient information. Also, foreign investors are restricted to buying B-shares on the Shenzhen and Shanghai markets, whereas cheaper A-share are reserved only for locals. Authorities know very well that if China's two-tier market system were abolished, foreign investment would pour in. Therefore, in 1999 more steps were taken towards opening financial sector to competition. In April 2000, Premier Zhu Rongji offered to allow foreign investors the opportunity to engage in full-service retail banking operations over the next several years, provided they take on a Chinese partner and hold no more than 50 per cent of the equity. And, more recently, Beijing announced that foreign firms would be allowed to list their shares on the mainland's stock exchanges. But no scheduling about it is known yet.

Strongly related with banking and securities is the insurance market. Even this important sector is, and will be, more and more heavily affected by the necessary changes due to the WTO integration. The provisions included in the agreement signed between China and US in November 1999 are indeed very similar for the two sectors. These will result in a slowly opening of the insurance market, with a few foreign companies entering the market every year, and in an important channel for insurance companies, chronically suffering from a lack of capital funds, so as to enable them to enlarge their financial assets.

And the effects start coming. The New China Life Insurance Co. Ltd., a major national-level life insurance company in China, became, in August 2000, the country's first insurance company to sell shares to foreign enterprises. This revolutionary agreement was signed between the company and five foreign financial institutions, including the Zurich Insurance Company, the International Finance Corporation and the Japan-based Meiji Life Insurance Company, for a purchase of 24.9 per cent of the total shares.[17]

2.4 Fiscal reform

The Chinese fiscal system is somehow archaic and still in rapid evolution.[18] Income tax law is amended almost every year, and there are so many exceptions to enacted laws, due to many special investment zones, that it is really difficult to paint a sound outlook of taxation in China. In spite of all the efforts in this sense, the level of revenue as a share of GDP still remains weak (12 per cent in 1998), even when compared with the 1980-level (26 per cent), and it explains somehow the stress authorities always put on increasing revenue news.[19] With the policy implemented by the government in 1999, which will continue in 2000 to sustain growth with public expenditures,[20] tax collection systems and a general strengthening of public finances will probably become one of the main issues on Zhu's agenda.

The law about the single investor enterprises (SIEs), imposes more changes. The business managers are subject to enterprise income tax. The self-employed are subject to personal income taxes since law regards them only as individuals. Before the tax laws are amended, if a self-employed person wants to start an SIE, he or she will have to pay both enterprise and personal income taxes. This is not only unfair but will also discourage those who want to shift from self-employment to an SIE. It is reported that tax authorities are now reviewing the issue. Hopefully, amendment will be made in the near future to create a more rational and friendly tax regime for private business.

Some important changes happened in 1999 about interest tax. For the first time, government taxed bank deposits, by imposing a 20 per cent tax on proceeds from bank savings. Only the interest on T-bonds is exempt from income tax, and in the year 2000, these were enthusiastically subscribed.

The greatest news of 2000 is the enacting of the inheritance tax. From the founding of New China in 1949 until 1990, China twice introduced the inheritance tax, but failed to actually collect it. This time government thinks that the tax will be effectively collected. In order to create healthy conditions for levying the inheritance tax, the government has imposed real name requirements on bank savings accounts, and is developing a standardised notary system. The rate of this inheritance tax may be as high as 50 per cent, but only the richest part of the population (between 1–3 per cent) will be subject to it. The Government intends that income tax, property tax, and inheritance tax will become important instruments to adjust individual incomes.

Improvements are expected in the field of foreign-related taxation systems, which will target not only overseas-funded firms in China, but also Chinese enterprises starting business overseas. At present, taxes levied on foreign-funded enterprises and foreign employees in China are ensured by legislation that does not apply to Chinese companies overseas. The amount of foreign-related taxes exceeded 160 billion yuan (US$19.3 billion) in 1999, rising in 2000 to more than 40 billion yuan (US$4.82 billion) and accounting for 16 per cent of China's total industrial and commercial tax revenue.

3. THE NEW OPPORTUNITIES

3.1 The decentralisation process

Chinese government has always seen regional autonomy as a great menace to its sovereignty and national integrity. The control of the centre has hence always been hard, discouraging all kinds of federalism. China might be the only and biggest country in the world that has a highly centralised structure, with virtually no administrative autonomies at all. Even if China has a very low degree of autonomy, it is certainly more apparent than substantial. In recent history China has faced a continuous swing between centralisation and decentralisation,[21] but the trend, anyway, has always been towards a bigger degree of autonomy, even if the reactions have sometimes been very harsh.

In order to maintain the whole country under control, the five-year plans have always shaped the economic growth by assigning different objectives for each region. The ninth Five-Year Plan, ending in 2000, and the long-term strategy up to 2010, divided China into seven economic zones, which will be characterised by different patterns of development:

1. The Yangtze River Zone, led by Pudong New Area in Shanghai, the Three Gorges Dam construction project and the industrial city of Chongqing, since 1997 the fourth state-level municipality.
2. The north-east area, including Beijing, Tianjing and Hebei province, with research and development facilities and abundant resources of coal, iron and steel.
3. The Pearl River Delta, including also Fujian Province – export-led, foreign-funded and the centre of Chinese light industry.
4. The south area – rich in both natural resources and tourist attractions – as Guizhou, Yunnan and Guangxi.
5. The Liaoning area, including the north – as Heilongjian, Jilin and Inner Mongolia – with a heavy industry that is a legacy of SOEs' system (Liaoning was the former centre of socialist era's heavy industry) and transport facilities.
6. The central area, for development of agriculture and raw material collections. A huge program of infrastructures is stated for these provinces, mainly railways.
7. Xinjiang's Uighur Autonomous Zone, abundant with energy, cotton and minerals.

One thing that involved both central and local government is the drastic reform of the bureaucratic system, announced by Li Peng in 1997 and carried out by Zhu since 1998. The reform on a provincial level would possibly represent a more arduous task. Actually, the central government has tried for many years to make changes in its overstaffed local organisations in order to improve their efficiency, but the results have always been far from satisfactory. In 2000, this task has been once more re-proposed, and with a new strength.

The local apparatus is affected by the same problems affecting the central one, but even more serious. The number of local civil servants far exceeds the one authorised by the central government,[22] according to official figures, among a total of 53 government offices in each province, 13 will be cut in the most part, while, in sparsely populated provinces, this number will rise to 23. Overall, the working staff of local governments will be divided almost in half.[23]

Reform must create an efficient and centre-loyal government, which can promote local economic development and safeguard social stability. The attention will focus on the separation of administrative management from business management[24] as well as on the establishing power and responsibility mechanism. At present, a deciding reason why local protectionism runs rampant in many areas of China is that many local officials have their own interests in local enterprises. A common practice indeed consists of Party and government officials occupying key positions in enterprises, this duality significantly increased the level of corruption and bad government.

In the decentralisation process, the poorest provinces although fiercely opposed to the project, have nonetheless always helped Beijing towards rich ones, like Guangdong. Guangdong is a brilliant example of a Chinese success story, started in 1979 with three of the four SEZs[25] and called in 1984, by Deng Xiaoping to become 'the fifth tiger of Asia'. It enjoys, in the greater Han ethnic group, a unique sub-regional culture, characterised by a similar level of per capita income, a shared history of international contacts for trade, and even a specific language, the Yueyu, or Cantonese. Now, after the two hand oversee of 1997 (Hong Kong) and 1999 (Macao), new and stronger ties are establishing in the region surrounding the Pearl River estuary, which is facing an increasingly tight relation between SAR's (Special Administrative Regions) and Guangdong's economies. The reasons for this growing partnership are easy to understand. The SAR is where the area's wealth is stored and manipulated, where international corporations plan their assaults on China's markets, where goods are loaded for distribution all over the world, while Guangdong's basic contribution is mainly cheap and abundant manpower, and land.

Guangdong has been working for SOE restructuring as well. To support SOE reform, the municipal authorities would soon set out a series of policies concerning SOEs' land use, easing access to capital for small SOEs, assisting employees laid off because of SOE reform, and setting up policies concerning local taxation. Statistics indicate that the stocks of 901 of Guangzhou's SOEs and enterprises which SOEs dominate, realised a gross industrial output value of 83.9 billion yuan (US$10.11 billion) in 1999, an increase of 10.8 per cent since 1998; and they yielded an industrial added value of 27.73 billion yuan (US$3.34 billion) last year, up 15.12 per cent.

A 'Pearl River Delta Authority' is unlikely to be formed for a long time to come, at least on a legislative level. But, for the moment, authorities can point to concrete, new examples of government co-operation across the border. Hong Kong is lending Guangdong money to upgrade the pipeline through which the province supplies the SAR with fresh water. And the two sides are working together to improve the water quality of the Dongjiang River. Hong Kong purchases most of its drinking water from a mainland state owned company. One question still unanswered is if Guangdong's continuous step towards globalisation on one hand, and stronger sub-regional co-operation on the other could loosen the ties with Beijing authorities, this could endanger the whole country's integrity. It is a real menace, even if the priority of

Guangdong leaders is not autonomy but maintaining the premiership of Chinese economic growth. But it is true that this is a delicate balance, and that excessive, hostile pressure by Beijing could provoke independentist claims. To manage this issue, both sides will need equal shares of luck and ability.

An important test of the effectiveness of SOE reform is constituted by Liaoning, with the Dalian hinterland, in Northeast China. This province always was a nerve centre of state economy, one of the principal locations of heavy industries in a socialist age. According to local government statistics, SOEs and state-controlled enterprises in the city turned over profits of 500 million yuan (US$60 million) in 1999, setting a record, and in the first two months of 2000, the industrial output value of SOEs and non state owned enterprises reached 11.29 billion yuan (US$1.36 billion), up 13.09 per cent over the same period in 1999. Exports value from these enterprises amounted in 1999 at 4.79 billion yuan (US$577 million), up 23.44 per cent from 1998 levels. Three key factors in these performances are: first, the reduction of corporate debts by closing about 100 small affiliate enterprises, second, the relevant upgrading of employed technology, and last but not least, the cutting of redundant workforces. The employment of the SOEs in Dalian had been cut from 200 000 to 110 000 people by the end of 1999, and the prevision for 2000 predicts the laying-off of an additional 10 000 units.

What about SOE restructuring in fairest provinces, such as the autonomous ones? Tibet, for example. The 37 state owned enterprises in Lhasa will probably be sold over the next three years, government said. City officials have made provision for a series of measures to encourage non-state enterprises to buy, merge or lease the SOEs. The city will first evaluate the assets of the retiring SOEs and then sell them, with their net assets, at rock bottom prices. Buyers who want to pay a lump sum will be given a 20 per cent discount. It will be possible to either acquire the firms with lease agreements or to transfer the entire property rights to the buyers. Northwest China's Gansu Province reported that the losses of state owned enterprises (SOEs) were reduced by half 1999. To enhance competitiveness of the state sector, the province has closed down 638 small coal mines and 176 simple oil-processing factories, which discharged heavy pollutants, while eliminating outmoded cotton spindles. It also set up 16 enterprise groups featuring socialised production with total assets of 25 billion yuan (US$3.01 billion), accounting for half of the combined assets of state owned enterprises in Gansu. The provincial government invested a record 8.5 billion yuan (US$1.02 billion) for upgrading existing equipment and developing new products last year.

But now, the need for a strong economic growth is forcing central government to partially release control over provinces. It is a fact that all the changes imposed by economic modernisation caused a certain degree of authority loss on provinces and local enterprise, as the story of the towns and villages enterprises demonstrated clearly.

3.2   Town and village enterprises success

TVEs are small and medium enterprises, operating in rural China over the last
two decades.[26] TVEs can have two different kind of ownership: there are some
collective enterprises and some private. The collective TVEs, run by local
committees, have readier access to credit (via bank or rural credit co-operative
loans), productive inputs, and information. The private TVEs are the ones run
by households either as individuals, named individual TVEs, with less than
eight employees, and named private if they have more than eight employees.
Since the main characteristic of the enterprises falling in the second category
is the 'collective' ownership of the assets, they are named as collective TVEs.
These are run by local governments (town, township, district and village
committees), or by rural households in co-operation with their local
government. Indeed, they have a specific 'Chinese nature' which is partially
derived from the Commune System. Most of the TVEs are in the industrial
sector, though they also operate in agriculture, construction, transportation,
commerce and foods services.

The TVEs sector is the most dynamic of the whole Chinese economy.
Between 1985–93, it was responsible for creating 54 million new jobs and the
annual average growth rate of gross output value of the industrial sector was
24.6 per cent at constant price. Moreover, in 1993, TVEs' contribution to total
gross output value of the industrial sector reached 44.5 per cent and they
accounted for one quarter of national exports in 1990. The outstanding
performance of the TVEs sector can be attributed to many economic, political
and socio-economic factors. Within the rural reforms (1979–84), agricultural
reform played an important role in removing economic stagnation in freeing-up
human and capital resources for the development of the TVEs. Because of the
existence of surplus labour in the agricultural sector,[27] TVEs have an unlimited
supply of labour. Some specific policies for TVEs have also been implemented.
The year 1984 may be considered a landmark year in terms of the main reforms
in the rural enterprises sector: the government approved the report on creating
a new situation in commune and brigade-run enterprises, which signalled a new
phase of development for such enterprises. Policies to promote economic
development in rural areas were implemented during the Seventh Five-Year
plan (1986–90), and from the early 1990s, in order to mitigate the strong
regional discrepancies, the general strategy became one of balanced regional
development with redistribution to help the poorest provinces.

Actions by provincial governments played an important role in the initial
phase of the development of TVEs. The role of local government is important
in promoting rural enterprises: since 1979, local governments have used the
revenue from TVEs to promote rural development and infrastructure. The
local authorities had great incentive to develop their administrative areas, to
increase their tax income, and to invest in new infrastructure. Collective

TVEs, run by the towns and village committees, have readier access to credit via bank or rural credit co-operative loans.

The private TVEs have grown on a large scale in the wake of two decades of development. According to Xinhua Agency,[28] by the end of 1999, the number of private enterprises has risen to 31.6 million with a total workforce of 62 million workers. A total of 1689 private enterprises have been set up, each enterprise has a registered capital of 681 800 yuan (US$82 145) on average. Most TVEs workers' contracts embody a higher degree of flexibility of employment than in the SOEs, with the result that employees put in a great deal of effort in order to keep their jobs and maintain their incomes.

However, there are some negative effects generated by the increase in the numbers of TVEs. Within the agricultural sector farmers are becoming more dependent on the TVEs sector. 'Perhaps the most damaging effect is that the low levels of investment and profitability, and increased uncertainty, have led to the channelling of investment funds, as well human resources, into the TVEs sector, with the result that the agricultural sector is relatively under funded' (Biggeri et al. 1999, p. 208). Also, a large proportion of TVEs employees still holds a piece of land as a safety net damaging real farmers. The rapid expansion of TVEs has also generated negative effects in the form of environmental problems in the rural area. In the absence of pollution regulations, TVEs contribute a lot to increase the level of air and water pollution.

3.3   The high-tech and new economy

China is heavily pursuing modernisation and is growing especially in all the sectors related to high-technology, from industries in the fields of aerospace, information technology and telecommunication, to the so-called 'New-economy', which includes companies linked to the Internet. High-tech product exports accounted for 13 per cent (US$24.7 billion) of the country's total export in 1999, two percentage points higher than in 1998.

The telecommunication sector in China is still in evolution, with efforts to restructure, merge, and improve performances. In 2000 emerged two giants of telecommunication, China Mobile Communications Corp and China Telecom Corp, resulting from a year of M&A, in the area of mobile (the former) and fixed-line communications (the latter). The registered capitals of China Telecom and China Mobile stand at 220 billion yuan (US$26.51 billion) and 51.8 billion yuan (US$24 billion) respectively. The history of the sector is as follows: to break up the monopoly of China Telecom (its unique competitor being China Unicom), and make telecommunication companies more competitive, the government, in March 2000, decided to split the country's largest telecom operator into four independent services. The mobile phone business, the most profitable arm of China Telecom, was reorganised into

Figure 1.1 China's top web sites (31 December, 1999)

---

1) Sina.Com.Cn
2) 163.Com
3) Sohu.Com
4) 163.Net
5) 263.Net
6) China.Com
7) 21cn.Com
8) East.Net.Cn
9) Online.Sh.Cn
10) Cpcw.Com

Source: China National Network Information Centre.

China Mobile, while the brand name of China Telecom remains limited to the fixed-line service.

A project that the authorities are strongly supporting is the creation of a network of high-tech development zones, whose aim is to build up a real Chinese 'Silicon Valley', and which they are willing to provide with a large amount of banking funding. According to internal sources, by the end of 1999, the main public banks[29] have provided 53 hi-tech industry development zones with a total of 75.8 billion yuan of loans, 18 billion yuan increase, up 31.23 per cent, 18.7 per cent growth over the country's loan amount compared to what had been planned for the year. The kernel of all is designed to be the Zhonguancun Science Technology Park in Western Beijing that, in accordance with 10-year planning of Beijing Municipality, was forecast to become one of the most important world centres for high technology research. Its origin goes back to June of 1999, when the State Council, China's cabinet, approved a proposal by the Beijing Municipal Government to speed up the park's development, expecting it to become the country's flagship in the sector of high technologies. A very popular saying in Beijing is that 'China will look to Zhongguancun in the 21st century as it did to the South Chinese open city of Shenzhen in the 1980s and Shanghai's new Pudong area in the 1990s'. The designated general manager is Duan Yongji, a member of the Ninth National Committee of the Chinese People's Political Consultative Conference (CPPCC), former president of the famous privately-owned Stone Company and, last but not least, a tycoon in China's IT sector. According to his forecast, the park's total output value is expected to exceed 600 billion yuan (72.3 billion US dollars) in 10 years' time.

The year 2000 will be recalled in the future as the year of the 'New Economy' boom in the entire world. China is not an exception at all. Internet is a revolution even there, where controls over information are strong and the attitude of authorities towards the net is still ambiguous. But government is aware of the enormous potential of the new economy, and tries not to be too strict about licences.

Every day, thousands of updated technological results and patent projects on many technical professional websites appear, enabling enterprises to go beyond the limits of time and space, and receive enormous technical information. Every type of corporation is approaching the net. Citic Pacific, for example, will launch a business-to-business portal, foodglobal.com that will operate into the mainland's food market. The portal, to be launched by its wholly owned subsidiary Neticom (Hong Kong) in the second half of 2000, aims to wire mainland food manufacturers to electronic trading platforms and collect global investors.

A similar company is eMarketplace, a business-to-business electronic trading platform to be launched by Cable & Wireless HKT and United States networking software provider Oracle. Citic Pacific will provide assistance to food companies that are not familiar with the mainland market. The existing portals catering only for the mainland food market were small-scale websites operated by mainland companies to cater for particular cities. Foodglobal.com at the beginning will cater for several large cities, such as Shanghai, Beijing and Guangzhou. Because the infrastructure in the mainland is not well developed, and the server's performance deteriorates badly with heavy transaction volume, Neticom will set up websites city by city. Neticom is the second portal by Neticom, which launched its first site, Carnet.com.hk, in March.

Another important item is the Internet-related IPOs: after the listing of the first and more successful Chinese portals, Sina.com, Netease and Sohu.com – respectively the second and third-largest portals – presented a registration statement with the U.S. Securities and Exchange Commission.

This statement would indicate that their IPOs on the tech-heavy Nasdaq exchange was imminent, but that there were still a lot of problems for foreign firms willing to be listed in China.

Beijing has been resistant all along to overseas listings because it would allow foreigners to hold stakes in the country's top Internet information providers. It is probable that only the offshore assets of the portals will be allowed access to foreign listing. It means that Sina.com, Sohu.com and Netease could go public only with their minor portals targeted at Chinese in Hong Kong, Taiwan and other countries – greatly undermining the price that stocks could fetch in an offering. It is almost the same business model as for Chinese web companies bidding for a US listing while complying with Chinese Government regulations. Sina.com and Netease.com are Cayman Island-registered, and Sohu.com was registered in Delaware, US company-haven.

The listing of Sina.com was attained in April 2000, one of the first pure Chinese Internet listings on the Nasdaq. Its performance is regarded with a lot of interest, because it represents an important test for other Chinese Internet operators who expect to go public this year. Sina.com rose almost 22 per cent on its first trading day on a stock market recently shaken by deep losses, and its shares gained US$3.69 to close at US$20.69 per share on Thursday.

There is a great expectation for these listings. Hong Kong-based Chinadotcom – which runs China's eighth-largest portal – listed on Nasdaq last summer achieved a market capitalisation of more than $7 billion, even though, with the recent turmoil in high-tech stock markets, it lost more than 60 per cent in the last five weeks.

Moreover, China is drafting laws and regulations on venture investments to facilitate the growth of Chinese high-tech companies; and this takes place right after last year's amendment of the Corporate Law, in order to encourage the development of high-tech companies and to help drawing foreign funds.

4. CHINA AND THE WTO

4.1 The agreements with US and EU

China has made a major effort to open up to world trade over recent years, cutting tariffs, reforming its currency and developing a legal system: now the country is coming back to the World Trade Organisation (WTO). China's re-entry into the WTO will shape the future evolution and direction of global economic relations.

The re-entry of China into the WTO is not far away. The agreement made with the US in November 1999 was followed by the agreement with the European Union in May 2000. Among the most important points of the agreements, is the willingness of China to reduce import duty by five percentage points (from 22.1 per cent to 17 per cent), with substantial decreases for some products, among which cars (the duties of which will come down from 80–100 per cent to 25 per cent before the of the year 2006), leather that will pass from 20–25 per cent to 10 per cent, ceramics (the import duty of which will be reduced from 24 to 15 per cent) and wine which will fall from 65 to 14 per cent.

Significant concessions are foreseen in the service sector with a remarkable growth of opportunities for foreign investors in telecommunications, in the banking and the distributions sector before the end of the year 2002. In practice the European Union has obtained that the agreement reached with the US in November 1999 for the opening up of the markets and for the foreign licences will be enacted in earlier and will cover bigger geographical areas. The agreement with the European Union has in a way anticipated two years ahead the agreement negotiated by Washington for the opening up of the Chinese market for mobile telecommunications. Furthermore, Beijing has promised to grant seven licences to European investors for the insurance sector within three months of the conclusion of the agreement, that is, before the admission to the WTO. On the subject of shares controlling, China did not want, however, to grant more to the Europeans than to the Americans: a holding no higher than 49 per cent in joint ventures in the sectors of services and telecommunications. In mobile telecommunications China will open the markets to the Europeans two years in advance and a greater number of cities compared to the agreement made with the US. The European investments in telecommunications will be of 25 per cent in the first year, 35 per cent in the second, and up to 49 per cent three years after the entry of China in the WTO. In the life-insurance sector, on the other hand, China will immediately grant seven new licences to European investors and the sector will be open to Europeans two years before it will be to the Americans. Foreign brokers operating in China will be free of joint-venture agreements five years after the Chinese entry in the WTO. The agreement made with the EU foresees, moreover, a gradual opening up to private trade of crude petroleum and fertilisers. Within the year 2005, the monopoly in the exportation of silk, that covers 70 per cent of the world's production, will be abolished.

The entry of China in the WTO should in theory favour the gradual elimination of some of the main obstacles to foreign investments: non-tariff borders, local protectionism, preferential relations between authorities and local enterprises and arbitrary norms imposed by local officials. There remains, however a diffuse scepticism on the real possibilities of fulfilment of the fundamental norms of the WTO, among which the transparent application of the regulations on trade and investments in an equal manner in all areas, as well as the principle according to which foreign enterprises have to receive the same treatment as local enterprises. These principles often tend not to be applied in China, where there are regions in which some local enterprises are favoured and protected to the detriment of not only foreign enterprises, but also enterprises from other areas of China. The respect for the rules of the WTO would be of secondary interest, should they be in contrast with the vital interests of the Chinese authorities, with the maintaining of social stability or with the supremacy of the communist party. Furthermore, it is probable that the Chinese bureaucracy will cause obstacles to the effective installation of the norms that come with the membership of the WTO. It seems particularly probable that the Ministry of Information Industry, which will face competition in the control of telecommunications and the Internet will oppose strongly. On the other hand, many observers maintain that the entry of China in the WTO cannot but bring a significant restructuring of the economy in the medium/long term.

4.2   The effects of the WTO on the domestic economy

The agreement for the re-entry of China into the WTO brings great perspectives to the opening up and transformation of the Chinese economy but also, in the short term, considerable risks for employment in the urban and rural areas. Looking at employment in the urban areas, the Chinese entry in the WTO and the consequent increase of competitive pressure on the state enterprises will make the already complex restructuring of the state enterprises increasingly difficult. According to the estimates of the World Bank, in the medium term, the Chinese entry in the WTO should make the rate of growth of the GNP increase by 2–3 per cent, followed by a development of five million new jobs per percentage point of growth (World Bank 2000). The growth of foreign direct investments should also contribute to the creation of new jobs. However, these are benefits that will be fulfilled only in the long run, it is therefore essential that the authorities prepare the structures necessary to face the consequences of the restructuring of state enterprises, so that the entry in the WTO does not generate social instability. The employment in the rural areas will also inevitably face growing competition that will follow the opening of the agricultural market, and this will increase the risk of expansion of the surplus of the work force. Furthermore, according to the previsions of the World Bank, it is probable that the entry of China in the WTO will favour migration into the urban areas.

The Chinese agricultural sector will be among the most profoundly influenced by the change. Vast reductions in prices are foreseen within the year 2004, and for some cases, key products like corn and wheat, the reductions might reach 14.5 per cent. A substantial rise in the import of wheat is foreseen, and therefore it is probable that vast areas in the north of China, at the moment devoted to the cultivation of wheat will be used for the cultivation of more profitable crops (vegetables and fruit) in order to allocate the existing resources more efficiently. The less efficient sectors, which until now have been protected from international competition will have difficulties. For example the car manufacturing sector: the agreements with the US and the EU foresee that the tariffs in the sector will be reduced from 80–100 per cent to 25 per cent, and that foreign producers will be granted the possibility to offer programs for financing the purchase of a car. Many local producers of the sector will most likely be forced to shut down.

The opening up of the banking sector to foreign banks will pose a big challenge to the local financial institutions, which will have to reassess their balances to be able to offer potential client services and above all, interest rates levelled with those offered by foreign banks. Some observers underline the danger that the benefits brought by the growing facility to enter the Chinese markets will be more than compensated by the growing competitiveness of the Chinese companies. From the point of view of commercial exchange, the short-term effects for the rest of the world will be positive owing to the reduction of tariffs and the removal of import quotas. In the long term, the impact will tend to vary more: the entry in the WTO implies a real restructuring of the economy, which brings along also the reform of the state owned sector. The Chinese companies that outlive the process of restructuring, characterised by high competitiveness and efficiency, might turn out to be a threat for the export companies from other countries (like the Korean producers of steel and chemical products), not only in the local market, but also globally.

The increased efficiency of the Chinese economy that will probably be realised in the medium/long term will bring about an increased pressure for competition, particularly for the rest of Asia.

4.3   Effects on East Asia

Concerning the effects on East Asia, Southeast Asian manufacture exporters are already subject to strong competitive pressure from China. One of the crucial problems will be the speed with which the Chinese producers in the area of assembling electronic goods grow, as this area represents the leading export industry to Malaysia, Singapore and the Philippines. However, natural resources exporters such as Indonesia, as well as those exporting agricultural products such as Thailand, could on the contrary profit from the greater possibilities of access to the Chinese market. Hong Kong could also benefit from the advantages of its admission, provided most of all by the expected opening of the Chinese financial sector. Many Chinese companies will come to Hong Kong to use financial services and obtain capital, keeping in mind that the renminbi is not freely convertible and probably will not be for a few more years. The Korean producers, and most of all those related to chemical and manufactured goods, might have to face growing competition in service industry markets, as important foreign companies will be able to build bigger establishments on Chinese territory to take advantage of economy of scale. Taiwan will probably be one of the economies which will benefit most from China's entry in the WTO. New enterprises will join the numerous others who already use China as a production base for export. Moreover, the process of admitting Taiwan in the organisation will now be speeded up. Indeed, it had been hindered until now by the requirement expressed by Beijing itself to admit preventively the PRC.

In September 2000, the twelfth session of the WTO's Working Party took place in Geneva. This working group presided over by the Swiss ambassador Pierre-Louis Girard is responsible for the compilation of a report containing the final conditions of China's entry into the World Trade Organisation. Beijing has been negotiating its return to the multilateral trade system for fourteen years. After the signing of the agreements with the United States and the European Union, which took place respectively in November 1999 and May 2000, the long membership process seems to have now reached the final phase, although a positive conclusion on a short-term basis cannot be taken as settled. The Geneva meeting was not easy. The main Chinese resistance came from the ministries who control the entrance of foreign businesses on the Chinese market and often obstruct the effective implementation of the WTO standards. There were, for example, delays in the concession of licences to European companies planned by the China-EU agreement concluded in May 2000. Besides, the Central Bank recently declared that they wanted to limit the amount of loans in yuan issued by foreign banks operating on Chinese territory. This decision would 'condemn' foreign agents to a marginal role. One of the inevitable arguments discussed in Geneva was, finally, the question of Taiwan. The Chinese negotiators, claiming Chinese sovereignty over Taiwan, called for the admission of the island to the WTO as a 'customs territory' of Continental China. On the other hand, the western negotiators, and most of all the United States, have declared an several occasions that Taiwan should join the WTO as an independent state.

Besides formal procedures, many uncertainties remain concerning China's total integration in the multilateral trade system: indeed, the acceptance of the accession request does not automatically imply a smooth implementation of the regulations. On one hand, the Chinese authorities now admit that a certain degree of liberalisation is necessary to promote growth and hence, obtain the people's support and capital to maintain power and political stability. But on the other hand, there is no certainty that China in the future will respect the conditions settled by the agreements. Following the rules of the WTO could in fact, be considered of secondary importance should they contrast with the vital interests of the Chinese authorities.

Therefore, one step away from the end of the negotiations, China still appears to be undecided between planned economy and free market. The entry in the WTO aims to speed up the transition process the Chinese economy is going through, by insisting on a real reform of state owned enterprises and of the banking and financial systems. The main obstacles to foreign investment will gradually be eliminated: consequently businesses and sectors of low efficiency, until now protected from international competition, will encounter difficulties. It is sensible to expect that the greater freedom of access to the Chinese market will benefit, on a short-term basis, China's business partners and the multilateral trading system as a whole.

The assessment of the effects in the long term, however, is a lot more complex. The pressures related to competition will increase, especially for East-Asian countries. The profits for the rest of the world could be largely compensated by the growing competitiveness of the Chinese enterprises. It is certain that the negotiations concerning the admission of China in the WTO will have an impact which exceeds the economic and commercial context, and could reveal fundamental security implications. China excluded from the multilateral trade organisation could show more hostility in its relations with neighbours, and particularly towards Taiwan. Vice versa, China actively involved in the international system should demonstrate more interest in the maintenance of peace in the region.

Joining the WTO is now a central issue in China political debates, but there is not a total consensus about the WTO entry. There are some preoccupations in most corporations representing sectors that may be damaged by the influx of foreign products. In the last National People's Congress a number of NPC and Chinese People's Political Consultative Conference deputies asked the authorities to postpone accession to the World Trade Organisation or make smooth its impact by boosting local subsidies, particularly for farming areas and industrial sectors that lack international competitiveness.

5. CONCLUSION

China seems most likely to continue consolidating the horizontal or fragmented authoritarianism model (Weber 1997), which is the most appropriate one for the consolidation of economic reforms, with a gradual extension of the decision-making base. Should this model hold sway in the coming years, it can be reasonably assumed that the forum for political participation will be extended and opened up to emerging social actors. Such a context would encourage an enlargement of the decision-making base to those political groups that accept the 'guiding role of the CCP' and are willing to contribute towards economic reforms. There is every reason to believe that the scenarios for the coming decades will be built on the consolidation of economic reforms and on political stability.

Furthermore, China will be able to get away with pragmatic political reforms, without much attention to real democracy, through the creation of a series of structures, which formally represent civil society. As we have observed, China is slowly moving in this direction, with the recent introduction of local elections in villages and townships. In other words the Chinese leadership seems willing to concede some formal powers to the localities as long as they do not question the central authority of Beijing and of the communist party. In this scenario, China would become a 'horizontal type authoritarian political system' or an 'Asian-style democracy' like Singapore, where one hegemonic party holds power and occupies all political ground, but accepts the political collaboration of all those who accept its supremacy and wish to co-operate in building society. In other words a political system in which pragmatism prevails, sustained by economic growth which allows the distribution of resources to the population, distracting it from making demands for real democracy (Weber 2000a).

China will be more integrated with the rest of the world, gradually complying with WTO rules and establishing relative hegemony within the Asian region, also thanks to the network of overseas Chinese. More specifically, one can say that the rise of China as a global power will reflect first of all its central positioning in the Asian equilibrium. But China is looking at Europe, too. The official visit of the Chinese Prime Minister Zhu Rongji in Europe in June 2000 lets us envisage that China has faith in Europe and in the Euro. 'Beijing wagers on Europe' ran Chinese newspapers as a headline at the beginning of the Chinese Prime Minister's long series of official meetings on the old continent. Zhu's trip started on the 27 June in Bulgaria and proceeded in Germany, Luxembourg, the Netherlands, Belgium, and ended with the visit to the EU headquarters in Brussels. During these two weeks of encounters and talks, the Chinese Prime Minister appeared engaged in consolidating the bilateral sino-european relationship in order to plead the cause of China's admittance into the WTO. The agreement with the European Union in particular has brought the moment of the opening of the Chinese market to mobile communications two years ahead compared to what had been decided in Washington. China trusts in Europe and in the Euro. Beijing's support reveals itself all the more important since the government led by Zhu Rongji controls in China and Hong Kong the greatest currency supplies in the world (around 230 billion dollars): it is estimated that 20 per cent or 30 per cent of this reserve is held in Euros.

The official meetings of the Prime Minister Zhu Rongji on European territory, in the context of the conclusion of the bilateral agreements with the United States and the European Union represent indisputably an important event in the perspective of a complete Chinese involvement in the global economic system. In this sense, the presence of China is relevant inside the ASEM (Asia-Europe Meeting), whose first summit took place in Bangkok one year before the Asian crisis burst out. At the Bangkok meeting, 1 and 2 March 1996, heads of state of all the European Union members and ten Asian countries (Brunei, China, South Korea, the Philippines, Japan, Indonesia, Malaysia, Singapore, Thailand and Vietnam) participated. On this occasion, the question of a special Asia-Europe partnership for the development of economic relations and for the promotion of a new political dialogue was brought up. The outbreak of the Asian crisis delayed the achievement of such a project for two years. The Asian crisis and the financial intervention in favour of the stricken countries occupied an important place in the talks of the second ASEM summit, which took place in London on 3 and 4 April 1998. In this reunion the countries' members have analysed the financial and economic situation of Asia approximately one year after the explosion of the crisis. They also prepared two specific initiatives with the intention of assisting the most affected countries: constitution of an ASEM financial fund (ASEM Trust Fund), operating since June 1998 from the World Bank, providing Asian members with financial resources, advice and assistance for restructuring the financial system and for the resolution of social problems caused by the crisis. The other initiative consists the creation of a network of European experts on systems and financial markets subjects, and to which Asian countries may have access to, in order to obtain assistance throughout the restructuring process of the financial sector.

The third ASEM summit of Seoul, South Korea, on 20 and 21 October 2000, has marked the consolidation of the dialogue between Asia and the European Union on questions of regional and global security, the development of an economic result-oriented co-operation, and, in a particular way, referring to social policies, intensification of exchanges in the education area, creation of co-operation networks on consumer protection concerns, possible broadening of the circle of participating countries to ASEM summits. Everything tends to show that dialogue and progressive co-operation between Asia and Europe puts the accent on the crucial role played by China. But unpredictable consequences can lie even in the most optimistic scenarios: for example, imagining China more and more integrated in the regional context is the best guarantee of the maintenance of peace in the area, although a strong and powerful China could well unbalance the already complex harmony existing between Japan, China and Southeast Asian countries.

NOTES

*   This paper is the result of joint work. Maria Weber wrote paragraphs 1.1, 1.2, 2.1, 2.2, 3.2, 4.1, 4.2, 4.3 and the conclusion. Stefania Paladini wrote paragraphs 1.3, 2.3, 2.4, 3.1 and 3.3.
1.   *China Daily*, 1 November, 2000.
2.   During the 15th National Congress of the Chinese Communist Party held in the fall of 1997, the central government decided to fully implement the shareholding system and to sell a large number of medium-sized and small state owned enterprises (SOEs) to the private sector. The government also encouraged the formation of conglomerates through mergers and acquisitions. The Chinese government believed that these moves were essential steps toward establishing what is being called a 'socialist market economy' in China.
3.   Zhu was nominated by the National Assembly, for the next five years, on March, 16, 1998. For a map of the State Council before and after 1998, the reference is: www.chinadaily.com.cn/highlights/gov/past.html.
4.   The Chinese socialist enterprise or *danwei* has been described neatly as a 'small society' in that it has provided everything social from health care, family planning (and control) and education to urban and commune populations. The *danwei* has also been a primary-order judicial organisation through mediating disputes between neighbours and colleagues, even investigating and punishing violations of the state criminal code. It has also often acted as the bottom rung of a socialist distribution network in times of crisis: organizing corvee labour to build and repair infrastructure and distributing scarce goods during times of rationing (Lewis 1999).
5.   See above, note 1.
6.   This document could be found on *China Daily* web server.
7.   Until 1999, 15.8 millions workers were covered by this fund.
8.   Nevertheless, private investments, which account for one fourth of the total fixed investment, have been slowing since 1996. And the excess capacities that ail many industrial sectors will discourage any significant increase in this field over the medium term.
9.   Under the supervision of Central bank (China Peoples Bank), there are four banks: the Industrial, the Commercial Bank, the Agricultural Bank, the Construction Bank. To make them more performing, in 1994/5 government created the 'policy banks', with the mission to

finance great infrastructure projects. They are the State Development Bank, the China Exim Bank and the Agricultural Development Bank.

10. Obviously, these are the most performing banks of the whole Chinese system. 'Last year, the 10 national shareholding banks in China had reported a total asset volume of 1.46 trillion yuan (US$175.9 billion) and a profit of 9.43 billion yuan (US$1.1 billion).' (April 16th 2000, *Business Weekly*).

11. Among regional banks, it is possible to include even the trust and investment companies (ITICs), which became very famous in 1999 for the wind-up of Gitic.

12. According to a survey by the Political and Economic Risk Consultancy (Perc) of Hong Kong, on a scale of zero to ten, China is edging towards the top of Asia's corruption league. The trend of corruption in the mainland, which scored 9.11 this year from nine a year ago, was deteriorating, By contrast, Singapore came in with 0.71 and Hong Kong was next with 2.49. 'No one knows how much of the more than six trillion yuan (about HK$5.5 trillion) of personal savings deposits in the banking system is black money siphoned off from state owned firms and government infrastructure projects. However, the sum is likely to be substantial. Li Jinhua, auditor-general of the National Audit Office, said as much as 125 billion yuan in funds for poverty relief, resettlement or water projects was misused or embezzled last year alone. The central bank itself could not put a figure on how many bank accounts had been opened under assumed identities, and since there was no requirement to show identification when opening accounts until this month, there was little way of checking.' (*South China Mornig Post*, April 10th 2000).

13. He was Governor of Central Bank in Li Peng's Government.

14. Starting from March 2001, Chinese investors have been allowed to trade B-shares, which were tradable, before, only by foreign investors. B-shares are listed in foreign currency, US$ at SHSE and HK$ at at SZSE. This measure aims at recovering B-shares, whose level has always been low. It is also a very important step towards the full convertibility of the yuan.

15. Companies listed in New York Exchange are: *1.* Beijing Yanhua Petrochemical Company Limited (BYH). It is a producer of resins, plastics, ethylene and a broad range of other petrochemical products in China. *2.* China Eastern Airlines Corporation Limited (CEA). China Eastern provides domestic, Hong Kong regional and international passenger, cargo and mail airline services in China (with Airbus and Boeing-MD aircrafts). *3.* China Southern Airlines Company Limited (ZNH) As with China Eastern, it is principally engaged in the provision of domestic, Hong Kong regional and international passenger and cargo and mail airline services in China and Southeast Asia. *4.* Guangshen Railway Company Limited (GSH) Owner of the railroad between Guangzhou and Shenzhen in the China's Pearl River Delta, with a connection to Hong Kong, providing passenger and freight transportation services. *5.* Huaneng Power International (HNP) HNP was established to construct and develop large coal-fired power plants throughout China. The company currently owns and operates eight power plants and acquired the Nanjing Power plant this year. *6.* Jilin Chemical Industrial Company Limited (JCC). JCC is a producer of basic chemicals and chemical raw materials, as petroleum products, organic chemical products and fertilizers. *7.* Shandong Huaneng Power Development Co. Ltd. (SH). It owns the Dezhou Plant, a coal-fired electrical power generating plant in Shandong Province, and 60 per cent and 75 per cent equity interests in the Weihai Plant and the Jining Plant. *8.* Shanghai Petrochemical Company Limited (SHI). It is a highly integrated petrochemical complex, which processes crude oil into synthetic fibres, resins and plastics, petrochemicals and petroleum products oil. *9.* Yanzhou Coal Mining Company Limited (YZC) This company mines prime-quality, low-sulphur coal from for sale to electric power plants, metallurgical producers and other customers located principally in China and East Asia.

16. See Paladini (1999) for a summary about oil corporation privatisation.

17. This sale will increase New China's net assets from the present 630 million yuan (US$75.9 million) to more than 1.6 billion yuan (US$192.8 million).

18. China introduced a somewhat modern system of taxation in 1994, to reduce the very high level of tax fraud at the provincial level, that itself collects taxes and then redistributes to centre, causing a serious tax evasion. The most important innovation of the tax reform was the introduction of a value added tax (VAT) – that is levied for 3/4 by the central government, and the imposition of unique corporation tax for all the companies, even joint-ventures (at a

rate of 33 per cent). Even the collection system was changed, and a double-stage system was introduced, carried out by both central and local authorities.

19. For example, the news about the 23.8 per cent jump in revenue in the first quarter of 2000.
20. But the accounting methods are slowly nearing the occidental ones. In fact, for the first time in history, the central government budget for the year has taken into account payment of debt interest as part of current expenditures.
21. For a efficient synthesis, see Van Kemenade (1997).
22. Statistics of 1999 show that the authorised number of staff in local government stand at 1.18 million while the actual number amounts to 5.48 million. Among these institutions, more than 90 per cent receive allocations from the state (the source here is the *China People's Daily's Surveys*, published in 2000).
23. In this case, as the other ones, the relocation of laid-off officials may be the toughest job, lacking China of autonomous medical care system, unemployment insurance and social security system. Moreover, the high prestige of these governmental departments and also the fact that the institutions they are diverted to – like research institutes and companies – are already full, make it worse.
24. The most well-known and serious problem in provincies, and a key issue for a successful economic and social reform, singled out and pursued, even if with scarce results, since 1980.
25. Special Economic Zones, a genial invention of Deng Xiaoping to open China to western foreign investments. Three of the first four were in Guangdong province, namely Zhuhai, Shantou and Shenzhen.
26. TVEs generated a large share of national industrial output, during the ninthies years. For a deeper analysis of the TVEs, see Biggeri (1999) and Biggeri et al. (1999).
27. The rural population was 850 million in 1993, about 72 per cent the total Chinese population and the surplus of labour force in the agriculture sector has been estimated during the period nearly 100 million workers (Gale 1988).
28. Xinhua Agency, *China Daily*, November 4th, 2000.
29. First of all, Industrial and Commercial Bank of China and China Construction Bank.

BIBLIOGRAPHY

AA.VV. (1994), *Doing Business with China*, London: Kogan Page.

Bai Gang (2000), 'Autonomy of Villages: Political Participation of Chinese Peasants', *Working paper of the Institute of Administrations Policies*, Chinese Academy of Social Science, April.

Baum, R. (1992), 'Political Stability in Post-Deng China: Problems and Prospects', *Asian Survey*, **32** (6), June, pp. 491–505.

Bell, M.W., H.E. Khor and K. Kockhar (1993), 'China at the Threshold of a Market Economy, International Monetary Fund', *Occasional paper*, 107, September.

Biggeri, M. (1999), 'Determinants of Chinese Provincial Economic Growth in the Last Decade', *Studi e discussioni*, 114, June, Dipartimento Scienze Economiche, Università di Firenze.

Biggeri M., D. Gambelli and C. Phillips (1999), 'Small and Medium Enterprises Theory: Evidence for Chinese TVEs', *Journal of International Development*, 11.

Bowles, P. and G. White (1993), *The Political Economy of China's Financial Reforms. Finance in Late Development*, Buolder: Westview Press.

Cavalieri, R. (1999), *La legge e il rito. Lineamenti di storia di diritto cinese*, Milano: Angeli.

Cavalieri, R. (1983), 'Costituzione cinese', *Mondo cinese*, 3.

Dassu, M. (eds) (1999), *Oriente in rosso. La Cina e la crisi asiatica*, Milano: Guerini Editore.

Dassù, M. and T. Saich (eds) (1991), *La Cina di Deng Xiaoping: il decennio delle riforme dalle speranze del dopo Mao alla crisi di Tienanmen*, Roma: CESPI.

Dornbusch, R. and F. Giavazzi (1999), 'Heading off China's financial crisis', *Strengthening the Banking System in China: Issue and Experience*, Bis policy papers, Basel, Banks of International Settlements.

Gale, J.D. (1988), *Economic Reforms in the People's Republic of China*, Chicago: Chicago University Press.

Garnaut, R. and L. Guoguang (eds) (1992), *Economic Reform and Internationalisation: China and the Pacific Region*, Sidney: Allen & Unwin.

Gibelli, M.C. and M. Weber (eds) (1983), *Una modernizzazione difficile: economia e società in Cina dopo Mao*, Milano: Angeli.

Goodman, D.S. and G. Segal (eds) (1994), *China Deconstructs. Politics, Trade and Regionalism*, London: Routledge.

Howell, J. (1993), *China Opens Its Doors, The Politics of Economic Transition*, Harvester Wheatsheaf: Lynne Rienner Publ.

Kapur, H. (1986), *China and the ECC: The New Connection*, Dordrecht: Martinus Nijhoff Publ.

Lardy, N.R. (1994), *China in the World Economy*, Institute for International Economics.

– (1998a), 'China and the Asian Financial Contagion', *Foreign Affairs*, Vol. 77, 4.

– (1998b), *The Unfinished Chinese Revolution*, Washington, Brookings Institutions;

– (1999a), 'The Challenge of Bank Restructuring in China', in 'Strengthening the Banking System in China: Issue and Experience', *Bis policy papers*, Basel, Banks of International Settlements.

– (1999b), *When will China's Financial System Meet China's Needs?*, paper presented at the Conference on Policy Reform in China, Center for Reasearch on Economic and Development and Policy Reform, Stanford University, November.

Lasserre, P. and H. Schutte (1999), *Strategies for Asia Pacific: Beyond the Crisis*, London: MacMillan.

Lawrence, S.V. (2000a), 'Privatization', *Far Eastern Economic Review*, 3 March.

– (2000b), 'They Say No Club', *Far Eastern Economic Review*, 13 January.

Lewis, S.W. (1999), *Privatizing China's State-Owned Oil Companies*, James A. Baker III Institute for Public Policy, Rice University, April.

Lieberthal, K.G. and D.M. Lampton (eds) (1992), *Bureaucracy, Politics, and Decision Making in Post-Mao China*, Berkeley: University of California Press.

Melis, G., G. Salvini, P. Sormani and M. Weber (1980), *La Cina dopo Mao*, Roma-Bari: Laterza.

Mills, M. and S. Nagel (1993), *Public Administration in China*, Westport: Greenwood Press.

Nolan, P. (1993), *State and Market in the Chinese Economy*, London: MacMillan.

Paladini, S. (1999), 'Le Soe: prospettive e possibili sviluppi dopo il 15° Congresso del CCP', *Quaderni Isesao*, 1.

Perkins, F.C. (1995), 'Productivity Performances and Priority for the Reform of China's State-Owned Enterprises', *Journal of Development Studies*, Vol. 31, 4.

Salomon Smith Barney (2000), 'Completing China's Transition: Enterprise and Bank Reforms', *Fiscal Sustainability, Economic and Market Analysis*, 30 June.

Samarani, G. (1994), *La Cina verso il 2000*, Venezia: Cafoscarina.

State Statistical Bureau (SSB) (1999), *China Statistical Yearbook*, Beijing: China.

Segal, G. (1992), 'Opening and Dividing China', *The World Today*, May, pp. 77–80.

Shapiro, J.A., J.N. Behrman, W.A. Fischer and S.G. Powell (1991), *Direct Investment and Joint Ventures in China*, New York: Quorum Books.

Tisdell, C. (1993), *Economic Development in the Context of China*, New York: St. Martin's Press.

Van Kemenade, W. (1999), *China, Hong Kong, Taiwan Inc.*, London: Abacus.

Weber, M. (1993a), 'Cina: la politica della porta aperta', *Relazioni Internazionali*, December, pp. 22–32.

– (1993b), 'Dalla Cina un nuovo modello di sviluppo: il socialismo di mercato', *Politica Internazionale*, 3.

– (ed) (1994), 'Cina', numero speciale di *Relazioni Internazionali*, September.

– (1995), *Rapporto Cina: il successo del socialismo di mercato e il futuro di Hong Kong*, Torino: Fondazione Agnelli.

– (1996), *Vele verso la Cina*, Milano: Edizioni Olivares.

– (1998), 'La Cina prossima ventura', *Sviluppo e Organizzazione*, 169, settembre-ottobre, pp. 15–23.

– (1999), 'La politica interna', in Marta Dassù (eds), *Oriente in rosso. La Cina e la crisi asiatica*, Milano: Guerini Editore, pp. 107–124.

– (ed) (2000a), *After the Asian Crises. Perspectives on Global Politics and Economics*, London: MacMillan, p. 214.

– (2000b), 'L'Asia oltre la crisi', *Sviluppo e organizzazione*, 178, aprile-giugno.

– (2001), *Il Miracolo Cinese*, Bologna: Il Mulino.

World Bank (1997), *China Engaged. Integration with the Global Economy*, Washington: The World Bank.

– (1997), *China 2020. Development challenges in the New Century*, Washington: The World Bank.

Xiao Xu (1998), *China's Financial System under Transition*, London: MacMillan.

Xiao Zhi Yue (1993), *The Ec and China, Current EC Legal Developments*, London: Butterworths.

2. Structural Reforms in Japan: the Attempt to Transform the Country's Economic System

Corrado Molteni

1. THE DISTINCTIVE CHARACTERISTICS OF THE JAPANESE ECONOMIC SYSTEM IN THE LATE 1980s

To understand how and why the Japanese economic system has changed in recent years and how it could change in the future, it is useful to start with a brief, schematic description of the main distinctive features of the Japanese market economy at the end of the 1980s. These were the years when Japan's economic juggernaut seemed unbeatable and the 'Japanese model' was widely praised and admired. Then, the collapse of the 'bubble economy' in the early 1990s, and the consequent financial and economic woes have dramatically shaken Japanese confidence in their economic institutions, unleashing demand for reform and change.

In short, these Japanese peculiar economic institutions include:

- a system of corporate governance favouring employees more than the shareholders,
- an employment system based on 'lifetime' employment (at least for the core-employees of large and medium sized firms), seniority-linked wages and enterprise unions,
- the prevalence in financial intermediation of the indirect (banking) channel,
- the existence of powerful business groups (financial keiretsu) kept together by cross-shareholding arrangements,
- the relative stability of inter-firm trading relations, and
- the discretionary but not discreet role of the state (the bureaucracy) in guiding and steering the economy of the country.

This is a fairly coherent system of interlocking and complementing institutions, which make the 'Japanese model' significantly different from the 'Anglo-Saxon' or 'Anglo-American' model. It is a system characterised first of all by the fact that the firm is viewed more as a community rather than a mere property of defined or undefined ('the market') owners. Consequently, the managers are expected to act and behave as the arbiters of the interests of both shareholders and employees. Second, banks play a dominant role as providers of funds to the corporate sector, while capital markets have a more marginal role. Third, it is based on stable and long term relations among individuals and institutions, relying on the commitment and the mutual obligations of the members of the community. Finally, it is a system in which firms and business groups compete among themselves in the final markets, but within the rules and the limits fixed by the 'visible hand' of the state bureaucracy.

Japan's distinctive economic institutions and practices have served well the country for many decades, allowing it to become the second economy in the world with a standard of living equal and often superior to that of many Western nations. However, in recent years, following the collapse of the asset price 'bubble', this system has come under severe criticism. Scholars, business leaders and policy-makers, both in Japan and abroad, have pointed to its flaws and weaknesses. In particular, critics believe that the system, on the one hand, has failed to prevent the occurrence of the bubble in the 1980s and, on the other hand, is an obstacle to both the process of economic restructuring and the development of information technology related sectors.

The main issues concern the degree and the scope of state intervention in the market, the power and the role of the bureaucracy, the functions of capital and labour markets, the system of corporate governance and the model of human resource management. In short, the main features of the Japanese model, whose efficacy and viability is now openly questioned.

In the following pages we analyse how the actual process of reform is developing in Japan, focusing on three main, critical reforms: of corporate governance, of the financial system and of the public administration. The intent is to provide a detailed picture of the content of the reforms in progress, but also of the constraints and the obstacles to their implementation. The questions we try to answer are whether these reforms can be successfully implemented and what will be their impact on the Japanese economic system.

2. THE REFORM OF THE SYSTEM OF CORPORATE GOVERNANCE

One of the cornerstones of the 'Japanese model' is the distinctive system of corporate governance. In fact, it is well known that, differing from what happens in other market economies and in Anglo-Saxon countries in particular, Japanese companies are not contestable and there are no possibilities of hostile acquisitions (only agreed mergers and acquisitions are conceivable). There are cultural reasons for this, but the main one is the fact that the controlling shareholders of large, listed corporations are a stable and, first of all, silent group of friendly institutions that are tied together by a complicated web of cross shareholding. Stable shareholders that are not supposed nor expected to interfere in the decisions taken by managers of other institutions or in their appointment.

As a consequence, the board of directors of Japanese firms is composed mainly of 'insiders': salaried managers who have climbed all the steps of the company ladder. Even large shareholders are not represented on the board. The only exception is the so-called main bank, the financial institution supplying funds to a firm and (supposed to) monitor and discipline its management.[1] This structure is again significantly different from the one prevailing in Anglo-Saxon countries like Britain and the US, where boards normally include outsiders who monitor the activities of top management on behalf of large shareholders. Moreover, in the Japanese system top managers are also freed from the short-term pressures of the stock market, as the network of stable and friendly shareholders prevent the capital markets from functioning as an effective device for controlling and disciplining firm management.

This arrangement has been very effective in protecting companies and their managers from external threats, providing stability to internal hierarchies and enabling managers to concentrate on long-term strategies and goals. However, the same arrangement could not prevent the speculative behaviour of many firms in the second half of the 1980s. Actually, the lack of effective control by the shareholders and the capital market has been identified as one of the main causes of the system's failure to monitor decisions over investment at the time of the bubble (Miyajima 1998).

The banks too were unable to check and restrain the managers of the firms to which they provided large amounts of funds. In the past, during the high growth period when corporate financing depended from the banking sector, banks (in reality the main bank of the firm) engaged in ex ante monitoring of their clients, intervening in the company management when financial performance deteriorated. However, with the financial deregulation in the 1980s, many firms have reduced their dependence from the banks and, as a result, the latter has seen their power to influence and discipline client firms' managers reduced. As shown by data collected by Hideaki Miyajima, the negative correlation between financial performance and several indicators of main bank intervention no longer applied during the 1980s (Miyajima 1998). Banks intervened only when there was clear evidence of financial distress but this normally happened ex post, when it was too late.

In sum, during the 'bubble' and afterwards, the Japanese system of corporate governance failed to provide effective mechanisms of control and discipline of managers' behaviour. And this fact has generated a strong movement in favour of a radical reform along the lines of the Anglo-Saxon model.

Reflecting this demand, in its 1998 'Manifesto', the Corporate Governance Forum, a body set up in 1994 by leading corporate executive, has declared that:

1. decisive emphasis is to be put on the notion of shareholders as the only owners and risk takers of the corporation;
2. other stakeholders of the corporation, such as employees, creditors, clients and regional communities are entitled to the pre-emptive benefits based, in principle, on the existing market;
3. company boards should be reformed by reducing the number and introducing independent directors (Okumura 1999).

These are revolutionary ideas and concepts in Japan, although – as mentioned below – in reality Japanese companies and managers have adopted a more pragmatic approach in introducing reforms, particularly at the company level.

Reforms, however, have been approved and implemented. In the name of shareholders' rights and of minority shareholders, in particular, in 1993 a law change made it easier and cheaper for shareholders to sue managers.[2] This move has been somehow successful since, in a country that is supposed to abhor litigation, shareholder suits have grown from almost nothing to about 200 a year (*The Economist*, November 18th 2000).[3] Then, in the summer of 1997, legislators have approved two more amendments: one authorising the use of stock options as a form of payment, and the other in favour of share buy-backs (Dore 2000).

But, in practical terms, more significant are the reforms of the accounting system, as they will contribute to increase transparency and accountability. Of these, the most important is the introduction from March 2000 of a system of consolidated accounts for listed firms, that have to incorporate in their accounts the assets and the liabilities of all the controlled firms, including those partly owned. This reform means that parent companies will no longer be able to hide losses and liabilities in the accounts of the subsidiaries, as it was common practice in the past. Moreover, from March 2001 listed companies will have to report on their balance sheet gains and losses on the securities and derivatives held in their portfolio (Nihon Keizai Shinbunsha 1998).

Other changes have been initiated and carried out by the companies themselves. For example, companies like Sony – a forerunner in the reform movement – have reduced the size of their board of directors. Sony has also decided to appoint as one of its independent directors a professor of economics of a national university: an unprecedented move in Japan that, by the way, has been opposed by the agency in charge of public officials.[4]

There are also signals of a change in the traditional pattern of ownership. Recent data shows that the share of corporate stocks held by stable shareholders has decreased, as financial institutions have reduced their holdings in favour of other, more aggressive and short-term oriented institutional investors such as investment funds and asset management companies. A growing role is also played by foreign investors, that in some cases have succeeded in acquiring a controlling stake in troubled financial and non-financial firms.[5] Financial keiretsu too are undergoing changes. Banks belonging to different groups have merged, while the horizontal linkages among non-financial firms seem to become weaker. Large firms continue on their path of independence from bank borrowing and increasingly rely on deregulated capital markets (Miyajima 1998).

Does all this mean that the Japanese system of corporate governance is really converging towards the Anglo-Saxon model? Maybe, but the evidence available also shows the strong resilience of the Japanese model. First of all, keiretsu are restructuring, but rather than dissolve it seems that they are regrouping in 3 or 4 even larger business groups, following the planned mergers of their respective banks.[6]

As for the lifetime employment, the system that lies at the core of the employees centred system, the evidence available is at least contradictory. The managers, including top managers, have adopted the language of the reformers, but the actual changes introduced in their companies are far from being radical and disruptive.

For example, Fujitsu has introduced a few years ago a new evaluation and reward system based on performance and not on seniority. But, following the traditional approach, the company has also been striving to provide job security to its employees, including those who were working in factories or offices negatively affected by technological change or the contraction of demand. For example, when it reduced the level of production at a semiconductor factory in Iwate Prefecture, Fujitsu started a program to match for re-training the workers, later transferred to other plants. It also set up a company providing jobs to senior employees (Akikusa 1999). Initiatives that clearly show that, while reforming, Japanese large companies continue to attach great importance to people and do maintain their commitment towards employees.

This pragmatic approach has been adopted also by Matsushita Electric, one of the strongholds of Japanese-style management. Like other businessmen, Yôichi Morishita, the President of the company, has joined those advocating structural reforms, saying that the reform of the management system is one of the major goals that should be achieved by Japanese companies in the years ahead (Morishita 1999). And, like Fujitsu, his company has introduced important innovations in the management of personnel and in the salary system. It has also introduced a stock-option scheme for its top managers, while other managers will receive a fixed bonus in case of an appreciation in the price of shares. Yet, what is interesting is that Morishita is also warning against the risk of being excessively concerned with the stock market and its signals. In his view, the basis of Japan's economic prowess rests in the manufacturing know-how, in the superior quality of its products, and in the accumulation of knowledge through research and development. And it is for this reason that he insists on the concept of 'people centred management' (Morishita 1999).

Thus, it seems that rather than a radical change what is actually occurring in Japan's system of corporate governance is a reassessment of priorities. In this process, shareholders are definitely gaining more attention and a higher profile than in the past, but the employees continue to remain a key resource of the company and as such an important stakeholder to be reckoned with and, therefore, to be properly rewarded. As for the managers, in the future too top positions in most Japanese corporations are likely to remain the prerogative of those who have spent their career within the same company, but competition will be tougher. At the same time, companies in different sectors will follow different paths. The result will be a further hybridisation of the Japanese model but, after all, in the course of its economic and social development has always adopted and adapted foreign elements. Reforms are introduced and the institutional set-up will change. Yet differences and peculiarities of its economic system are not going to disappear.

3.   THE REFORM OF THE FINANCIAL SYSTEM

The second element of the Japanese model that is undergoing a thorough reform is the financial sector, which in post-war Japan has developed under the closed supervision and control of the Ministry of Finance (MOF).[7]

The existence of a strong Ministry meant that until the 1970s Japan's financial system was tightly and minutely regulated, protected from international competition, and segmented in three principal sectors: securities, banking and insurance. In particular, the Ministry has exercised its extensive power[8] to restrict and control entry and capital flows, approve or reject innovations, regulate interest rates, fix commissions, and facilitate the establishments of the so-called 'convoy system'. This meant that the Japanese financial industry – like wartime naval convoys – was expected to proceed at the same speed, that is the pace of the less efficient institution, in order to guarantee the safety and the stability of the whole system. To this end, the financial authorities limited competition among firms and prevented the most efficient ones to gain advantage over competitors. Specifically, in the case of the banking sector, the MOF used the Interest Control Law of 1948 to regulate interest rates through the device of advisory councils that, in reality, were a bank cartel. This scheme allowed banks to keep low the cost of raising funds, while raising toward but still below market clearing levels the interest rates on bank loans. On the other hand, bank deposits and saving were safe and guaranteed. The MOF would not allow financial institutions to fail no matter how poorly they were managed. If a firm risked insolvency, the authorities would intervene, arranging for mergers or acquisitions by other institutions. However, MOF intervention was not based on transparent criteria and procedures, but the Ministry exercised its power in a very discretionary way, preferring to rely on its expertise and judgement.

For several decades this financial system, controlled by MOF and dominated by the banking sector, succeeded in effectively transferring the savings of Japanese household to the private sector and, in particular, to the strategic, export-oriented industries designated by the Ministry of International Trade and Industry (MITI). As pointed out by Akiyoshi Horiuchi of Tokyo University, the fragility of the system did not surface during the high-growth era, because the regulations restricting competition guaranteed protection to the less competitive institutions and conspicuous rents for the better managed institutions (Horiuchi 1977). Moreover, the existence of rents induced bank managers to refrain from excessive risk-taking. Indeed, Japanese banks were known more for their conservatism than for their innovative behaviour.

However, the constraints and the limits of the system appeared already in the early 1970s. At that time, the government was forced to adopt an expansionary fiscal policy as a remedy against the contraction of domestic demand caused by the hike in oil prices. This brought about a surge of Japan's fiscal deficit, which in turn determined an increase of interest rates on loans. The cost of financial protection became evident and so did the pressure for change. To cope with this demand, the MOF began to authorise a larger number of companies to float eurobonds, enabling them to raise funds in foreign markets at lower rates. Then, deregulation progressively gathered pace.

In 1981 came into effect a major amendment to the Foreign Exchange and Foreign Trade Control Law of 1947, which, in principle, prohibited all international financial transactions, with exception granted on a case-by-case basis. The new amendment, instead, reversed this principle, allowing all cross-border transactions unless specifically prohibited (Flath 1998). In the following years the internationalisation of the yen continued and by the end of the decade the euroyen and yen-denominated foreign bond markets were on the whole liberalised (Nakamura 2000). Furthermore, the market was gradually opened to foreign firms. Japanese banks and securities companies too began to establish branches abroad as the yen's value soared and Japan needed to recycle its huge trade surplus abroad. Interest rates were also gradually deregulated, while new instruments and new markets were developed and introduced. However, it should be underlined the fact that in this period most of the reforms were still the result of foreign (Western and, in particular, American) pressure and demands for market opening and liberalisation. The Japanese financial authorities were not yet entirely convinced and continued to guide the system with the old methods, failing to realise that the gradual but steady process of liberalisation and deregulation was changing the rules of the game.

In the new environment large firms became less and less dependent from the banks, issuing corporate bond and tapping new financing sources both in Japan and in foreign markets. Having lost their best clients, banks were forced to extend credit more aggressively to new customers and to enter new, more risky and less familiar fields of activities.[9] In this period, for example, large city banks began to extend loans to small and medium sized enterprises, a sector left in the past to regional smaller banks. Then, the easy monetary policy of the second half of the 1980s just provided additional, cheap fuel. The result was the unprecedented asset price 'bubble' (Molteni 2000a).

The lack of an effective system for monitoring bank activities became evident when the bubble collapsed and Japan plunged in the worst financial crisis of the post-war period. This was a systemic crisis. Not just a few badly managed institutions, but many of Japan's banks, securities firms and insurance companies were on the verge of collapse. Having heavily financed speculative transaction in the stock market and the real estate sector, Japanese financial institutions found themselves burdened by a huge and growing amount of bad loans. Moreover, their problems were exacerbated by the fact they had generously financed what turned out to be excessive, unprofitable capital investment by manufacturing firms affiliated to their keiretsu.[10]

Table 2.1 Total bad loans and disposed bad loans of 16 major banks (as of end of March, 2000)

Bank	Total bad debts (¥ bn)	Disposed bad debts (¥ bn)
Sumitomo Bank	1917	681
Bank of Tokyo-Mitsubishi	1841	504
Sakura Bank	1723	464
Sanwa Bank	1300	405
Fuji Bank	1314	344
Tokai Bank	678	322
Dai-Ichi kangyo Bank	1768	282
Asahi Bank	863	204
Daiwa Bank	1035	164

Source: Asahi Shinbun 2000.

In this situation, short-term remedies such as disguising loss trough loopholes in the accounting system were of no avail. Several financial institutions, including well-reputed ones, actually went under.[11]

The crisis was perceived as a failure of the MOF centred system of financial supervision and control. The numerous bankruptcies and a series of scandals brought to the attention of the public and the media the conflicting roles exercised by MOF and its incapacity to perform effectively as the supervising authority. Indeed the MOF was not only the supervisory agent, but also functioned as regulator, inspector and frequently even as managers of financial institutions, since many retired MOF officials are hired as directors or top managers by a large number of financial institutions: a practice called amakudari or 'descent from heaven'. This practice is supposed to improve communication and information flows between the financial authorities and the market. However it also produced a complex and at times incestuous web of relations that further reduced the efficacy of the MOF safety net while raising the moral hazard.

To cope with the unprecedented crisis, the government had to intervene. Using massive resources (taxpayer money), it had to bail out and often nationalise (temporary nationalisation) all kind of financial institutions, from the jusen housing loan companies to once prestigious and powerful institutions like the Long Term Credit Bank of Japan (LTCB) and the Nippon Credit Bank (NCB). It also had to concede the take-over of important institutions by foreign firms, and to re-capitalise the once powerful city-banks trough the injection of public funds: a task assigned to the newly set up Financial Reconstruction Commission (FRC). In addition, by amending the Deposit Insurance Law, the government extended until the end of March 2002 (instead of March 2001 as originally scheduled) the special measures to fully protect deposits and other claims on failed financial institutions (Bank of Japan 2000).

Furthermore, in March 1997 the Cabinet established a new supervisory body: the Financial Supervisory Agency (FSA)[12] that started its activities in June 1998. This new institution is in charge of supervision and licensing, but its approach is expected to be different from the MOF (although currently FSA is staffed with former MOF officials). In fact, it will have to rely on transparent and standardised procedures, making use of the prudential criteria and rules recently adopted (see below).

While tackling the problem of insolvent institutions and reorganising its supervisory functions, the government also decided to focus on the process of reform. The first step was the Financial System Reform Act of 1993: an important but still limited reform in the direction of allowing firms to overcome the traditional boundaries (with the exception of the insurance industry) through the establishment of separated subsidiaries (Harner 2000).

It was in November 1996 that the Hashimoto administration announced at last a bold program to match of deregulation and liberalisation known as the

Japanese version of the 'Big Bang'.[13] After one year of intensive deliberation, five councils composed of government and business representatives drafted concrete and detailed plans. These were incorporated in the Financial System Reform Law, which was finally approved on 1 December 1998 and is currently being implemented.[14]

Basically the provisions of the new law can be grouped under five categories:

a) those designed to expand user choice;
b) those designed to improve the quality of the services and to promote competition among intermediaries;
c) those designed to ensure the development of an 'easy' to use market;
d) those designed to establish a fair market;
e) those designed to preserve financial stability (Hall 1998).

Looking at the content, it is possible to say that this time the reform was a real and bold step in the direction of deregulation and liberalisation. As Maximiliam Hall, a scholar of Japan's financial system, and Stephen Harner,[15] a banker, write, the programme 'was labelled the "Big Bang", but it was vastly more sweeping and profound than the similarly named securities related reforms introduced in London in 1986' (Harner 2000).

The reform aims to restructure Japan's financial market in order to make it more free, transparent and first of all competitive with those of New York and London.

In practical terms, the idea of a free market implies the lifting of many restrictions such as those on derivative and cross-border transactions. It also means the liberalisation of many financial activities previously restricted such as the opening of accounts abroad by Japanese residents, the lowering of entry barriers (for example, by allowing banks to trade in stocks and sell insurance policies), and the total deregulation of brokerage commissions: measures enhancing competition.

A fair market means greater transparency and the enforcement of stricter rules concerning, for example, conflict of interests, insider trading and consumer and investor protection. Fairness also means more stringent rules and criteria regarding disclosure requirements. As for global, it implies the adoption of international (but often this means American) standards and practices.

The reform has also authorised the establishment of holding companies, an institution that will facilitate the process of restructuring and re-organisation of the financial system through the creation of universal banks.

And, last but not least, the Big Bang has introduced a new scheme for preserving financial stability in a liberalised and deregulated market. This scheme known as 'prompt corrective action' is based on capital adequacy ratios, that should enable financial authorities to intervene and take administrative actions before the actual occurrence of a financial institution insolvency (Hall 1998). This is a scheme that, as already pointed out, implies that financial authorities will have to abandon their discretionary approach in guiding the market.

In sum, it is an articulated reform that is gradually but profoundly changing the Japanese financial system. Indeed, the reform has already attracted into Japan a large number of foreign financial firms, particularly from the United States, which are bringing into Japan innovative methods and techniques, while taking advantage of the weakness and damaged reputation of Japanese competitors. For example, in consumer banking, Citibank has been innovating and gaining market share, while in the insurance sector, companies like AIG have been making inroads into this very conservative and tightly regulated market by introducing new products and services specifically designed for Japanese customers (Harner 2000).

The effects of the reform will become more evident when the burden of bad loans is completely removed. For the time being, new services and new opportunities have been made available for the Japanese public. One evident result is the establishment of several holding companies, under whose umbrella different financial institutions have joined hands. For example, this is the case of the Mizuho Financial Group, the holding company set up by Dai-Ichi Kangyo Bank, Fuji Bank and the Industrial Bank of Japan, three major players which have joined forces to restructure and to regain competitiveness (*Nikkei Weekly*, April 20th 2000).

However, apart from the problem of bad loans, there are other factors that might hamper or delay the transition to the new environment. First, in Japan there is a serious problem with the training of human resources. Indeed, so far specialised education in financial engineering and advanced finance topics is almost non-existent at the graduate level.[16] Second, Japanese financial institutions themselves have insufficient know-how and expertise in innovative financial methods and techniques.[17] (Nakamura 2000). Third, they have problems with risk management. The Japanese tradition of avoiding conflicts and favouring personal relationships has in fact been an obstacle to the development of a culture that attaches importance to objective risk assessment and pricing: tools that are essential in the new competitive environment (Harner 2000). Finally and more important, the reform requires the support and the commitment of bureaucrats if it has to produce those radical changes that have been envisaged by those who designed it. From this point of view, the fate of the reform largely depends on the successful implementation of the other major reform envisaged by Hashimoto: the reform of Japan's public administration and of its bureaucracy.

4.   THE REFORM OF PUBLIC ADMINISTRATION[18]

As already mentioned, in 1996 Prime Minister Ryutaro Hashimoto committed himself to the task of reforming six crucial areas of Japan's socioeconomic system, among which public administration was the top priority. In November of the same year the Administrative Reform Council was established under the chairmanship of the Prime Minister himself: an unprecedented arrangement that shows the overall importance of the issue. In December 1997, the Council submitted its Final Report, whose recommendations were accepted by the Cabinet and, after lengthy discussions,[19] finally approved by the Diet on 8 July, 1999 as the Basic Law for Administrative Reform (BLAR).

The main points of the re-organisation plan, to be enforced from January 2001, can be summarised as follows:

1. Reduction of the number of departments (ministries and agencies) almost by half: from 22 units to 12 units.
2. Strengthening of Cabinet's functions and Prime Minister's leadership, through the creation of a new co-ordinating, planning and supervising body, the Cabinet Office. This new body is in charge of promoting comprehensive co-ordination and politically led initiatives to overcome ministerial sectionalism and bureaucratic inertia. Within the Cabinet Office various permanent committees are to be created to deal with cross-sector issues, such as the Council on Economy and Fiscal Policy, the Council on Arts and Sciences and Technology, the Central Disaster Prevention Council and the Council for Gender Equality.
3. Transfer of functions related to the drafting of annual budgets from the Budget Bureau of the Ministry of Finance (MOF) to the newly created Council on Economy and Fiscal Policy. Moreover, in order to stress the on-going process of revision of the role and functions of MOF – a process that, as already seen, has begun in 1998 with the creation of the Financial Supervisory Agency – the name of the ministry will be changed into Ministry of the Treasury.
4. Introduction of a new system of policy evaluation across the government, in order to satisfy the growing demand of accountability.
5. Strengthening of inter-ministerial co-ordination mechanisms.
6. Appointment within each Ministry of up to three deputy-ministers (politically appointed) with the task of supporting the Minister in the exercise of political leadership.[20]
7. Creation of Independent Administrative Corporations (IAC) that will take over non policy-related governmental functions.
8. Streamlining of administration: reduction of the number of government employees by 25 per cent in ten years, starting from 2001; reduction of the number of bureau, from 128 to 90; reduction of the number of divisions (the

units within each bureau) by about 15 per cent. However, the Prime Minister's personal staff will be increased.

The key objective of the reform is to change the relation between bureaucracy and elected politicians, in response to a growing demand for 'political leadership' in general and policy-making, in particular. Indeed, the policy-making process in Japan has been, until now, dominated by the bureaucrats, who played the roles of both drafting policy options and choosing among them. According to Jun Iio, a Japanese scholar, in Japan there is still a strong tendency to view ministers just as the spokesmen of bureaucrats, and the Cabinet as an organisation whose primary function is to rubber-stamp whatever the bureaucrats have decided (Iio 1999). In reality, in recent years members of the ruling party (or coalition) have attempted to intervene in decision-making processes and achieved some success, thus establishing a sort of 'dual system'. The reform aims at overcoming this dualism by placing the policy-making function firmly within the Cabinet. In particular, an amendment of the Cabinet Law has reinforced the Prime Minister's authority and power in the fields of security, foreign policy, fiscal management, budget planning, personnel administration and organisation. The Diet has also decided to reduce the number of policy councils (from 211 to 90) and to exclude former bureaucrats from these bodies, which has been an important instrument of policy-making on behalf of the bureaucracy.

Moreover, for the first time, the re-organisation changes the internal structure of the central administration, until now considered as a sort of 'political sanctuary' that could not be touched (Ito 2000). The reform reorganises the internal structure of the central bureaucracy in wider functional areas and redefines the boundaries of each ministry's jurisdiction. The real aim is to change the traditional vertical structure of the central bureaucracy into a more integrated, horizontal structure, capable of dealing effectively with cross-sector issues.

In particular, it changes the role and the functions of the Ministry of Finance. As already mentioned, the BLAR contains a provision concerning the transfer of power and competence related to budget drafting from the Budget Bureau of the Ministry to the Council on Economy and Fiscal Policy. To fully understand the meaning of this power transfer, it is necessary to consider the importance of the budgetary process in Japan. In fact, in Japan most of the political decisions are made as part of the budgetary process, controlled by the bureaucrats of the Budget Bureau and not by the government, as stated in the Constitution (Campbell 1977). A previous attempt to transfer the powers of budget decisions from the MOF to the Cabinet had failed (Ito 1988). But the financial crisis and the prolonged recession in the 1990s have created a real need to change the system. When resources are scarce it is necessary to make clear-cut choices among competing alternatives, based on a set of priorities.

Table 2.2 Long-term debt* (¥ bn)

Fiscal Year	FY 1996	FY 1997	FY 1998	FY 1999 Est.	FY 2000 Est.
Debt	449 000	492 000	553 000	608 000	645 000
% of GDP	89.2	97.4	111.2	122.7	129.3

* *National and Local Debt.*

Source: Ministry of Finance.

Transferring the powers related to budget drafting to the Cabinet Office, the new 'heart' of Cabinet, is a way to give back to the government the authority to decide the country's priorities. The Ministry's loss of this power is actually the clearest signal of the declining fortunes of this institution, which – as discussed above – has lost ground also as the country's regulator and supervisor of the financial system.

The reform will also introduce a new system of policy evaluation, getting rid of the traditional principle of the 'infallibility' of the bureaucracy. It is worth mentioning, in this context, two other relevant measures, which are not included in the BLAR, but are strictly related to the issue of transparency.

The first is the Administrative Procedure Law (APL) approved in 1993, a general document concerning transparency in the administrative procedures. In its fourth chapter the APL contains, for the first time in the history of Japanese law, provisions to regulate the use of administrative guidance.

In brief, the provisions prohibit the infliction of a disadvantage or a sanction to those who do not comply with the guidance. In addition, the institution exercising the guidance has to furnish, upon request, documents stating its purpose and contents, and has to issue a public notice in advance when its action is directed to more than one person or institution. In sum, the law puts a limit on possible abuse and arbitrariness in the exercise of administrative guidance and introduces the principle of transparency even in the informal sphere of administrative power and action (APL 1993).[21]

The second measure is the Freedom of Information Law (FIL), approved in May 1999 and to be enforced by May 2001. Its introduction arises from the awareness that lack of transparency was one of the main weaknesses of the Japanese system.

Along with administrative reform, the government has promoted various deregulation measures. Indeed, regulatory reform has been discussed in Japan since the early 1980s. However, only since 1995 was it promoted as a key policy for economic recovery and essential for the transformation to a market-led system. In particular, the Deregulation Program of 1998 (to be implemented by March 2001) has restricted government's intervention in the private sector through the imposition of regulations, authorisations and permissions. The granting of subsidies is to be reviewed. The system for the assignment of public works is also to be comprehensively reviewed and entrusted to a limited number of offices within each Ministry. Deregulation is also to be achieved by the privatisation and outsourcing of the government functions (Connors 2000).

From the above, it is possible to say that a pragmatic reformist mood is prevailing and reforms are actually implemented. At this stage, there is no data available on the actual results and their effects. Yet the overall impression is that administrative reforms are not only taking place but are also going in a welcome direction for Japan and its market economy (Connors 2000). The relation between the mighty bureaucracy and the politicians is changing in a way that could benefit both sides; the bureaucracy's discretionary and often arbitrary intervention is being reined in by the adoption of more transparent and clear rules. And, in general, pragmatic reformism is prevailing over both conservatism and radical reformism.

Of course, there was and there is strong resistance and dissatisfaction in bureaucratic circles, which fear to loose power and prestige. When the interim report on administrative reform was officially announced, opposition to the proposals incorporated was raised by vested interests and, in particular, by senior bureaucrats and conservative politicians who have traditionally colluded with them (Ito 2000). However, it should be pointed out that part of the bureaucracy – particularly relatively young career officials – actively participated and contributed to the reform process. These junior bureaucrats were ready to renounce some of their political power and influence, because they saw the reform as an opportunity to strengthen their role as 'professionals' with specific knowledge and competence. Moreover, these junior bureaucrats resented the lack of clear functional demarcation in the Japanese administrative structure. Thus they saw the reform as an opportunity for the creation of a new, more clearly defined and more effective system of administrative jurisdiction that they are expected to run and manage. Young bureaucrats have contributed to reform the old system in the belief that they will be able to a play a different but still major role in the new one.[22]

5. CONCLUSION

In the previous sections, we have argued that following the burst of the 'bubble' the distinctive characteristics of the 'Japanese model' (employees-centered corporate governance, the main bank system, administrative guidance and bureaucratic-led government) have been gradually transformed. Even the fundamental institution of 'lifetime' employment is questioned. Financial markets and shareholder values are becoming more important and more influential as the traditional system of corporate governance has failed. Deregulation too is advancing, while the supremacy of the bureaucracy is weakening.

Is Japan too adopting the Anglo-Saxon version of market economy?

To some extent yes, though it is difficult to imagine that the process will bring, in the end, a social and economic set-up similar to the one which characterises the United States and the United Kingdom.

First of all, the cultural divide is still too wide for Japan to adopt American or British ways indiscriminately. The process will continue in a gradual, piecemeal fashion as it has developed so far. And Western (American) pressure for further and more radical reforms might even backfire, as the Japanese public's resentment and annoyance toward outside pressure is becoming more pronounced. Second, Japanese firms' tradition of caring for their 'core' employees is so entrenched that it is unlikely to be easily abandoned. As seen in paragraph 2, Japanese top managers continue to treasure their employees: a policy that might prove right in the long run as human resources are after all the key of the firm competitiveness.

NOTES

1. A good example is that of Nissan, the troubled car maker that has been recently 'rescued' by Renault. In 1997, before the partial French take-over, Nissan's board of directors was composed of 40 (sic) members, of which only three were outsiders. The other 37 were 'inbred' Nissan managers who had spent at least 27 years in the company. It is interesting to note that all the three outsiders came from banks: one from Fuji Bank, one from IBJ – the Industrial Bank of Japan and one from the Japan Development Bank, a public financial institution (Nissan Jidôsha 1997).
2. As pointed out by Ronald Dore, the amendment was actually the result of the Structural Impediments Initiative, a round of trade negotiations between Japan and the US (Dore 2000).
3. According to The Economist, the law change has been so successful that the government now wants to change again the law in order to place some limit to the shareholders' claims (*The Economist*, November 18th, 2000). However, for Ronald Dore the amendment has not produced such significant changes.
4. As a result of the agency's opposition the professor has moved from the national university to a private one.
5. In 1999 the amount of foreign direct investment in Japan has been four times higher than the previous year, reaching 12.7 billion US dollars (JETRO 2000). In the financial sector, an American firm has acquired for the first time a major bank, The Long Term Credit Bank of Japan, that had been previously rescued by the Japanese government. In the manufacturing sector, well known are the cases of Nissan and Mitsubishi, the two car makers now partly controlled by Renault and Daimler-Chrysler (Molteni 2000b).
6. The process of re-organisation is still going on, but there are many signs that the Mitsui group is integrating with the Sumitomo group, while DKB companies might regroup with firms of the Fuji and IBJ groups.
7. Actually, the Ministry of Finance's significant regulation and control of the Japanese financial system dates back to the financial crisis of 1927. The new Bank Law approved in 1928, in the immediate wake of the crisis, gave the MOF extensive powers to regulate banks' activities.
8. No other ministry in any market economy had such extensive powers as MOF, which had responsibilities for the national and local budgets, customs, taxation, and the supervision of the financial industry (banking, insurance and securities).

9. According to the Bank of Japan, the average annual growth in bank loans to the real estate sector climbed from 7 per cent in the 1976–1980 period to 18 per cent in the first half of the 1980s and to 20 per cent in the years from 1986 to 1990. Meanwhile, the total annual growth rate of increase was 9 per cent in 1976–1980 and 11 per cent in the following two periods (Lincoln 1998)
10. According to statistics provided by the Financial Supervision Agency, in September 1999 the bad loans of the whole banking sector still accounted for 62 000 billion yen or 11.6 per cent of the credit extended. In the case of major banks (city banks, long term banks and trust banks) bad loans amounted to 39 600 billion yen.
11. Yamaichi Securities, Hokkaido Takushoku Bank, Nippon Credit Bank and the Long Term Credit Bank of Japan are among the large financial institutions that failed in the second half of the 1990s.
12. Later renamed in English as Financial Service Agency.
13. This program is one of the six major structural reforms that Hashimoto wanted to implement. Beside the financial system reform, the six structural reforms (*roku daikôzô kaikaku*) concern education, economic structures, social security, public finance and the overall important reform of the public administration (on the latter see section 4).
14. The reform will be completed in 2001 at the end of a three-year period. Among the last reforms to be implemented is the opening of the insurance sector to banks and securities companies.
15. S. Harner was the chief representative of Merrill Lynch International Bank in Tokyo from 1991 to 1993.
16. Only 2 prestigious universities like Hitotsubashi and Keio have started innovative courses for the training of financial experts that will probably generate widespread emulation in the next few years.
17. To acquire the necessary know-how and expertise several Japanese firms have entered into co-operative agreements with American and European financial institutions.
18. The author would like to thank Silvia Zanazzi for her assistance in writing paragraph 4.
19. The debate in the Diet lasted 90 hours (Connors 2000).
20. Deputy-ministers will be responsible for responding to questions in the Diet, a task that, in the past, was left to senior bureaucrats.
21. Management and Coordination Agency, *Administrative Procedure Law*, November 1993.
22. This process reminds what happened at the time of the Meiji Restoration, when young warriors took the lead in reforming the country's institutions, including the abolition of the privileges of their own class.

REFERENCES

Akikusa, N. (1999), Fujitsu de wa Shareki, Nenrei ni Imi wa nai (At Fujitsu Past Career and Age have no Meaning), 'Bungei Shunju', November.
Asahi Shinbun (2000), *Japan Almanac 2001*, Tokyo.
Bank of Japan (2000), *Annual review 2000*, Tokyo.
Campbell, J.C. (1977), *Contemporary Japanese Budget Politics*, Los Angeles: University of California Press.
Carlile, L.E. and M.C. Tilton (eds) (1988), *Is Japan Really Changing Its Ways?*, Regulatory Reform and the Japanese Economy, Washington: Brooking Institution Press.
Connors, L. (2000), Administering Reform of the Japanese Model, paper presented at Conference on the 'Japanese Model', Kuala Lumpur, Malaysia, March 29–30.
Dore, R. (2000), *Stock Market Capitalism: Welfare Capitalism - Japan and Germany versus the Anglo-Saxons*, Oxford: Oxford University Press.
Flath, D. (1998), *The Japanese Economy*, Oxford: Oxford University Press.
Hall, M.J.B. (1998), *Financial Reform in Japan: Causes and Consequences*, London: Edward Elgar.

Harner, S.M. (2000), *Japan's Financial Revolution and how American Firms are Profiting*, Armonk: M.E. Sharpe.

Horiuchi, A. (1977), Financial Fragility and Recent Development in the Japanese Safety Net, paper presented at the Conference on 'Regulation and Deregulation: Japan and Europe in the Global Economy', Florence, European University Institute, November 27–29.

Iio, J. (1999), 'Down From The Pedestal: The Changing Role of Japan's Bureaucrats', in *Nira Review*, Vol. 6, Spring.

Ito, D. (1988), 'Policy Implications of Administrative Reform', in *Dynamic and Immobilist Politics in Japan*, Oxford: Macmillan.

Ito, D. (2000), Administrative Reform. The Road to Democratic Accoun-tability, paper presented at the EU-Japan Club Symposium on 'What is the Future of Global Society', Florence, European University Institute, October 27–29.

JETRO (Japan External Trade Organisation) (2000), *Jetro white paper on foreign direct investment*, Tokyo.

Lincoln, E.J. (1998), 'Japan's Financial Problems', *Brookings Papers on Economic Activity*, Washington, 2, pp. 347–385.

Miyajima, H. (1998), 'The Impact of Deregulation on Corporate Governance and Finance', in Carlile, L.E. and M.C. Tilton (eds), *Is Japan Really Changing Its Ways? Regulatory Reform and the Japanese Economy*, Washington: Brookings Institution Press, pp. 33–75.

Molteni, C. (1999), 'Il Giappone dalla sconfitta dei liberal-democratici alla ricerca di nuovi equilibri politici', in Borsa, G. and M. Torri (eds), *Asia Major 1999. L'incerta vigilia del nuovo secolo in Asia*, Bologna: Il Mulino, pp. 15–33.

– (2000a), 'The Crisis in Northeast Asia: the Cases of Japan and South Korea', in Weber, M. (ed), *After the Asian Crises. Perspectives on Global Politics and Economics*, London: MacMillan, pp. 28–49.

– (2000b), 'Il Giappone tra riforme strutturali e politiche conservatrici', in Borsa, G., C. Molteni and F. Montessoro (eds), *Asia Major 2000. Crescita economica e tensioni politiche in Asia all'alba del nuovo millennio*, Bologna: Il Mulino.

Morishita, Y. (1999), *Matsushita de wa Akubyodo o mitomenai (At Matsushita Bad Equality ios not Allowed)*, in *Bungei Shunju*, November.

Nakamura, H.R. (2000), *Japanese Financial Market Liberalisation? Institutional Transparency before and after the April 1998 'Big Bang'*, paper presented at the EAJS (European Association of Japanese Studies) Conference in Lahti (Finland), 23–26 August 2000.

Nihon Keizai Shinbunsha (ed) (1998), *Nikkei Daiyosoku 2001nenban* (Major Forecast of the Japanese Economy - 2001 Edition), Tokyo: Nihon KeizaiShinbun.

Nissan Jidôsha (1997), *Yûkashôkenhôkokusho* (Financial Report), Tokyo: Ministry of Finance Printing Bureau.

Okumura, A. (1999), *Corporate Governance from Japanese Perspective - Summary Statement*, paper presented at the Conference on the 'Political Economy of Corporate Governance in Japan and Europe', Florence, European University Institute, 10–11 June.

Vogel, E.F. (2000), *Is Japan Still Number One?*, Subang Jaya: Pelanduk Publications.

3.   Something New, Something Old: the South Korean Economy after the Financial Crisis*

Vasco Molini and Roberta Rabellotti

---

1.   INTRODUCTION

In 1960, South Korea was poorer than many sub-Saharan African countries with a per capita GDP of 883 US (1985) dollars when in Mozambique, for instance, it was 1128. Since then, Korea has grown at an average rate of 8 per cent (from 1962 to 1997), leaving behind not only African countries but also others like Mexico and Argentina, much richer in 1960 (respectively, 2798 and 3294US$).

Much has been said about the reasons explaining this outstanding growth[1], but on one aspect there is a wide agreement in the literature: the role played by the government was crucial, in positive or in negative, in the development of the economic system.

We agree with Rodrick (1995), who stresses the crucial co-ordinating role of the government to encourage private (and public) investments in sectors where, due to the existence of economies of scale and externalities, market allocation of resources would have failed. This government-led model of development was rather successful in mobilising and allocating resources until the 1970s, allowing the creation from scrap of an industrial base, dominated by large firms, named *chaebol*.[2]

Nevertheless, a significant side effect of this was the development of an intricate system of relationships among the government, the large conglomerates and the financial sector. Over the years the effectiveness of this structure waned progressively in the rapidly changing market and technology environments of the 1980s and 1990s (Kim 1997).

The shift towards a more market oriented economic system has been under discussion in Korea during all the last decade. Some reforms were implemented and Korea was also forced from the outside, the USA, its largest trading partner, the WTO and the OECD after joining in 1996, to begin opening its domestic market to international competition.

But before the financial crisis in 1997 the implementation of reforms was slow and its impact on the economic system was marginal. President Dae-Jung Kim, interviewed by the New York Times after the outset of the crisis, said that the 'crisis can be a blessing in disguise', a unique opportunity for a real change in Korean economy and society.

The aim of this paper is to analyse how far the implementation of reforms has gone, attempting to understand if the expected renewal is really starting to take place. In the next two sections we analyse the main causes behind the 1997 crisis and the explosion of the financial turmoil. Then, after considering the first impact of the IMF bailout, we analyse the implementation and the first results of reforms in the corporate sector, the financial system, the public sector, the good capital and labour markets. Besides, the boom in the new economy is considered to be the most interesting novelty in the Korean economic system. Finally, some conclusions are drawn in the last section.

2. AT THE ROOTS OF THE KOREAN CRISIS: MACROECONOMIC PERFORMANCE AND LONG RUN WEAKNESSES

Just before the slowdown of 1997 the Korean macroeconomic performance was not showing many signals of adversity and it is therefore unsurprising why such a deep crisis was not forecasted. Throughout the first half of the 1990s the yearly growth rate averaged over 7 per cent, the inflation was under control due to a tight monetary policy and the 3 year corporate bond yield declined from an average 15 per cent during the first half of 1990s to 12.5 per cent in 1996. Even the unemployment rate was very low and did not rise above 3 per cent. The situation of public balance was also under control and in 1997 the fiscal deficit was 1.5 per cent of GDP (Table 3.1).[3]

Nevertheless, although the situation of the main macroeconomic indicators was good, in the backstage of a generally fine performance, remained some unsolved issues, both at the macro and at the structural level. In the rest of this section we analyse these weaknesses.

2.1   The current account imbalance

The main sign of macroeconomic imbalance was the deficit of current account, primarily due to the gap between imports and exports. Since the beginning of its process of economic growth, Korea has known long periods of sizeable current account deficit, because of its structural dependence on technological and high value added imports. Nevertheless, during the first half of the 1990s the deficit began to progressively reduce and on average from 1990 to 1995 was less than 1 per cent of GDP (Table 3.1). This improvement

Table 3.1 Macroeconomic indicators: 1990–2000 (%)

	1990–95	**1996**	**1997**	**1998**	**1999**	**2000***
GDP growth rate	7.8	6.8	5.0	–6.7	10.7	7.5
Inflation (CPI index)	6.6	4.9	4.5	7.5	0.8	3.2
Interest rates						
(3 year corporate bonds)	14.9	12.5	24.3	15.1	8.9	n.a.
Current account (% of GDP)	–2.0	–4.4	–1.7	12.8	6.1	2.4
Public budget balance						
(% of GDP)	0.5	0.3	–1.5	–4.2	–2.9	n.a.
Unemployment rate	2.2	2.0	2.6	6.8	6.3	4.4

* *estimates.*

Source: Asian Development Bank 2000; World Bank 1999; Bank of Korea 2000.

was made possible by increasing expenses in research and financing hi-tech projects in co-operation with foreign investors, within the framework of an important public plan aimed at reducing the traditional Korean know-how and technological dependence on external sources. But suddenly, in 1996 the deficit began to grow very fast, approaching 4.2 per cent of GDP. The imbalances stemmed primarily from commercial deficit and were caused by three combined factors: a fall in the price of semiconductors, a rise in the import of fuels and an increasing dependence on imported machinery.

Plunging prices for semiconductors[4], that accounted for almost 17 per cent (776 in Table 3.2) of Korean exports, laid bare the structural problems of the

Table 3.2 Main products on total manufacturing export: 1992–1998 (%)

SITC Rev. 3		**1992**	**1993**	**1994**	**1995**	**1996**	**1997**	**1998**
653	Fabrics, woven, of man-made fabrics	5.9	6.1	6.4	5.7	5.4	5.0	4.0
752	Automatic data processing machines	3.0	3.3	3.1	3.4	4.1	4.4	3.9
764	Telecommunication equipment, & parts	3.3	3.8	4.1	3.7	3.8	3.8	3.9
776	Cathode valves & tubes; diodes; integrated circuits	10.9	10.5	13.3	16.9	15.0	16.6	17.0
793	Ships, boats & floating structures	5.8	5.3	5.5	4.8	6.2	5.5	7.0
Tot Main Products on Tot Mfg. Export		28.9	29.0	32.4	34.5	34.5	35.3	35.8

Source: PC/TAS 1992–1998.

Korean specialisation model. The excessive reliance on few products and the inability to break out with a pattern of pure imitation, particularly in high tech productions, have traditionally affected Korean exports but the situation strongly deteriorated when new competitors broke into the market.

Korea abandoned labour-intensive productions to lower costs manufacturers in China, Vietnam and other new Asian emerging countries, trying to specialise in capital intensive and technological sectors, with success in some markets like semiconductors and unsuccessfully in others like personal computers. Tables 3.3 and 3.4 show that during the 1990s, sectors like clothing and leather products Korean exports registered negative rate of growth and a decreasing weight on total manufacturing exports. (Table 3.5 shows the aggregation of macro-sectors).

Table 3.3 Korean selected exports rate of growth: 1992–1998 (%)

	1993	1994	1995	1996	1997	1998
Chemicals	10.1	24.5	34.6	4.2	13.0	–2.8
Yarn, fabrics and textiles	9.1	19.4	15.1	3.2	4.8	–15.4
Leather and leather products	–15.7	–6.7	–2.1	–8.5	–10.8	–22.8
Metal and other basic manuf. prod.	15.0	–5.8	24.9	–13.4	8.9	13.6
Non electric machinery	17.1	33.3	37.4	3.9	4.5	–6.8
Computers, telecomm; consumer electronics	9.7	12.0	16.9	5.1	–2.4	–12.6
Electronics components	15.2	46.7	57.3	–10.5	1.1	–4.9
Transport equipment	14.1	17.2	35.8	24.4	1.2	2.9
Clothing	–8.9	–8.3	–12.3	–14.8	–0.6	–10.9

Source: PC/TAS 1992–1998.

Table 3.4 Korean selected exports on total manufacturing exports: 1992–1998 (%)

	1992	1993	1994	1995	1996	1997	1998
Chemicals	7.9	8.1	8.7	9.1	9.4	10.4	10.4
Yarn, fabrics and textiles	11.5	11.7	12.0	10.7	11.0	11.2	9.8
Leather and leather products	6.8	5.3	4.2	3.2	2.9	2.5	2.0
Metal and other basic manufact.	10.2	10.9	8.8	8.5	7.3	7.8	9.1
Non electric machinery	4.7	5.1	5.9	6.3	6.5	6.6	6.4
Computers, telecomm; consumer electronics	13.5	13.8	13.3	12.1	12.6	12.0	10.8
Electronics components	15.1	16.2	20.3	24.9	22.2	21.8	21.5
Transport equipment	12.4	13.2	13.2	14.0	17.3	17.1	18.2
Clothing	9.5	8.0	6.3	4.3	3.6	3.5	4.0
Others mfg. products	8.4	7.7	7.3	6.9	7.2	7.1	7.8

Source: PC/TAS 1992–1998.

Table 3.5 Concordance for macro-sectors

Macro-sectors	Sectors (SITC Rev. 3)
Total Manufacturing	5-8
Chemicals	51-59, 62 excluded 232, 266, 267
Yarn, fabrics and textiles	65
Leather and leather products	61, 831, 851
Metal and other basic manuf. products	66-69
Non electric machinery	71-74
Computers, telecomm; cons. electronics	75-76
Electronics components	77
Transport equipment	78-79
Clothing	84
Others manufactured products	551, 63, 64, 667, 81, 87-89

Source: International Trade Center 2000.

In this way, Korea quickly lost competitiveness in the low value added markets but it did not so rapidly compensate the losses in high value added markets. An indicator of competitiveness, the index of *Revealed Comparative Advantage*[5] (RCA) (Balassa 1965) is presented in Table 3.6. Among labour-intensive sectors, leather products saw a decrease of RCA from 3.74 in 1992 to 1.31 in 1998, clothing from 2.12 to 1.01; while among more advanced sectors, only electronic components registered an RCA over 1, while computers and telecommunications saw a decrease from 1.28 to 0.91. Finally, transport equipment registered an increase, but from further calculations (not reported here) it appears that the largest contribution to exports comes from products like ships.[6]

On the import side, we can notice that the growing volume of some commodities is mainly related to the deep changes occurred in the Korean

Table 3.6 RCAs: manufacturing sectors

	1992	1993	1994	1995	1996	1997	1998
Chemicals	0.59	0.62	0.67	0.69	0.71	0.80	0.77
Yarn fabrics and textiles	2.76	2.92	3.01	2.79	2.98	3.07	2.84
Leather and leather products	3.74	2.84	2.29	1.86	1.68	1.52	1.31
Metal and other basic mfg. prod.	0.71	0.75	0.75	0.80	0.88	0.96	0.90
Non electric machinery	0.73	0.70	0.63	0.59	0.67	0.64	0.67
Computers, telecomm;							
consumer electronics	1.28	1.15	1.08	1.04	1.05	0.92	0.91
Electronics components	1.71	1.66	1.93	2.17	1.94	1.87	1.88
Transport equipment	1.81	1.93	1.99	2.18	2.71	2.70	2.94
Clothing	2.12	1.81	1.48	1.1	0.92	0.84	1.01

Source: PC/TAS 1992–1998.

internal demand. The increasing level of wealth, the higher wages and the end of the 'austerity policy' generated a substantial increase in the domestic demand of luxury goods, cars, electronic appliances (Tables 3.7 and 3.8). Most of this demand was in fact satisfied by made-in-Korea goods, but the increase in domestic production determined a rising demand of energy, doubling fuel imports from 1990 to 1997 (World Bank 1999).

The same applies to capital goods imports, which doubled in six years (World Bank 1999) suggesting that Korea was not yet able to produce its own equipment and that the level of imports for use in domestic production still reflected a strong high dependence on imported inputs (Tables 3.7 and 3.8 and Figure 3.1).

Table 3.7 Korean selected imports rate of growth: 1992–1998 (%)

	1993	1994	1995	1996	1997	1998
Chemicals	10.3	19.4	74.7	1.0	–1.1	–30.4
Yarn, fabrics and textiles	0.6	28.1	16.7	–3.0	–7.2	–37.6
Leather and leather products	7.6	30.7	–52.1	16.7	–14.4	–57.7
Metal and other basic manuf. prod.	–2.5	40.0	12.1	3.1	–11.9	–47.3
Non electric machinery	–4.6	27.8	99.4	7.2	–23.1	–52.3
Computers, telecomm; consumer electronics	–12.2	43.0	28.8	13.0	–6.4	–43.5
Electronics components	8.0	28.3	28.1	13.9	16.6	–15.1
Transport equipment	2.1	26.0	–47.8	12.4	–40.0	–48.1
Clothing	–6.8	41.8	–73.1	40.3	–7.4	–63.8

Source: PC/TAS 1992–1998.

Table 3.8 Korean selected imports on total manufacturing imports: 1992–1998 (%)

	1992	1993	1994	1995	1996	1997	1998
Chemicals	11.0	11.9	11.0	14.7	13.7	14.9	16.8
Yarn, fabrics and textiles	5.0	4.9	4.9	4.4	3.9	4.0	4.0
Leather and leather products	3.8	4.0	4.0	1.5	1.6	1.5	1.0
Metal and other basic mfg. prod.	11.9	11.4	12.3	10.6	10.2	9.9	8.4
Non electric machinery	17.3	16.3	16.0	24.5	24.5	20.7	15.9
Computers, telecomm; consumer electronics	7.8	6.7	7.4	7.4	7.7	8.0	7.3
Electronics components	5.3	5.6	5.5	16.2	17.2	22.0	30.2
Transport equipment	17.8	17.8	17.3	6.9	7.2	4.8	4.0
Clothing	5.8	5.3	5.8	1.2	1.5	1.5	0.9
Other mfg. products	14.3	16.1	15.8	12.6	12.5	12.7	11.5

Source: PC/TAS 1992–1998.

Figure 3.1 Manufacturing exports and machinery and transport equipment import rate of growth: 1993–1998 (%)

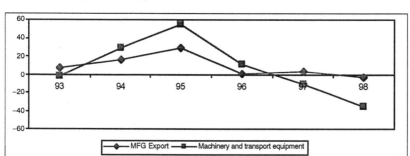

Source: PC/TAS 1992–1998.

Given the structural and continuous current account deficit of the Korean economy, its sustainability has also to be taken into analysis. A large current account deficit can be sustainable when it reflects continuous capital accumulation, high GDP growth, with expectation of high profitability and could therefore imply a sharp trade balance reversal in the long run. In the Korean case we can say that the trade imbalance was sustainable until 1996 when the country experienced a slowdown in GDP growth, together with an increasing trade deficit. Nevertheless, this event was generally not interpreted as a warning signal of an imminent unsustainability of the debt, because in the country the belief that economic expansion would be permanent was still very diffused.

As a matter of fact, during the 1990s the debt to GDP ratio grew very rapidly, in particular domestic banks borrowed heavily from foreign financial institutions in order to finance domestic investors. In general, it should be said that the high debt burden was not a new phenomenon in Korea and in fact the debt to GDP ratio was much higher in 1980 (48.5 per cent) than in 1996 (22.3 per cent) (World Bank 2000).

But there are some important differences in the debt structure, with the ratio of short-term debt increasing during the 1990s and in 1995 exceeding the long term ratio and within the longterm debt, the public or publicly guaranteed debt decreasing in favour of the private not guaranteed debt (Table 3.9).

The predominance of short term debt weakened the domestic financial system, increasing its dependence on the fluctuations of the international financial market. Moreover, the financial situation was aggravated by the peculiar role played by the banking system because foreign lending was not directly to firms, but went through national banks. Korean banks borrowed heavily short-term funds from foreign banks in foreign currency lending long term to the corporate sector in national currency. According to Kim (1999) in

Table 3.9 The structure of foreign debt (US$ million)

	1992	1993	1994	1995	1996	1997	1998
Total debt stock (EDT)	44156	47202	72414	85810	115803	136984	139097
Long-term debt (%)	74.1	75.2	56.7	46.0	42.5	59.8	87.0
Short-term debt (%)	26.9	25.8	43.3	54.0	57.5	39.2	13.0
EDT/GDP (%)	14.1	13.7	18.0	46.0	22.3	28.9	44.0
EDT/EXPORT (%)	49.1	42.0	63.1	56.7	73.7	81.1	86.9

Source: World Bank 2000.

October 1997, 64.4 per cent of the funds borrowed by merchant banks were short-term loans and 83.3 per cent of these funds were in long-term investments.

2.2   The main structural weaknesses of the financial and corporate sectors

The Korean financial system was affected by several structural distortions that emerged dramatically during the crisis. At the end of 1989, the liberalisation of capital markets, aimed at providing low-cost funds to finance the process of internationalisation of the corporate sector, was not matched with the creation of a solid framework of controls and supervision in order to push domestic financial institutions towards more appropriate international standards.

The list of inefficiencies of the Korean financial and banking sector could be very long, in general we can say that one of the main problems and the origin of most of the weaknesses was the substantial subordination of the financial sector to the corporate sector. This was the heritage of the process of bank privatisation, resulting in several cases in private banks effectively controlled by *chaebol*. Too often banks did not care very much about their own profitability, over-lending to large conglomerates outside traditional market criteria of credit allocation and financing investments of dubious profitability. The ultimate result was that the financial system never really checked the financial conditions of conglomerates reliant on short-term loans and did not watch over investment returns.

The result of this system is a pre-crisis share of non-performing loans (NPLs) as a proportion of total lending at 8 per cent (Corsetti, Pesenti, Roubini 1998). It may be worth to add that in Korea loans are classified as non-performing when they are six months or longer in arrears and only with insufficient collateral, while for instance in the USA, NPLs are loans three months or longer overdue, irrespective of collateral.

Moving on to the corporate sector, it is well known that Korea's biggest *chaebol* account for a very large part of the country's output and exports. From the 1970s to overcome the disadvantage of a small domestic market and to exploit the stable nature of mature technologies on which initial industrialisation strategy was to be built, the Korean government intentionally sustained the growth of large firms (Kim 1997). Moreover, the growing economy of the 1960s and 1970s provided opportunities to expand into new markets. The extent of diversification of Korean conglomerates is striking if compared with industrialised countries: 57 per cent of firms are diversified into unrelated sectors (while for instance in Germany the share is 18 per cent and in Japan 6.8 per cent) (World Bank 1999).

The government helped the capital formation as well as the diversification process, with little attention to long run profitability and strongly reducing *chaebol*'s incentives for efficiency. Entry barriers limited competition and credit was made available at a rate below the market.

Combining high investment rates and low profitability required an high degree of financing in the form of debt, because of the low capability of self-financing and the unwillingness of the main shareholders (often the founders or their relatives) to confront with the market. For all these reasons, Korean firms have been traditionally excessively leveraged as can be seen in Table 10. In 1996, the average debt-to-equity ratio for the top 30 *chaebol* was 333 per cent, much higher than in other advanced countries (the comparable figure for the USA is close to 100 per cent) (Corsetti, Pesenti, Roubini 1998). Given this excess of debt, *chaebol* were highly vulnerable to the fluctuation of the international economic environment and even a slight rise in interest rate or fall in sales was enough to damage profitability and generate anxiety among creditors.

Furthermore, the corporate sector was weakened by an intricate system of cross debt guarantees among affiliates of *chaebol*, with the result that well performing companies in the group were exposed to the effects of group's

Table 3.10 Financial conditions of top Korean chaebol at the end of 1996 (hundred million won and %)

Chaebol	Total asset	Debt	Sales	Net Profit	Debt/Equity Ratio
Samsung	508.6	370.4	601.1	1.8	268.2
Hyundai	531.8	433.2	680.1	1.8	439.1
Daewoo	342.1	263.8	382.5	3.6	337.3
LG	370.7	287.7	466.7	3.6	346.5
Hanjin	139.0	117.9	87.0	−1.9	556.9
Kia	141.6	118.9	121.0	−1.3	523.6
Ssangyong	158.1	127.0	194.5	−1.0	409.0

Source: Corsetti, Pesenti, Roubini 1998.

group's poor performance. According to Kim (1999) before the crisis, the cross debt guarantees of the 30 major conglomerates reached 67.5 trillion won.

In such a system, managers and controlling shareholders had little interest in improving the efficiency of their companies because they became accustomed to the government overprotection. Besides, internal supervision remained weak and minority shareholders did not have enough power to play any real checking role.

To conclude, in the pre-crisis Korean economic system the tight relationships among the largest conglomerates, the financial sector and a benevolent government boosted both domestically and internationally the conviction that *chaebol* were 'too big to fail', generating a moral hazard problem which has magnified the financial vulnerability of the country.

3. THE CRISIS AND THE IMF INTERVENTION

At the beginning of 1997, Korea disclosed the first evident signals of economic distress during the strong struggle between workers and government on the new labour bill. Moreover, on January 1997 the 14th largest *chaebol*, Hanbo, went bankrupt, opening a period of several breakdowns of other important groups like Sammi, Jinro, Daiong and Ssangyong Motor. Immediately, the crisis extended to the financial sector as well, due to the increase in non-performing loans.

Meanwhile, the international investors' concern was raised by the deterioration of macroeconomic conditions in Thailand, Indonesia and Malaysia. A series of speculative attacks generated a diffused financial panic in the region. The announcement of the intention by the Korean government to guarantee foreign liabilities of domestic banks was not enough for reassuring investors. After that the KIA group, the 8th largest *chaebol*, was also put under protection, being unable to pay 370 million US$ worth of liabilities, the speculative pressure became very heavy and in November the won plunged by 25 per cent during the month.

Following the rapid devaluation of won, banks and non banking financial institutions had to cope with foreign lenders refusing the roll-over of short-term credits and domestic borrowers unable to pay interests and to repay loans. In early December, the crisis rapid degeneration led the Korean government to sign a 60b US$ IMF-led rescue package, the biggest in the history of stand-by-credits.

The stand-by agreement (IMF 1997 and IMF-Letter of Intent 1997) included three macro points (Macroeconomic Policies, Structural Policies, Other Structural Measures) aimed at solving two different levels of problems: first of all, the immediate objective was to stabilise the exchange rate and restore market confidence after the turmoil; secondly, it was designed to address the underlying structural weaknesses of Korean economy. The main measures prescribed by the IMF can be summarised as follows:

- **Macroeconomic Policies.** To stabilise the exchange rate and prevent any second round inflationary effects from the depreciation of the won, the IMF imposed monetary tightening, high interest rates and fiscal tightening.
- **Structural Policies.** These included measures aimed at restructuring and reforming the financial sector and the corporate sector, increasing transparency and market orientation, improving supervision in the case of the financial sector and promoting greater foreign competition in both sectors.
- **Other structural measures.** These incorporated the reform of labour market to enhance flexibility and the improvement of social protection to mitigate the impact of the crisis. Besides, IMF required the elimination of most of trade and capital barriers, giving up all protectionist policies adopted by Korea to preserve the internal market and the domestic ownership.

4. THE LOOSENING OF MONETARY AND FISCAL POLICY AND THE MACROECONOMIC RECOVERY

At the early stages of the crisis, the IMF demanded the central bank to fix the call-rate at 30 per cent and to bring down the growth of total liquidity from 18 per cent to 13.5 per cent (IMF-Letter of Intent 1997). Those measures were intended to improve trade balance through reduced imports, to encourage foreign capital inflows by re-establishing market confidence and to stabilise the exchange rate. The strategy implemented was to intervene on credit and interest rate rather than exchange rate because the level of foreign reserves was too low for pegging the currency to an established level (IMF 1999).

But the tightening of monetary policy generated unforeseen events. In fact, it was effective to control the borrowing of highly loan dependent enterprises and to push out of the market low profit marginal companies but at the same time it generated a credit crunch, affecting profitable enterprises with cash flow problems and deteriorated the debt structure of many groups, delaying in some cases the restructuring process and increasing the burden of NPLs (SERI 1999; Feldstein 1998).

The collateral effects of monetary policy have been the subject of an intense debate between economists. On one side, there are those who blamed the tight monetary policy for deteriorating the economic situation and leading to a vicious cycle of high interest rates, causing a worsening of the enterprise debt structure. This led to a deterioration of financial institution performance, which caused a credit crunch, delayed business restructuring and brought on widespread banking and corporate bankruptcies (SERI 1999; Kim 1999).

On the other side, there are those who defended the high interest rate policy, because first of all, it reduced excessive financing of conglomerates, second it favoured an increase in foreign investments and prevented further outflows of domestic ones and finally, it improved the current account balance by reducing imports (Corsetti, Pesenti, Roubini 1998). The IMF itself defended stubbornly its policy, arguing that it had contained the explosion of inflation, without causing a collapse of credit volumes and expediting the stabilisation of won (IMF 1999).

Clearly, the high interest rate policy has contributed to the stabilisation of the foreign exchange market, preventing domestic financial institutions from purchasing dollars on the domestic exchange market borrowing low interest won. Nevertheless, as the situation progressively deteriorated, the requests of the IMF became less and less restrictive over time (IMF-Letters of Intent 1998). In 1998, the Korean economy experienced the severest recession in thirty years. Output growth plunged to negative 6.7 per cent and unemployment more than tripled (Table 3.1). From the second quarter of 1998, concerned with the deep recession and the string of bankruptcies in the bank and corporate sectors, the IMF revised the inflation targets and eased the monetary policy by allowing the central bank to lower the call rate. On October 1998, the IMF handed over the control on monetary policy to the Bank of Korea (BOK), which progressively pursued an expansionary monetary policy.

Moving on to fiscal policy, initially the IMF required a tightening in order to counter the expected deterioration of the fiscal balance and to build room for a non inflationary financing of the financial sector restructuring. The fiscal policy was formulated within an expected contest of positive, although reduced, growth. The unexpected deepness of economic recession changed dramatically the assessment of the situation and the role of fiscal policy shifted immediately to support the internal demand and to counter the large fall of private consumption and investments. Furthermore, the severity of fiscal policy was relaxed to counter the huge unemployment rate with social policies and public investments.[7]

Also concerning fiscal policy, analysts tend to disagree about the adequacy of the IMF interventions. Some argued that the Korean low ratio of public debt to GDP did not justify the strictness of the IMF requirements for fiscal policy. Moreover, they criticised the excessive slowness in revising the established plans when the situation drastically changed and anti-cycle policies became unavoidable (SERI 1999). On the other hand, IMF supporters underlined the negative effect that a loose fiscal policy would have caused in markets' confidence, in credibility and in policy makers' commitments to reduce current account imbalances (Corsetti, Pesenti, Roubini 1998).

In 1999, thanks to looser monetary and fiscal policies and a more robust international demand, Korean economy began to recover. GDP grew by 10.7 per cent, unemployment fell slightly and private consumption and investment grew steadily (Table 3.1 and Figure 3.2). Furthermore, inflation increased only

Figure 3.2 Consumption, investment and GDP rate of growth: 1997–1999 (%)

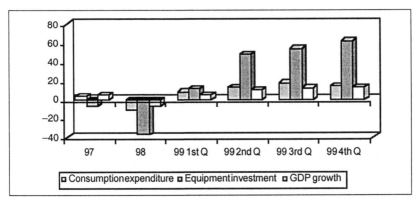

Source: BOK 2000.

by 0.8 per cent, kept under control thanks to the progressive appreciation of won on the dollar registered during 1999.

Manufacturing export, the engine of the recovery, climbed by 12 per cent and Korea recorded an impressive trade surplus of 24.5 billions of dollars even if imports begin to soar (29 per cent) after the 1998 slowdown (Figure 3.3). The sectors showing a sustained trend in exports are cars, computers and telecommunications.

On the capital side, after the success of liberalisation process, foreign inflows increased, mostly under the form of foreign direct investments (FDI's) or purchase of Korean assets (Figure 3.4). This process underpins a steady rise in foreign exchange reserves, hardly reduced during the crisis.

Figure 3.3 Import and export values: 1996–2000 2nd Q (million US$)

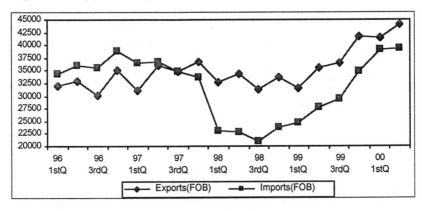

Source: BOK 2000.

Figure 3.4 Foreign direct investment: 1996–2000 (million US$)

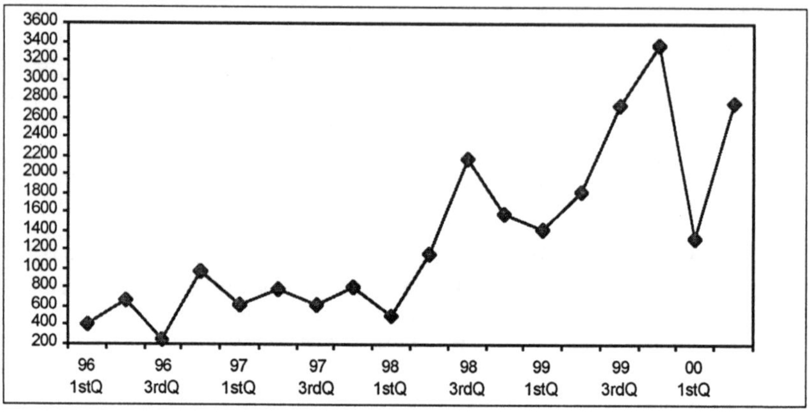

Source: BOK 2000.

Given these early positive signs of macroeconomic recovery, a frequently asked question is the contribution to economic upturn of structural reforms which were part of the agreement signed with IMF. In the next paragraph we will analyse how far the implementation of these reforms has gone.

5. STRUCTURAL REFORMS: WHERE ARE THEY NOW?

The structural reform plan is based on two fundamental principles: a) exposing the economy more fully to world competition and b) introducing more effective governance structures into financial institutions and the corporate sector. Its implementation is therefore aimed at substituting the interventionist role of the government of the past with a market-based paradigm. Establishing such a paradigm requires first a rehabilitation of the corporate and the financial sectors, a reform of the public sector as well as an increased liberalisation in goods and capital markets and improvement in labour market regulations.

5.1 The corporate sector reform

At the beginning of 1998 the government and the chairmen of the five top *chaebol* (Hyundai, Samsung, Daewoo, LG and SK) agreed upon five major principles for corporate restructuring: 1) enhancing the transparency of corporate management, 2) clearing cross debt guarantees between affiliate companies, 3) improving the financial structure of companies, 4) concentrating on core businesses and encouraging co-operation among large conglomerates and small and medium-sized enterprises and 5) strengthening the responsibility of major shareholders and managers (SERI 2000).

Given these general tasks, different restructuring approaches were applied according to the scale of the conglomerates: the top five *chaebol* were to follow a program named the 'Big Deal' while for the 6th to 64th largest conglomerates the program was named the 'Workout Program'. The main reason for dividing small from top conglomerates in their reform efforts is that smaller *chaebol* and small and medium-sized companies suffered very strongly from credit crunch during the financial crisis and therefore the government's first efforts were to restore their creditworthiness. While in the case of the top five, the most important reasons to reform were other than creditworthiness, given that they did not have problems obtaining funds, even during the financial crisis (Kim 1999).

In the rest of this paragraph we analyse first of all some of the general changes introduced in the legal and regulatory framework aimed at improving the incentive system for debt restructuring and removing impediments to corporate reform and then we examine the implementation of restructuring in the 6-64 *chaebol* and finally in the top five conglomerates.

5.1.1 The reform of the legal and regulatory framework

Starting from February 1998 over the course of the next twelve months the government laid out a quick succession of measures aimed at fulfilling the five tasks initially agreed with the corporate sector.

Concerning the enhancement of transparency, the government required the appointment of external auditors, strengthening their responsibility and the introduction of consolidated financial statements conforming with international standards, especially to the top five *chaebol*.

On financial structure side, from April 1998 cross debt guarantees among affiliates were forbidden and accordingly financial institutions were prohibited from demanding cross guarantees from corporate borrowers. The common practice of cross debt guarantees among affiliates belonging to the same conglomerate was in fact considered both by the government and the IMF as one of the major causes for banks' huge losses during the financial crisis, because a company's financial trouble might lead to the bankruptcy of the entire group (Kim 1999). In addition in order to pressurise firms to seek workouts, prudential limits on large exposures were tightened and emergency or rescue loans were curtailed (World Bank 1999).

The Korean government provided incentives for financial restructuring as well. Key changes include: quality improvement of bankruptcy act, liberalisation of the mergers and acquisitions (M&A) regime (including allowing hostile take over by foreigners); introduction of tax incentives on asset sales and opening of the real estate market to foreigners' firms.

Finally concerning the responsibility of major shareholders and managers, the government required enterprises listed on the stock exchange to appoint and empower outside directors and it approved the right of institutional investors to vote (Kim 1999). Within the first year, 752 listed companies had assigned outside directors. Nevertheless according to Kim (2000a), many companies hired their friends to the board but hopefully in the future it will be different if institutional investors and minority shareholders will have the right to recommend outside directors.

5.1.2   The 6-64 reform

As said before, for the *chaebol* ranking from 6th to 64th and for small and medium-sized enterprises the main objective of intervention has been to restore creditworthiness. In the Korean government opinion, the 6-64 *chaebol* and the other smaller companies were too weak to reform, so it was decided that the financial sector should take the lead in promoting the workout plans, providing needed financial support (Kim 1999).

A Corporate Restructuring Agreement (CRA), concerning the workout procedures, was signed on June 1998 by some 200 Korean banks and non-bank financial institutions. These procedures included the appointment of a lead bank negotiating the workouts with the major corporate groups and the establishment of a control body in the form of the Corporate Restructuring Co-ordination Committee (CRCC). The companies were called to agree a Capital Structure Improvement Plan (CSIP) with their banks in order to reduce the debt-to-equity ratio to 200 per cent by the end of 1999. If financial institutions could not agree on a workout strategy among themselves, or the lead bank and the debtor could not reach an agreement, the CRCC had to resolve these differences. The Financial Supervisory Commission (FSC) monitored the restructuring plans agreed under the CRA to ensure consistency with the guidelines issued for the workouts.

As underlined by the World Bank (1999), since the threat of bankruptcy became likely as a consequence of the new legal framework, the CRA process succeeded in encouraging corporate restructuring: by mid 1999, 90 companies had applied to the formal workout program within the CRCC framework. About half of them were subsidiaries of 16 *chaebol*; 7 out of 90 companies dropped out at some point, leaving 83 companies in the program. All but 2 of the 83 companies have by now reached an agreement on a debt resolution plan. These plans were based on the London rules type of out-of-court settlement (Kawai 2000).

The terms of the workouts have featured a combination of interest rate reduction (65 per cent of the transactions), capitalisation of interest and deferral of the principal with very little conversion of debt into equity (5 per cent) or convertible bonds (7 per cent). These last measures were in fact strongly sponsored by government in order to increase the banking system control on the corporate sector. Nevertheless in practice, they were constrained by several disincentives: first of all, banks could not dispose freely of equity stakes and distressed assets; second, they had to offer excessively generous conditions of buyback, hampering the growth of a secondary market for these bonds; and finally, in most of the cases outside investors were excluded from acquiring stakes because conglomerates did not want to lose control of their shares.

Given that the restructuring has been mainly based on rescheduling and interest reduction, according to the World Bank (1999) it is unlikely to lead to sustainable financial positions. Moreover, most of the operational reforms have been obtained through a pure reduction of labour costs, with little sale of assets and disposition of affiliates, confirming the reservations with regard to long term sustainability of the reform.

5.1.3 The reform of the top five chaebol

Differently from other restructuring programs, the top five bailout began later and produced evidences only from the beginning of 1999. There are many reasons for this delay, in particular it is important to stress a point we made before: the credit crunch and the tight monetary policy forced the smaller *chaebol* to agree to the workout program because otherwise many of them could not avoid the bankruptcy but they did not produce the same effect on the biggest conglomerates. At the end of 1998, the top five *chaebol* still controlled 30 per cent of total loans (KIEP 1998) and did not suffer from the credit crunch because banks and non financial institutions did not give up lending to them.

Since their privatisation in the 1980s, the banking and non banking systems fell progressively under the control of the main corporate groups (Seo 2000), through a complex mechanism of cross ownership that allowed the large *chaebol* to purchase shares well above the legal 5 per cent. In this way, the subordination of the financial system to the corporate sector continued also after the end of public ownership of the banking system. Large groups obtained funds through almost unlimited banking lending, without risking any contest by foreign or domestic capital. Furthermore, profitability and viability of the financial sector have been systematically overlooked in order to sustain the *chaebol* expansion.

At the end of 1998, it was clear that the voluntary top 5 workout had failed and that the government should take the initiative (Kim 1999). The Korean government, fearing another financial crisis, was finally persuaded to get a move on with the restructuring process of the top five *chaebol* and to try to end the dangerous liaison between financial institutions and conglomerates.

In December 1998, the government jointly with the Financial Supervisory Commission, the Fair Trade Commission, the main creditor banks and the 5 top conglomerates reached an agreement, amending the previous ones and outlining a specific program of restructuring based on *chaebol*'s problems and necessities.

First of all, the top five agreed on a heavy reduction of their debt accepting the target of reducing the debt-to-equity ratio to 200 per cent by the end of 1999 (World Bank 1999). The objective could be reached by selling off affiliates, attracting foreign capital as well as converting part of their banking loans into equity capital (debt-to-equity swap) in order to strengthen banking control on debt restructuring.

Second, the top five were recommended to eliminate all the existing cross debt guarantees by March 2000, while banks have refused them since the end of 1998. Accordingly, the top five and their banks should revise the Capital Structure Improvement Plan including the new targets for debt, cross guarantees and business restructuring. Furthermore, they should disclose as much as possible the contents of these CSIPs in order to ease controls.

Third, they agreed on a re-organisation plan, the so-called 'Big Deal', aimed at redefining core competencies of each group, reducing and rationalising the areas of overlapping investments. The top 5 had to select from among 3 to 5 core sectors and focus their investment plans on these areas, selling affiliates in the other sectors. The government specifically requested a re-organisation in the following strategic sectors: semiconductors, railroad rolling stocks, petrochemicals, aerospace, power generation facilities, ship engines, oil refining, cars and electronics.

Finally, large *chaebol* also accepted to enhance management transparency, to increase the power of their board of directors and to strengthen the minority shareholders' rights.

The assessment of the restructuring process is a very hard task because not all targets have been reached and when there are results it is difficult to judge their real impact on the corporate system (Kim 1999). The first important consideration is that from 1999 the top 5 were reduced to 4 after the crisis of Daewoo, the second largest conglomerate with businesses in cars, heavy industries, electronics, telecommunications, construction, trade, finance and hotels. Daewoo did not meet the debt reduction targets or financially restructure, thus collapsing under a spectacular debt of 80 billion dollars. As a consequence of the default, Daewoo was broken up into 12 separate independent businesses.

In the government opinion, the most advanced part of restructuring is the re-organisation of the strategic sectors. The process involved 16 companies, belonging to 4 among the five top conglomerates and 3 non-top five *chaebol* (SERI 2000). At the end of March 2000, mergers and take-overs were completed in semiconductors, oil refining, aerospace and railways while in other industries like cars and electronics progress was slower (MOFE 2000) (Table 3.11).

Nevertheless, the program did not go through in the form of business swaps, as initially intended by the government, but it rather ended up with a mere consolidation in which companies took over other companies or jointly

Table 3.11 The 'Big Deal'

Chaebol	Hyundai	Samsung	Daewoo	LG	SK
Core sectors	Cars, electronics, heavy chemicals, constructions, financial services	Electronics, financial services, trade	Trade, constructions, cars, heavy industry, financial services	Chemical products energy, electronics, telecommu- nications, financial services	Chemical products, energy, financial services, information and telecommu- nications, constructions, whole sale trade
No. of affiliates before the bailout	63	65	41	53	42
No. of affiliates after the bailout	30	40	10	30	20

Source: KIEP 1998.

created a new company (SERI 2000). Another problem stressed by Kim (1999) is the abuse of mergers as an instrument for simply reducing the number of affiliates and in this way showing a willingness to reform to obtain economic incentives, without really implementing restructuring.

Furthermore, and very significantly, mergers and acquisitions within *chaebol* have not encouraged the creation of a competitive environment but rather in some cases they have increased monopolistic concentration of markets. For this reason the attempt, strongly supported by financial institutions, to reduce the power of large conglomerates enhancing competition, has failed and in some cases obtained the opposite result of increasing market concentration.

With regard to debt restructuring process, there is not agreement on achievements among governmental sources and other observers. According to the government, the debt reduction problem is over, because, excluding Daewoo, the other top conglomerates have more or less reached the target, but it is not specified if results were obtained with or without assets revaluation (MOFE 2000).

According to the World Bank (1999) the situation is less optimistic: it agrees with the government about the success of debt reduction in 4 *chaebol* (again except Daewoo) but it is quite sceptical about the way in which the conglomerates reduced their debt, underlining that there is a gap between debt to equity ratio with (235 per cent) and without assets revaluation (302 per cent). Furthermore, the World Bank expresses some concern regarding the over-expansion of the largest *chaebol* in the non-banking sector, and particularly in investment trust companies, through which the conglomerates have been able to collect increasing funds.

In agreement Kim (1999) argues that the *chaebol* expansion in the non-banking sector has been the most successful way for conglomerates to reduce their debt to equity ratio. Since the abolition of the limit on cross-shareholding, investment trust companies provided financial support to affiliated companies to purchase stocks in other affiliates, instead of using the money to pay off their debt. Without consolidated statements and controls on non-banking financial institutions, the mechanism of cross-shareholding has allowed conglomerates and their affiliates to reduce their debt-to-equity ratio increasing the denominator instead of reducing debt. The system is that everybody, it seems, will sink or swim together: if company A, an affiliate in conglomerate X, uses cash to increase its equity holdings in company B, a co-affiliate in X, and company B does the same in co-affiliate C and company C does likewise in A, the result should show an improvement in the debt-to-equity ratio of all three companies.

Analysing Fair Trade Commission data, Kim (1999) shows that *chaebol* have in fact greatly reduced debt-to-equity ratio, but the total amount of debt is increased during 1999, suggesting that the mechanism described above is supported by strong evidence.

More concrete results have been obtained in cross-guaranteed debt reduction. The top five conglomerates have been able to reduce 11 trillion won debt from April 1997 to December 1999 by repayment of loans as well as by paying higher interest rates to creditor banks and converting the cross guaranteed debt to creditor loans given their high credit rating (SERI 2000).

Finally, analysing improvement in management style within family-centred conglomerates there are some positive signals of change. A significant case is the succession at Hyundai, Korean biggest *chaebol*, where after a long family fight the old founder took the very un-Confucian step of appointing the younger son to succeed him. Immediately, the new chairman announced that he would fill half Hyundai's board with outside directors and from then onwards this board would decide management issues.

In conclusion it could be said that it is quite premature to claim that the reforming process is ended, because the main structural problems that affected the Korean corporate sector are still unsolved and still unclear are the consequences of the increasing monopolistic structure of the Korean economic system. Large conglomerates continue to have enormous economic power and are still structures too much diversified in many unrelated business areas.

The legal framework has been undoubtedly amended, shareholders are more protected and their opinion formally should be considered by management, which now, theoretically, it is less dependent on ownership, but it remains a large distance between law and the common practice, and a long and deep cultural revolution will be necessary in order to break with previous customs.

On the supervision side, the Financial Supervisory Commission and the Fair Trade Commission have acquired more power and have more instruments for enhancing market transparency and competitiveness but it is yet not clear if these independent commissions could really pursue their targets openly and without constraints.

It is difficult to say if new elements, introduced in the Korean corporate system consequently to the crisis will prevail over old elements and how the renewed system will perform, but such a broad restructuring process for giving important results will definitely require more time than the 3 years of IMF tutelage.

5.2   The financial sector restructuring

The financial sector, hardly hurt by the crisis explosion, was indicated by many parts as the weakest element of the Korean economic system. Therefore, all financial institutions, banking and non banking, were involved in a deep and broad restructuring program aimed at modifying the most peculiar characteristic of Korean capitalism: the tangled web of relationships among financial and corporate sectors. As said before, the process of bank privatisation of the 1980s generated as a side effect the total subordination of the financial sector to the corporate sector, obstructing its autonomy and the pursuing of its own profitability.

A particularly serious problem was the lack of supervision and control on financial systems. Only in April 1998, by unifying all control agencies, an autonomous agency was set up, the Financial Supervisory Commission (FSC), aimed at supervising the financial system as well as the financial activities of the corporate sector, avoiding the fragmentation of competencies that affected the previous system of supervision.

During 1998, the government pressed ahead energetically with financial restructuring because it recognised that, in the wake of the currency crisis, the first priority was the stabilisation of the financial market and the restoration of external confidence. For this reason, financial institutions no longer viable because excessive non-performing loans (NPLs) were closed down and those still profitable were quickly restructured through re-capitalisation and the purchase of their NPLs by the government.

For carrying out the restructuring of the financial sector the government set up the Korean Asset Manger Corporation (KAMCO) which bought the worst non-performing loans at a favourable price, giving in exchange to banks KAMCO bonds, saleable in the market. KAMCO mandate also included corporate restructuring, asset recovery and asset sales. In 1998 in order to promote the re-capitalisation of banks and to buy NPLs problems, the government injected more than 30 trillion won through KAMCO. Nevertheless also according to the World Bank (1999), KAMCO has been very effective in purchasing bad loans, but the process of asset disposal has been quite slow.

Moving on to the banking system, the reform was very rapidly implemented because of the extreme gravity of the situation (Kawai 2000). On 30 December 1997, all banks were required to present a credible restructuring plan for meeting standards set by the Bank of International Settlements in terms of capitalisation to an evaluation committee, composed by experts of the Bank of Korea and by the end of June the Capital Adequacy Ratio had to reach 6 per cent (IMF-Letters of Intent 1997, 1998). The institutions which did not meet the required standards were immediately shut down. The government immediately gave a strong signal in this direction by shutting down 14 insolvent merchant banks and after a second round of bank evaluation as other 9 merchant banks were closed. Furthermore at the end of June 1998, 5 commercial banks were deemed non viable and subsequently acquired by 5 stronger banks. In early 1999, two main commercial banks in distress, Korea First and Seoul, were nationalised. Later a controlling stake of 51 per cent of one of them, Korea First, was sold by the government to US based Newbridge Capital. At the end of July 1999, 252 financial institutions, or 12 per cent of the total number of domestic financial institutions went out of existence as a results of restructuring measures (Table 3.12).

Table 3.12 Number of out-of-business financial institutions as a result of financial sector restructuring (at the end of July 1999)

	Total no. of institutions (at the end of 1997)	Out of business
Banks	33	10
Merchant Banks	30	19
Securities Firms	36	6
Insurance Co.	50	5
Investment Trust Co.	31	7
Leasing Co.	25	5
Mutual Savings & Finance Co.	231	36
Credit Unions	1666	164
Total	2102	252

Source: SERI 2000.

After the first round of reform mainly concentrated on emergency measures, the government announced the beginning of a second stage aimed more at long-period transformations and, according with the new targets of monetary policy, it provided a huge injection of funds. By the end of 1999 the amount of public funds injected in the financial system reached 64 trillion won (US$49.2 billion or 14 per cent of GDP) and 69.5 per cent went into commercial banks (SERI 2000).

The second stage is characterised by an accelerated process of mergers with healthier banks, promoted and financially sustained by the government and at the end of 1999 four mergers were successfully completed (SERI 2000).

Foreign capital has also been actively advancing into the domestic financial system. In the commercial banking industry, the market share of those banks, in terms of deposits and loans, in which foreigners are the number one majority shareholder, amounts to 42 per cent (SERI 2000). Foreign equity participation in commercial banks may play a crucial role in introducing more modern market-oriented techniques, accountability and transparency in the financial sector.

With regard to non-banking financial institutions, in 1998 the FSC announced a restructuring plan for insurance, investment trusts, leasing and securities companies. By the end of November 1998, the total number of non-banking financial institutions shut down was 39 but a large number of insolvent institutions were still operating. Since the beginning of 1999, governmental directions for the non-banking sector followed the same path of bank restructuring, shifting its attention from short term and emergency to enhancing competitiveness and strengthening of capital structure. As happened for the banking sector, mergers, foreign capital attraction and asset sales were therefore encouraged.

Nevertheless, it is opportune to stress that the implementation of reforms in the non-financial institutions has been rather effective in securities and insurance companies, but less so in leasing and investment trust companies. Particularly, the reform was postponed several times and never really implemented in investment trust companies, strongly bounded by cross-shareholdings to the conglomerates and characterised by over lending to the corporate sector and huge capital losses.

Attempting a general assessment of the financial reform, we agree with the World Bank (1999) that the restructuring is far from complete. A very important result is a clear signal to the market that the myth of Korean banks never going bankrupt is over. Banks appear financially healthier thanks to their re-capitalisation, the sale of NPLs and the strong infusion of public and foreign funds but long term reforms such as the rationalisation of staff and branches, the improvement of corporate governance have at best just begun. Operational restructuring is a necessary condition if banks want to become profitable as they move forward. Moreover, in the non-banking financial sector restructuring efforts have been rather limited to date and most of these institutions are still distressed.

There are also doubts about the regime of rescheduled and restructured loans because the common practice in Korea is to consider them as performing unless the borrower defaults again, while internationally they are not considered under control until the borrower has made a minimum number of payments. Therefore, there are risks of loading again the banking system with potentially non-performing loans and of a general weakening of prudential rules.

We also agree with other studies (Kim 1999; SERI 2000; Kim 2000a) warning about the excessive role of the government in the restructuring process. To stop the deterioration of the financial sector and end the credit crunch, the government had to intervene with a huge infusion of public funds; there is a risk that this could continue to stimulate moral hazard behaviour and limit the growth of managerial autonomy and accountability in financial institutions.

In addition, banks have in the past not really been free to allocate credit according to market criteria because the government has several times forced them to prop up companies facing difficulties. In the case of Daewoo, before it defaulted, banks had to roll over their bonds for quite some time with losses estimated at 10.4 billion of dollars (Asian Development Bank 2000). Had the banks been allowed to call in loans sooner, they might have lost less. The recent default of Daewoo Motors (November 2000) following the refusal of the state-owned Korea Development Bank, their biggest creditor, to supply any more loans, may be a signal that the government now intends to step out of lending even if this involves letting insolvent companies go bust.

To conclude, as underlined for the corporate sector it will take some time for new practices to consolidate but Korean banks strongly need to build a stronger credit culture – sound corporate governance, prudent risk management and sound lending practices. Without these measures, re-capitalisation of banks can simply result in a repetition of inefficient injections of capital (Kawai 2000).

5.3   The public sector reform

Many attempts have been made to reform public sector administration before the onset of the crisis but they were not very successful. Despite radical changes in the political and economic environment since the beginning of the Korean economic development, the government continued to function as a development state, intervening frequently in the market and hampering continuously the development of a real free market economy.

After the election of President Kim Dae Jung in 1998, the new administration set as a priority the public sector reform and the simplification of the regulatory system. The explosion of the crisis and the big consensus accorded to the first really democratic administration represented the opportunity to bring about major reforms in the public sector. The government established a reform office with the precise purpose of engineering public sector reform and placed it directly under the Minister of Planning and Budget.

The reform has been undertaken in a new way, first of all, during the working out process, the government consulted private organisations, breaking with a tradition of not transparent and 'not in partnership' reform path. Second, in contrast with previous attempts, the government enhanced a really comprehensive reform which concerned simultaneously: a) central and local government, b) state owned enterprises (SOEs) and c) quasi-governmental organisations, excluding only political and judiciary division.

a) The administration tried to reorganise itself, selecting four specific goals: the principle of customer orientation, entrepreneurial government management in order to raise productivity, flexible and transparent administration and empowerment of civil servants.

Two ways were pursued: a structural adjustment to enhance particular functions or eliminate duplications and a progressive transfer of central government functions to local governments even through the outsourcing and the privatisation of some activities.

The first solution has implied a massive reduction of expenses (US$3 billion) and also a huge downsizing of employees. According to Kim (2000b) the elimination of duplicated functions and restructuring in local and central governments will result respectively in 19 per cent and 16 per cent reduction of workforce by the end of 2001.

The second one is still a work in progress, but the first results are: 23 functions of central government are being transferred to local government and 88 functions have already been outsourced (Kim 2000b).

After a year of structural reforms, the government is now focusing on the operating system reform which includes a new more performance-based management career system, an increasing ministry autonomy, the introduction of various measures to improve flexibility and efficiency and finally the increased adoption of information technology.

b) Korea had a far smaller number of state owned enterprises than other newly industrialised countries, in 1998 there were 26 SOEs and 82 subsidiaries, with a total of 166 000 employees (Kim 2000b).

Public enterprises were affected by the typical problems owed to the state ownership: inefficiency because of the monopolistic structure, subordination to bureaucracy control rather than market mechanisms, organisational rigidity, low attention to profitability and excessive reliance on state help and a consequent moral hazard attitude.

The government has tried to privatise about 40 per cent of total SOEs and by the end of 2000 this process will be concluded. For the remaining 60 per cent the government has undertaken a management reform that implied a drastic reduction of unprofitable and overlapping investments and a withdrawal from sectors where the private sector is performing well. The government tried to give more autonomy to SOEs management, to incentive performance evaluation and to encourage management renewal. The recruitment is now managed by selected committees and not directly by the government, in order to hire the most qualified and independent persons (Kim 2000b).

c) In the quasi-governmental sector, which includes government supported research institutes, public organisations such as the Consumer Protection Agency and agencies with different tasks on behalf of the government, the new administration intervened immediately after the crisis, reorganising the management, closing agencies with redundant tasks and trying to encourage self-financing.

The restructuring process is not yet completed and it is possible to quantify the effect of the reform only in the case of research institutes: according to Kim (2000b), in 1999 almost 100 million US$ has been saved.

The first stage of reforms is now concluded with more or less success. According to Linsu Kim (2000b) the incumbent administration has accomplished more changes in the SOEs and quasi-governmental organisations than in the government sector, because of internal resistance and the bureaucracy strength to delay the restructuring process.

From the end of 2000, the government will pursue a second stage with new challenges. After the restructuring process, a deep change is now necessary in the organisational culture of public sector, more compatible with the logic of the new management systems, introduced in the past years. The risk is that without a cultural change, the new organisational framework will not be implemented and the public sector will regress back to an inefficient and expensive bureaucracy.

5.4   The capital and goods liberalisation

Traditionally, Korean markets have been characterised by a low degree of competition, largely closed to foreign goods access and capitals. Since the 1980s, there had been a steady, albeit selective and very slow, liberalisation of the trade regime. The simple effective tariff rate declined from nearly 7 per cent in 1988 to about 4.5 per cent in 1996 (World Bank 1999).

Nonetheless, Korea maintained formal non-tariff barriers, including a set of quantitative restrictions and a second set under the Import Diversification Program that protected domestic producers by restricting imports from specific countries.

Concerning foreign direct investments, they were not allowed in some strategic sectors, listed in the so called 'negative list' and in general foreign control on Korean firms had always been discouraged by imposing ceilings on foreign equity ownership.

The 1997 crisis changed radically the situation given that the acceleration of deregulation and trade liberalisation were among the priority issues on the IMF reform agenda. By the end of 1998, the aggregated ceiling on foreign investment in Korean equities was removed and from then foreign investors can buy freely equities in the domestic stock market for the purpose of mergers and acquisitions.[8] As a matter of fact, Korean companies quoted in the stock market are for the first time contestable.

Furthermore, important changes have been also introduced in financing, because since the end of December 1997 restrictions on foreign borrowing were removed and Korean firms can now borrow directly abroad, avoiding brokerage of the domestic banking system, and foreign banks and brokerage houses can establish subsidiaries in Korea.

Also in the trade sector the impact of the crisis has been an acceleration of liberalisation reforms. All trade related subsidies have been abolished and the Import Diversification Program has been phased out at the end of 1999, giving place to a progressive harmonisation of Korean trade procedures to WTO standards.

In general, international financial organisations have positively assessed the efforts made by the Korean government in liberalising markets, but they have also stressed the importance to keep on with more liberalisation for instance in the service sector, which is still highly protected from foreign competition (World Bank 1999). Furthermore, many markets are still burdened by cumbersome and complex regulations, like redundant tests, imposition of more stringent requirements on imports than on domestic products, and delays in product certifications.

To conclude, it may be useful to refer to a concern of the World Bank (1999), underlining that the deregulation process should eliminate rents and encourage competition but it should be careful not to dismantle useful regulations, particularly in the field of health, environment and product standards.

5.5 The labour market reform

Some efforts for enhancing labour market flexibility had been already undertaken early before the crisis, when the parliament approved a reform of the labour bill that provoked an explosion of strikes and the strong opposition of the two main trade unions. After three months of tough social strife, an agreement was reached, liberalising substantially the labour market in exchange for the legalisation of the second main Korean trade union.

The period between the end of this social conflict and the intervention of the IMF was a difficult one for workers, because the increasingly bad situation in the corporate sector threatened many jobs. Furthermore, the situation was made even worse by the fact that mass unemployment was a new experience in Korea and there did not yet exist a social safety net scheme.

The IMF requirements for labour market changes did not introduce any dramatic novelty in the pre-crisis plan of reform. The IMF simply suggested an acceleration of the process by allowing immediately layoffs due to managerial reasons and to mergers and acquisitions and by legalising the temporary work contracts.

In the meantime, the impact of the crisis on employment was particularly strong and following the long series of bankruptcies, the unemployment rate rose from 2.6 per cent in the second quarter of 1997 to an average 7 per cent in 1998, peaking to 8.7 per cent in February 1999 (Economist Intelligence Unit 2000).

The structure of unemployment reflected directly the path of reforms. The first wave came from small and medium enterprises, hardly hurt by the credit crunch of 1998; according to the World Bank (1999) three-quarters of the newly unemployed were temporary, daily, self-employed and unpaid family workers, while the second wave was mainly composed of workers of large conglomerates, fired after the beginning of the reform in 1999.

A consequence of the increasing unemployment was of course a sharp decline in incomes and an explosion in urban poverty. In absolute terms, the number of poor surged from 2.9 million in 1997 to a peak of 7.7 million a year later (World Bank 1999). Moreover, there was also a negative impact on income distribution with the Gini coefficient[9] rising at 0.3 in 1998, its highest level since the government started recording the index in 1979 (Economist Intelligence Unit 2000).

Given this serious deterioration in the social situation, the government had to intervene tripling the expenditure on social protection, which reached 2 per cent of GDP in 1999. The main instruments adopted by the government for facing the diffused social distress were the creation of a broader unemployment insurance scheme, increasing the number of beneficiaries from 18 000 in 1998 to 174 000 in 1999; the implementation of a policy of public works that provided more than 400 000 new jobs and the reintroduction of a livelihood program for partially compensating income reductions.

Recently, the effectiveness of the government action together with the recovery have contributed to reduce unemployment at an average rate around 4 per cent. Nevertheless, the structure of the labour market is deeply changed: the long-term contracts, once the most typical form of employment, are progressively substituted by new forms of temporary and flexible contracts and most of the new jobs are created within a framework of high flexibility.

6. THE BOOMING NEW ECONOMY

One of the most positive side effects of the financial crisis in Korea is the boom of the new economy. Following the down-scoping and down-sizing in *chaebol* and the promotion of venture businesses by the government, through tax breaks and other incentives, Korea has seen a major surge of high technology venture firms. Kim (2000a) reports a remarkable increase from a mere 100 companies before the crisis to 5000 by the end of 1999, reaching more than 7000 by June 2000. For the first time, executives are defecting from the huge conglomerates to strike out on their own, applying their high tech expertise to start up businesses in everything from telecommunications to liquid-crystal displays. There are even cases of government officials moving to venture companies. Many *chaebol* have already introduced a performance-based wage system and stock options as a means to retain their core employees (SERI 2000).

New companies like mobile-phone maker Appeal Telecom, a venture firm set up by a former Samsung engineer, are teaming up with global leaders such as Motorola. Furthermore, some multinationals (MNCs) recently established local R&D centres in Korea. Other MNCs, like Hewlett-Packard and Philips, have purchased a large stake in their Korean subsidiaries. The drastic increase in FDIs is mainly focused on information technology and will lead to some transfer of technology but also and mainly to transfer of management know how and more transparency and accountability (Kim 2000a).

To sustain this jump into the new economy Korea has recently invested a lot of resources in R&D activities. In fact, although its external dependence on technology imports, particularly from USA and Japan has not decreased, R&D domestic investments have seen a continuous increase, apart from the worst moments of the financial crisis. In 1998, R&D as a percentage of GDP reached 2.5 per cent, surpassing many Western European countries (Table 3.13) (Kim 2000a).

After the crisis, large *chaebol* reduced their R&D activities but this reduction was in part compensated by an increase in government expenditures, to some degree directed to promote venture businesses and therefore responsible for the boom of technology-based small firms. A recent paper,

Table 3.13 Research and development expenditures: 1970–1998 (billion of won)

	1970	1975	1980	1985	1990	1995	1998
R&D expenditure	10.5	42.7	282.5	1237.1	3349.9	9440.6	11 336
Government	9.2	30.3	180.0	306.8	651.0	1780.9	3051
Private Sector	1.3	12.3	102.5	930.3	2698.9	7659.7	8276
R&D/GNP %	0.38	0.42	0.77	1.58	1.95	2.51	2.52

Source: Ministry of Science and Technology (data quoted in Kim 2000a).

already quoted, by Kim (2000a) accounts an increase from 3060 R&D corporate centres at the time of the crisis to 5200 two years later, 95 per cent of which is due to SMEs.

A further indicator of the improved quality of R&D activities is the increase in the number of patents, which more than tripled in two years after the crisis, from 8642 to 24 579 in 1999. Korea is now fifth in the world in terms of the number of industrial property applications, after Japan, USA, China and Germany (Kim 2000a).

For the first time, Korean companies are trying hard to innovate in emerging areas such as plasma display panels, mobile phones and digital television, rather than just reverse-engineering copies of products manufactured by other firms. Some results of these efforts are already visible in the export market. Equipment like mobile phones, satellite receivers and liquid-crystal displays are increasing their weight in exports and also in memory chips, the biggest export category, Korean companies are trying to move towards higher-end products, less prone to boom-and-bust cycles.

But Koreans are not only increasingly producing and exporting high tech goods, they are also using them. South Korea is already the most wired nation in Asia and is a world leader with regard to online stock trading (more than 60 per cent of all trading is now done online) and broadband access (EIU 2000). About 60 per cent of its 46 million people already use mobile phones (EIU 2000). In high-speed Internet connections, Korea is even more advanced than the USA: by 2002 more than 3 million Korean households are expected to be using these very advanced facilities, vs. 2 million in the USA and only 300 000 in Japan (EIU 2000). A further indicator of Korean enthusiasm with the Internet is that there are three Korean web sites among the world 10th most visited sites.

Nevertheless, the vibrant Korean IT revolution may be in danger because of the difficulties occurring to the old economy. The recent bankruptcy of Daewoo Motor and the financial problems at Hyundai Engineering and Construction are not helping to restore international confidence in Korean economy. The Seoul stock market has fallen by 50 per cent already this year, and it could fall further as the clouds continue to gather over the *chaebol*. Even worse is the performance of Kosdaq market, modelled on the US's Nasdaq, having lost 60 per cent since the beginning of the year. The Kosdaq collapse is a common outcome of tech bourses from Asia to Europe to the USA, but definitely its performance has not been assisted by the slow restructuring and the defaults in major *chaebol*.

The unanswered question is whether the flowering of an Internet economy in Korea can really help to break with the past. Certainly, the success of Korea's vibrant sector of small and medium-size companies is a completely new phenomenon in the domestic panorama and its transformation would have been much slower but for the financial crisis.

7. CONCLUSIONS

During the last 4 years many things have been changing in Korea: first, at the end of 1997 there was a financial crisis, followed by the worst depression after the Korean war in the 1950s, second, very rapidly the economic system began to recover. As said before, in 1999 GDP grew by 10.7 per cent, unemployment fell and inflation remained under control.

In these positive signs of upturn many observers have seen a risk of undermining reform efforts. In a way, although the rapid recovery is accidentally mitigating the pain of economic and social depression there is a diffused concern that, without the strong incentive of crisis ('blessing in disguise'), as the economy gets better stakeholders will be less willing to accept painful and long-overdue reforms (Kim 2000a).

Nonetheless as seen in this paper, Korea has made substantial progress toward improving and restructuring but there is much more to be done. A result of weakening and slowing the reform process is the immediate reaction of foreign investors; the huge financial difficulties at Daewoo and Hyundai are definitely not assisting the need for capital of the booming new high tech sector. Moreover, there are other signs of market difficulties: the moderate appreciation of the won on the US dollar, which will not help the balance of current accounts, the oil price explosion, which is expected to have an impact on inflation, the weight of public direct involvement in financial restructuring on fiscal deficit and also, the bad performance, worse than in the rest of Asia, of the Korean stock market.

There is a general agreement that reforms must go on at a fast pace and for the time needed not only to sustain the actual economic recovery but also to carry on the structural transformation of the Korean economy. Up to now, positive results have been obtained in several fields like the setting up of a regulatory and legal framework adequate to a more open and market-oriented economic system; a significant opening to international competition of capital and goods markets, the introduction of increasing flexibility in labour markets and some important changes in the public sector.

Particularly complicated is the assessment of what has been done in the financial and corporate sectors. As said before, banks are financially healthier above all thanks to a huge infusion of public funds, the amount of NPLs has decreased but it could rise significantly as a result of corporate restructuring and still unreformed is a part of the non banking financial system, namely investment trust companies, which are even more than before strongly tied with the corporate sector. In a market oriented economic system a financial sector should play a crucial role in resource allocation, something that Korean financial institutions are actually learning to do with an important contribution from foreign investors. The possibility to apply what they learn will very much depend on the state's willingness to step out of lending. Moreover, Korea, together with other Asian countries which went through the crisis (Plummer and Trivellato 2000), strongly needs to develop an efficient domestic financial market, able to channel long term savings into profitable economic projects.

With regard to corporate reform, probably the most evident result is the concentration of the biggest *chaebol* in some strategic sectors, overcoming their excessive diversification before the financial crisis; nevertheless, this policy has led in most of the sectors to strengthening oligopolistic positions, contrasting with the declared reform intent of increasing market competition. Also in corporate governance there are some significant results: rights of minority shareholders are better protected, there is increasing accountability and transparency, outside directors have been appointed, but most of them are still strongly related with the family owners. Recently, some opposition to *chaebol* restructuring has also come from labour unions: at Daewoo Motor trade unions had rejected demands from creditor banks for 3500 jobs to be cut. In order to reduce labour opposition to restructuring, it is crucial that effective actions and plans are required to guarantee adequate protection for workers who may lose their job security (Kawai 2000).

In the reform process the leading role of the government has up to now been central and its strong commitment to implement restructuring has probably contributed significantly to restore market confidence and therefore to sustain the rapid economic recovery. Nonetheless, the main driving principle of the reform process is to transform Korea in a market-oriented system. For this to become a reality, the state should stop directly intervening in resource allocation and concentrate on its regulatory and co-ordinating role. Up to now, there are signals of its resolute intention to advance in this direction.

NOTES

*   The paper is the result of thoroughly joint work; however, Rabellotti wrote sections 1, 6 and 7 and the two authors wrote the remaining sections together. The two authors would like to thank Stefano Chiarlone, Alessia Amighini and Matteo Picariello (ICE Seoul) for kindly providing data.

1.   About how Korea and other East Asian countries managed to grow at a such a high and continuous rate there is a very wide debate, culminating in the publication of 'The East Asian Miracle' by the World Bank in 1993 and more recently, since Krugman article in 1994, focused on its long-run sustainability. Krugman, founding his analysis on empirical evidence provided by Young (1992), asserts that there is not an economic miracle behind East Asian growth but simply a process of physical and human capital accumulation, bound to decreasing returns. This interpretation of the Asian growth process generated many econometric exercises trying to measure the extent to which output growth is due to factors accumulation as opposed to total factor productivity (TFP) growth.

2.   Kim (1997) defines a *chaebol* as a business group consisting of several corporate enterprises engaged in diversified business areas and typically owned and managed by one or two interrelated family groups.

3.   Some caution should be taken in analysing the situation of the public sector because Korea adopts different criteria from international standards to measure public expenditures. The public deficit is underestimated because, for example, pension funds of public employees or

bonds issued by government-operated financial institutions and foundations are not included in the consolidated accounts. Kim (1999) recalculated the public balance between 1971 to 1992 on the basis of international standards and the deficit average to GDP expanded from 1.98 to 4.19.

4.   Korean chipmakers have focused on the volatile market for D-Ram memory chips, which has continued to suffer from price declines. In June 1998, the price of 16M D-Ram plunged to a level under 2 dollars and that of 64M D-Ram fell to below 8 dollars (SERI 2000).

5.   The Balassa index is calculated as: $RCA=(x_j/x)/(X_j/X)$, and x_i and X_i are respectively country *j* and world exports in sector *i* while x and X are respectively total manufacturing exports in country j and in all world. If $0<RCA<1$, country *j* does not reveal comparative advantage in sector *i*, while if $RCA>1$ there is a comparative advantage in the sector.

6.   Two recent interesting papers discussing Korean international specialisation in relation with other East Asian countries are Chiarlone and Amighini (2000) and Helg (1999).

7.   The Korean government perceives the deficit expansion as a temporary situation and it has prepared a medium and long-term plan (2000–2006) for managing and reducing the fiscal imbalance through a deep reform of the tax system.

8.   At present, only twenty categories remain restricted to FDI's, mainly in the service sector (World Bank 1999).

9.   The Gini coefficient is a measure of income equality, in which a coefficient of zero implies perfect income equality and a coefficient of 1 implies perfect inequality.

BIBLIOGRAPHY

Asian Development Bank (2000), *Asian Development Outlook*, Manila: Asian Development Bank.

Balassa, B. (1965), 'Exports and Economic Growth: Further Evidence', *Journal of Development Economics*, **5** (2), 181–189.

Bank of Korea (BOK) (2000), *Annual Statistical Bulletin*, Seoul, available at BOK web site. (www.bok.go.kr)

Chiarlone, S. and A. Amighini (2000), *Growth Potential in East Asia: Evidence from International Trade Flows*, mimeo, Milan: Bocconi University.

Corsetti, G., P. Pesenti and N. Roubini (1998), *What caused the Asian currency and financial crisis? Part I: A macroeconomic overview*, mimeo.

Economist Intelligence Unit (2000), *Country Report-South Korea*, London: EIU.

Feldstein, M. (1998), 'Refocusing the IMF', *Foreign Affairs*, March/April, Washington D.C.

Helg, R. (1999), *East and South-East Asian economies and the EU: Pattern of Specialisation and Intra-Industry Trade*, in Chirathivat, S. and C. Molteni (eds), *ASEAN-EU economic relations: the impact of the Asian crisis on the European economy and the long term potential*, AESS, Nomos Publ., Baden-Baden.

International Monetary Fund (IMF) (1997), *Stand By Arrangement, Summary of the Economic Program*, available at IMF web site, Washington D.C. (www.imf.org)

International Monetary Fund (IMF) (various years), *Korea, Letter of Intent and Memorandum of Economic Policies*, 1997, 1998, available at IMF web site, Washington D.C.

International Monetary Fund (IMF) (1999), *IMF-Supported Programs in Indonesia, Korea and Thailand, A preliminary Assessment*, available at IMF web site, Washington D.C.

International Trade Centre (ITC) (2000), *The trade performance index, background paper ITC*, mimeo, available at ITC web site, Geneva. (www.intracen.org)

Kawai, M. (2000), 'The resolution of the East Asian crisis: financial and corporate sector restructuring', *Journal of East Asian Economics*, 11, 133–168.

Korean Institute for Economic Policy (KIEP) (1998), *Agreement for the restructuring of the top 5 chaebol*, mimeo, Seoul.

Kim, D. (1999), 'IMF Bailout and Financial and Corporate Restructuring in the Republic of Korea', *The Developing Economies*, 28, 4.

Kim, L. (1997), *Imitation to innovation*, Boston Mass.: Harvard Business School Press.

Kim, L. (2000a), *Crisis and national innovation system: its re-engineering in Korea*, mimeo, Seoul: Korea University.

Kim, L. (2000b), *Public sector reform in Korea*, mimeo, Seoul: Korea University.

Krugman, P. (1994), 'The myth of Asia's miracle', *Foreign Affairs*, December, 62–78, Washington D.C.

Ministry of Finance and Economy (MOFE) (2000), *Korea Economic Update-newsletter*, various issues, available at MOFE web site, Seoul.

Plummer, M. and B. Trivellato (2000), *Economic Policy Convergence in ASEAN: Malaysia and Thailand Compared*, mimeo, Milan: ISPI.

Rodrick, D. (1995), 'Getting Interventions Right: How South Korea and Taiwan Grew Rich', *Economic Policy*.

Samsung Economic Research Institute (SERI) (1999), *One Year after the IMF Bailout*, available at SERI web site, Seoul.

Samsung Economic Research Institute (SERI) (2000), *Two Years after the IMF Bailout*, available at SERI web site, Seoul.

Seo, I.J. (2000), *La Corée du Sud-Une Analyse Historique du Processus de Développement*, Paris: L'Harmattan.

UNCTAD/WTO (1999), *PC/TAS Trade analysis system on Personal computer* (Cd-Rom) 1992–1996 and update 1997–1998, United Nations Statistics Division: Geneva.

World Bank (1993), *The East Asian Miracle: Economic Growth and Public Policy*, Washington D.C.: Oxford University Press for the World Bank

World Bank (1999), *Republic of Korea Establishing a New Foundation for Sustained Growth*, November, World Bank, Washington D.C.

World Bank (2000), *Global Development Finance-Analysis. Summary Tables and Country Tables*, World Bank, Washington D.C.

Young, A. (1992), *A tale of two cities: factor accumulation and technical change in Honk Kong and Singapore*, NBER Macroeconomics Annual, MIT Press.

4. Economic and Policy Convergence in ASEAN: Malaysia and Thailand Compared

Michael G. Plummer and Benedetta Trivellato[*]

1. INTRODUCTION

Prior to the Asian crisis, there existed a perceived process of economic and policy convergence in Asia generally and in ASEAN particularly.

In the post-crisis era, some have argued that this convergence is breaking down. The goal of this paper is to test this latter hypothesis, using a comparison of Malaysia and Thailand as a case study.

Malaysia and Thailand are excellent candidates for such a comparison, in that each appeared to share a common policy stance prior to the crisis and experienced common results: rapid growth, strong macroeconomic fundamentals, reduction in poverty: brief, economic development. In fact, they constituted the backbone of the 'ASEAN Success Story' and graduated to the ranks of 'Dynamic Asian Economies' (DAEs) in the late 1980s/early 1990s. However, during the crisis and so far in the post-crisis era, there is a common impression that policy and economic convergence may be going in opposite directions. If so, this could have important implications for economic development in the region, as well as international policy initiatives.

Hence, this chapter focuses on questions surrounding 'real' and policy convergence between Malaysia and Thailand in the context of economic interdependence and co-operation. In order to do this, we begin by defining what is meant by 'convergence', proposing various indicators and followed by an application to the cases of Malaysia and Thailand. As the questions surrounding 'convergence' between Malaysia and Thailand tend to be more on the policy side, we focus much of the paper on this area.

2.   DEFINING AND GAUGING CONVERGENCE

From economic and political perspectives, evaluation of the process of convergence is significant for a number of reasons. We focus here on the economic and political economy aspects of convergence, leaving actual 'politics' and specific international-relations-related topics, such as peace issues, to other contributions.

First, convergence is important in that the greater the economic integration between countries, the more dependent they will be on the economic growth of their partner countries. This type of convergence is the most direct; a recession in other ASEAN countries would have little effect on Singapore if it did not trade much with ASEAN. But because it does, Singapore is to some degree dependent on ASEAN (and, of course, has an incentive to urge its partners to embrace sound economic policies). Hence, because of this real convergence, there exists a second (and related) reason why convergence is important: policy externalities. As policies in the region will affect a specific country according to the degree to which it 'converges' with its neighbours, it has a strong incentive to co-operate with them. This type of argument can also be applied independent of convergence if one expands the analysis to the sphere of political relations: if a country pursues potentially-destabilising economic policies or a dangerous foreign policy, the instability that might be created could have critical spill-over effects with negative implications for regional development, even if that country has not converged economically with its neighbours.

Third, greater economic convergence makes it easier to launch initiatives, both with economic and political intentions, in regional forums when countries are closely integrated. For example, one could argue that the ASEAN Free Trade Area (AFTA) would have been impossible if the ASEAN countries had not already attained a certain degree of economic (and policy) convergence. The fact that a few of the new member-states were not highly integrated with ASEAN – either in terms of economics or politics – has made it more difficult for these countries to fully co-operate in AFTA and other initiatives. Moreover, the Single Market Program in Europe and, especially, monetary union would not have been possible without highly advanced degrees of convergence in Western Europe. The Maastricht Treaty even required a considerable degree of convergence in measurable quantitative macroeconomic indicators (the 'Maastricht Criteria') before countries could qualify for monetary union.

Fourth, convergence makes it easier for countries to co-operate in international organisations. If countries have not 'converged' sufficiently, they may have diverse economic interests, and if they do not share a common policy approach to international economics and development, they will have fewer common interests and, hence, less incentive and motivation to advocate common policies. Convergence in ASEAN made it easier for member-states to participate in various aspects of the Uruguay Round, and ASEAN has tried hard to launch a joint approach to activities in APEC, albeit with mixed success (and possibly the result of insufficient convergence).

Finally, one can argue that convergence is important from the perspective of a 'demonstration' effect. The more two countries 'converge', the more they will be familiar with each other and perceive to share a common fate. As these countries become closer, they will have greater exposure to each other's economic policies. If one country is doing far better than the other, then a 'demonstration' effect may occur, in which the latter attempts to learn from the former's model of economic development. For instance, the many meetings between ASEAN officials in the late 1970s and 1980s served at least to some degree as a showcase for the successful policies of the region's dynamic member-states, which prompted more inward-looking countries, such as Indonesia, to adopt more outward-oriented policies.

2.1   Definitions of Convergence

Thus far, we have used the term 'convergence' in a way that suggested that there exists a commonly accepted definition. This is not necessarily true. It is important especially in light of the goals of this paper to be specific in defining what we mean by 'convergence'. In particular, it is crucial to differentiate between policy convergence, which we define to be common policy stances embraced by governments, and real convergence, which are responses of the economy to these initiatives in national marketplace. Clearly, the two will be interdependent: greater real convergence will likely lead to greater policy convergence and vice versa.

Policy convergence

We define 'policy convergence' to cover various symmetries in approaches to macroeconomic and microeconomic policies. For example, in the case of the EU, in addition to specifying convergence criteria, the Maastricht Treaty de facto imposed a set of common macroeconomic goals and approaches to policy formation, which, on the road to integration, may be perceived as the logical follow-up to the many common microeconomic policies required by the Single Market Program. We might specify three types of symmetry under the rubric of 'policy convergence':

1. Symmetry of macroeconomic goals and policies to reach them (e.g., common inflation targets, unemployment-rate 'warnings', exchange-rate stability, government expenditure restrictions, current account/financing issues).
2. Symmetry of microeconomic goals and policies (e.g., government involvement in the private sector, trade-policy orientation, export diversification

policies, foreign investment policies, regulation of the financial sector, competitions policies, intellectual property protection).
3. Symmetry of multilateral co-operation policies (positions in bilateral, sub-regional, and multilateral forums).

Real convergence

We define real convergence quite simply to be the actual integration that takes place between two or more countries. There are a plethora of indicators that may be used to gauge the degree of 'real' convergence, all of which are imprecise and explain different aspects of real convergence. Myriad methodologies exist to capture various manifestations of integration, but while the idea is clear and unambiguous, the applications are difficult and subject to dispute (which is often the case in economics). We offer here two approaches to 'real' convergence that differ in the types of questions they address:

1. Symmetry of economic structure
   a) Have economic structures become more similar (as proxied by similarities in sectoral production shares, export structure, 'revealed' comparative advantage, etc.)?
   b) Do external shocks affect the countries' economies in a similar way (e.g., extent to which changes in, say, product prices, productivity, etc., affect relative macroeconomic performance)?
2. Economic convergence through interdependence
   a) To what degree has integration occurred with respect to trade and investment (e.g., changes in bilateral trade shares, investment flows, labour flows)?
   b) Are real business cycles correlated, that is, are external shocks 'symmetric'?

3. APPLICATIONS TO THE CASE OF MALAYSIA AND THAILAND: REAL CONVERGENCE

In the aftermath of the Asian crisis, as was true before it, most developing countries in Asia continue to accept the proposition that open trade and investment policies are necessary for sustained economic development. We will argue below that this is also the case in both Malaysia and Thailand, though the question of openness with respect to finance may be a different story. Much of the emerging literature on Asian policy reform is naturally present- and forward-looking, perhaps taking for granted the liberalisation trend without acknowledging that reform is part of a volatile process of change (in some cases truly radical; in others, less so). Even before the onset of the Asian crisis, certain social elements in ASEAN were setting up obstacles to reform.

In fact, it was not long ago that Malaysia and Thailand embraced policies that are diametrically opposed to those that now guide their development strategies. From the 1950s until arguably the mid-1980s, they adopted policies designed to limit exposure to international interactive variables such as imports and, in a number of sectors, foreign direct investment (FDI). According to what became known as the 'import-substitution' paradigm, countries were thought to be better off limiting imports to those that were absolutely necessary (e.g., advanced capital equipment or necessary agriculture commodities). The position vis-à-vis exports was more ambivalent; every country needed to export a minimum amount of goods and services in order to finance requisite imports, but anything beyond that would depend on the circumstances of the country in question. Countries with more diversified economic structures might use the international marketplace as an additional source of demand for domestic production, though preferential treatment of import-competing goods and often the perpetuation of overvalued exchange rates usually limited the success of these countries on international markets.

The shortcomings of the import-substitution model have been widely documented, and it is beyond the scope of this paper (as well as being redundant) to survey them. But in a nutshell, the main problems relate to the critical inefficiencies that are spawned by inward-looking policies at the domestic level, and the failure to exploit the ample opportunities available from the international marketplace, including expanded market demand, 'forced efficiencies', additional capital (especially FDI), and new technologies. Malaysia and Thailand reached their decisions to open to the international marketplace at different speeds, albeit at approximately the same time (mid-1980s), arguably spurred by economic crisis, unsustainable macroeconomic and microeconomic policies, in short, the realisation of bankrupt policies of the past.

In the first year of the Asian crisis (1997), Thailand was hit hard, and Malaysia began to show signs of losing momentum later in the year. As can be seen in Table 4.1, Thailand contracted by almost 2 per cent in 1997, and Malaysian growth, albeit positive, fell to 5.4 per cent. However, 1998 was a terrible year for both countries; Thailand contracted by 10 per cent and Malaysia by 8 per cent, one of the worst years in their respective modern economic histories. In response to the depths of this crisis, Thailand followed strictly the standard IMF package that it had negotiated. Malaysia never took IMF money, but had agreed on a policy framework and indicators that would 'mirror' an IMF plan. However, in September 1998, Malaysia decided to go a different route: it imposed severe capital and currency controls, lowered its domestic interest rates, and fixed its exchange rate (something that would have been impossible to do with an open capital account). Thus, at this point, Malaysian and Thai economic policies diverged substantially, while they had previously been quite symmetrical. This is what makes the Thai-Malaysian example an appropriate case study for this paper.

There are a number of ways in which we can gauge the degree of 'real' convergence between Malaysia and Thailand. First, the share of bilateral exports in each other's trade has increased over the past 10 years, though it continues to remain at less than 5 per cent of total exports (ICSEAD 2000). In essence, this small share can be traced to the fact that Malaysia and Thailand, as developing countries, continue to engage substantially in inter-industry trade, have relatively small markets, and rely on traditional, high-income trading partners (i.e., the United States, the EU, and Japan). Hence, at least in terms of trade, while Malaysia and Thailand have become more interdependent, they are still far more affected by changes in the economies of developed countries than each other.

Second, we might consider an alternative form of estimating the degree of integration that would allow us to control for the biases inherent in market size: measures of trade-bias or 'gravity coefficient' calculations. As noted by Petri (1993), increases in intra-regional trade signify an increase in inter-dependence but do not give a strong indication of the 'bias' toward regionalisation, as it may reflect changes in other variables, especially income growth. To control for this effect, a 'double-density' measure can be used, which normalises bilateral or intra-regional trade shares by the importance of the country or region in total trade. Results for the years 1980, 1986 and 1994 are presented in Table 4.2. By this measure, Malaysia and Thailand in 1994 traded with each other more than double what one would expect, suggesting significant interaction at least on a relative basis. However, it is important to note that the share actually decreased from a multiple of approximately five in 1980 and seven in 1986. Thus, while trade share analysis shows that integration

Table 4.1 ASEAN countries growth rate of GDP (per cent per year)

Asean Countries	1994	1995	1996	1997	1998	1999	2000[a]	2001[b]
Cambodia	3.9	6.7	5.5	2.6	1.3	5	6	7
Indonesia	7.5	8.2	7.8	4.7	−13.2	0.2	4	5
Laos	8.1	7	6.9	6.9	4	4	4.5	5
Malaysia	9.2	9.8	10	7.5	−7.5	5.4	6	6.1
Myanmar	7.5	6.9	6.4	5.7	5	4.5	NA	NA
Philippines	4.4	4.7	5.8	5.2	−0.5	3.2	3.8	4.3
Singapore	11.2	8.4	7.5	8	1.5	5.4	5.9	6.2
Thailand	9	8.9	5.9	−1.8	−10.4	4.1	4.5	4.6
Vietnam	8.8	9.5	9.3	8.2	4.4	4.4	5	6

a. forecasted; b. forecasted.

Source: Asian Development Outlook 2000, Asian Development Bank.

Table 4.2a Trade bias calculations for ASEAN and selected countries (1980)*

	US	Sing	Indo	Malay	Phil	Thai	ASEAN	EU 15	APEC
Singapore	1.126	0.00	NA	23.479	2.215	7.453	5.483	0.304	2.018
Indonesia	1.458	9.314	0.000	0.478	2.282	2.411	3.745	0.225	2.756
Malaysia	1.315	14.034	0.574	0.000	3.528	5.245	5.863	0.425	2.368
Philippines	2.110	1.517	2.474	2.977	0.000	1.478	1.869	0.346	2.270
Thailand	1.261	6.007	2.080	4.677	1.719	0.000	3.600	0.477	1.938
ASEAN	1.367	5.812	0.627	8.869	2.171	4.220	4.492	0.332	2.286
EU15	0.581	0.260	0.274	0.456	0.381	0.460	0.343	1.370	0.458
APEC	1.498	1.741	2.708	2.618	2.351	1.759	2.222	0.397	1.893

Table 4.2b Trade bias calculations for ASEAN and selected countries (1986)*

	US	Sing	Indo	Malay	Phil	Thai	ASEAN	EU 15	APEC
Singapore	1.316	0.000	NA	23.201	3.597	7.390	5.863	0.274	1.860
Indonesia	1.194	7.300	0.000	0.863	2.153	1.384	3.360	0.302	2.117
Malaysia	1.222	13.670	1.288	0.000	6.058	7.294	7.004	0.346	2.062
Philippines	2.087	2.274	2.637	5.051	0.000	2.191	2.702	0.352	1.995
Thailand	1.128	6.508	1.055	6.988	2.203	0.000	4.234	0.439	1.735
ASEAN	1.309	5.251	0.613	10.393	3.297	4.687	5.093	0.324	1.944
EU15	0.556	0.253	0.331	0.364	0.412	0.493	0.341	1.397	0.438
APEC	1.499	1.563	1.871	2.264	2.198	1.649	1.836	0.401	1.793

Table 4.2c Trade bias calculations for ASEAN and selected countries (1994)*

	US	Sing	Indo	Malay	Phil	Thai	ASEAN	EU 15	APEC
Singapore	1.235	0.000	NA	13.018	2.765	5.248	4.211	0.351	1.775
Indonesia	0.950	3.488	0.000	1.323	1.409	1.141	2.036	0.461	1.729
Malaysia	1.387	7.395	1.656	0.000	1.879	3.208	3.834	0.381	1.859
Philippines	1.897	2.498	1.536	1.356	0.000	1.628	1.815	0.346	1.830
Thailand	1.168	3.771	1.008	2.359	1.071	0.000	2.283	0.448	1.632
ASEAN	1.266	2.997	0.656	5.779	1.894	3.077	3.329	0.389	1.768
EU15	0.548	0.294	0.464	0.356	0.361	0.499	0.381	1.627	0.444
APEC	1.495	1.344	1.527	1.936	1.803	1.820	1.651	0.401	1.716

* *formula used to calculate double-density ratio was $(Trade_{ij}/Total_j)/(Total_i/World)$, where i = partner country, j = host country; ASEAN includes Indonesia, Malaysia, Singapore, Thailand, and the Philippines; APEC: missing Papua New Guinea, Brunei, and Taiwan.*

Sources: United Nations, Commodity Trade Statistics, Various Years; IMF, International Financial Statistics.

is actually small but rising, the trade bias approach would lead one to conclude that it is fairly large but falling.

Third, we might consider the 'structure' of output and exports, under the assumption that greater similarity suggests greater macroeconomic symmetry and, hence, each country would be susceptible (and would wish to react similarly) to the same types of economic shocks. Trends in Thailand and Malaysia are similar in this regard: over the 1960–1984 period, on average Malaysia and Thailand dedicated about 30 per cent of output to agriculture, which fell to 15 per cent or less over the 1985–1996 period (Kose, Kim, and Plummer 2000). By 1999, the share of industry, agriculture, and services in output were almost exactly the same in Malaysia and Thailand (Table 4.3).

Finally, it is possible to consider symmetry of economic structures by focusing on the correlation of business cycles, an exercise that was used frequently in the case of European countries wishing to join in monetary union. The correlation of macroeconomic variables throughout the business cycle permit us to examine the degree to which countries exhibit common responses to international trends and shocks. Using a first-difference filter,[1] one finds that the correlation of the business cycles in Thailand and Malaysia has increased substantially: over the 1960–1996 period, the correlation was 0.35; over 1985–1996 (i.e., the new period of economic liberalisation), the correlation almost doubled to 0.66 (Kose, Kim, and Plummer 2000). It is also noteworthy that each country's growth correlation with Asia in general also increased substantially over this period and was even greater than the bilateral correlation estimation in both periods (rising to over 0.70 for each country). This suggests that there is evidence of increasing symmetry of the economies of Thailand and Malaysia at the macroeconomic level.

Table 4.3 ASEAN sectoral share of GDP (per cent)

Economy	Agriculture			Industry			Services		
	1970	1980	1999	1970	1980	1999	1970	1980	1999
Asean Countries									
Cambodia	NA	NA	37.4	NA	NA	22.1	NA	NA	35.5
Indonesia	35	24.4	17.4	28	41.3	42.8	37	34.3	39.8
Laos	NA	NA	51.2	NA	NA	22.9	NA	NA	25.9
Malaysia	NA	22.9	8.9	NA	35.8	42.8	NA	41.3	48.4
Myanmar	49.5	47.9	41.9	12	12.3	17.2	38.5	39.8	41
Philippines	28.2	23.5	20	33.7	40.5	34.5	38.1	36	45.5
Singapore	2.2	1.1	0.1	36.4	38.8	32.2	61.4	60	67.7
Thailand	30.2	20.2	10.2	25.7	30.1	42.9	44.1	49.7	46.9
Viet Nam	NA	42.7	23.9	NA	26.3	34.7	NA	31	41.4

Source: Asian Development Outlook 2000, Asian Development Bank.

In sum, while Thailand and Malaysia have quite different factor endowments and traditions that have created substantially different initial conditions, there appear to be significant increases in the symmetry of their economic structures. Prior to the crisis, each experienced high rates of economic growth; impressive levels of savings and investment relative to GDP; strong fiscal balances (Table 4.4); strong inward FDI flows through the mid-1990s (Table 4.5); robust increases in exports, creating an important 'engine' of growth; significant diversification out of agriculture and into manufacturing and services; considerable diversification of export structure (especially toward manufacturing, e.g., electronics is now one of the largest exports in each country); and large current account deficits financed in similar ways. In fact, there is empirical evidence of a strong positive correlation between inward FDI flows into Thailand and those going to Malaysia,

Table 4.4 Overall budget surplus or deficit of central government (percentage of GDP)

Asean Countries	1994	1995	1996	1997	1998	1999
Cambodia	−6.8	−7.5	−8.3	−4.2	−6.1	−3.7
Indonesia	0.4	0.6	0.2	0	−3.7	−2.2
Laos	−11.5	−9.7	−9.1	−8.8	−13.9	−9.3
Malaysia	2.3	0.8	0.7	2.6	−1.5	−3.8
Myanmar	−2.4	−3.1	−1	NA	NA	NA
Philippines	1	0.6	0.3	0.1	−1.8	−3.6
Singapore	9.1	6.6	8.6	9.6	1.6	2.5
Thailand	1.9	3	2.4	−0.9	−3.4	−3
Viet Nam	−2.3	−1.5	−1.3	−1.7	−1.6	−2

Source: Asian Development Outlook 2000, Asian Development Bank.

Table 4.5 Foreign direct investment ($million)

Asean Countries	1993	1994	1995	1996	1997	1998
Cambodia	54	69	151	294	204	140
Indonesia	2004	2109	4346	6194	4673	−356
Laos	36	59	88	128	86	45
Malaysia	5006	4342	4178	5078	5106	3727
Myanmar	149	91	115	38	124	40
Philippines	1238	1591	1478	1517	1222	1713
Singapore	4686	8550	7206	7884	9710	7218
Thailand	1805	1364	2068	2336	3733	6969
Viet Nam	1002	1500	2000	2500	2950	1900

Source: Asian Development Outlook 2000, Asian Development Bank.

suggesting significant 'policy externalities'. Each has been successful at mobilising domestic factors of production but with disappointing rates of productivity growth, which emerged as an important policy priority in both countries, along with the need to address infrastructural policies.

Also prior to the crisis, economic integration with respect to trade has increased (though is still small) if gauged by a trade-shares approach, and when evaluated on a relative basis (the 'double-density' measure), is actually quite high (but declining). Finally, proxies for similar changes in economic structure and macroeconomic 'symmetry' reveal significant convergence between Thailand and Malaysia.

4.   APPLICATIONS TO THE CASE OF MALAYSIA AND THAILAND: POLICY CONVERGENCE

As noted above, the two countries did experience significant policy convergence prior to the crisis, at least with respect to economic policy. Malaysia and Thailand, though quite different in terms of socio-political institutional development, adopted similar macroeconomic and microeconomic policies, though, of course, there were differences. Inflation was low in both countries, averaging approximately 3.5 per cent in Malaysia and 5.4 per cent in Thailand in the year leading up to the crisis.[2] Malaysia has had traditionally fewer restrictions on trade than Thailand, but both followed a similar pattern of liberalisation beginning in the mid-late 1980s. Fiscal reform was more important in the case of Malaysia, which brought down a double-digit central government deficit (as a percentage of GDP) in the early 1980s to almost a surplus of one per cent by 1996, whereas Thailand had actually achieved a significant surplus in the 1990s (Table 4.4). The gap in relative shares of government spending in GDP had substantially narrowed by the 1990s, with the Malaysian share hovering around 22 per cent, and Thailand, 17 per cent (Asian Development Bank 2000). Exchange-rate policies were similar; each eventually adopted open capital accounts and essentially fixed their currency to the US dollar, allowing some flexibility. Table 4.6 shows very stable exchange rates for Thailand and Malaysia until the crisis. As can be seen in Table 4.7, each country ran very high current account deficits in the years leading up to the crisis (5–8 per cent of GDP in Thailand and 6–10 per cent in Malaysia for the period 1994–96) and did little if anything to correct them (see 'Lawson Doctrine'). Direct foreign investment policies were similar in that each adopted 'negative lists' (rather than the more restrictive 'positive' lists) and created one-stop investment centres. Inflows of FDI were among the largest in the developing world in the 1980s, but had slowed considerably by the mid-1990s (at least relative to GDP growth), whereas short-term portfolio flows boomed. Each country experienced salient speculative financial bubbles leading up to the crisis.

Table 4.6 Exchange rate to the Dollar (local currency/US$, average of period)

Asean Countries	Currency	1994	1995	1996	1997	1998	1999
Cambodia	Riel	2567	2464	2635	2952	3756	3809
Indonesia	Rupiah	2160.8	2248.6	2342.3	2909.6	10013.7	7853.9
Laos	Kip	717.5	818.6	926.2	1259.6	3296.2	7108.2
Malaysia	Ringgit	2,6	2,5	2,5	2,8	3,9	3,8
Myanmar	Kyat	5,9	5,6	5,9	6,2	6,2	6,3
Philippines	Peso	26,4	25,7	26,2	29,5	40,9	38,9
Singapore	S$	1,5	1,4	1,4	1,5	1,7	1,7
Thailand	Bath	25,1	24,9	25,3	31,3	41,3	37,8
Viet Nam	Dong	10978	11037	11032	11683	13297	14028

Source: Asian Development Outlook 2000, Asian Development Bank.

Table 4.7 Balance of payments on current account (percentage of GDP)

Asean Countries	1994	1995	1996	1997	1998	1999	2000[a]	2001[b]
Cambodia	−15.2	−14.5	−17.3	−8.8	−8	−8.4	−9	−10
Indonesia	−1.7	−3.3	−3.4	−2.3	4.1	3.5	2.2	0.5
Laos	−14.4	−13	−16.6	−16.8	−10.6	−10.3	−11	−12
Malaysia	−6.1	−9.8	−4.9	−5	12.9	14	11.3	8.1
Myanmar	−0.1	−0.2	−0.2	−0.2	−0.2	NA	NA	NA
Philippines	−4.6	−4.5	−4.7	−5.3	1.7	9.1	6.3	5.6
Singapore	16.4	17.3	15.9	15.8	20.9	18.5	17.8	16
Thailand	−5.4	−7.9	−7.9	−2.1	12.7	9.1	5.5	1.9
Viet Nam	−8	−11	−10.3	−6.5	−4.4	2.3	0.8	−1.4

a. forecasted; b. forecasted.

Source: Asian Development Outlook 2000, Asian Development Bank.

4.1 Financial and corporate sector reform in Malaysia

Malaysia's experience of financial restructuring differed from the other crisis countries in two aspects. First, Malaysia began with a stronger financial sector. Before the crisis it had developed more effective bankruptcy and foreclosure laws, as well as a stronger supervisory capacity. The banking sector was also well capitalised, with capital-asset ratios exceeding 10 per cent. Nonetheless, the deepness of the regional financial crisis, and its effects on the domestic economy, together with the high level of non-performing loans (NPLs), led the authorities to introduce a number of measures to promote the consolidation of the industry and enhance its competitiveness. Second, as noted above, Malaysia altered its macro-economic course in September 1998, choosing to impose capital controls rather than accept an IMF rescue package (ADB 2000).

Prior to the crisis, official indicators of the Malaysian financial system's soundness had actually improved significantly during the years: the ratio of NPL's to total loans in banks and finance companies fell from 20 per cent in 1990 to about 3.8 per cent for banks and 4.7 per cent for finance companies in 1996 (Lindgren et al. 1999). However, the persistent pace of credit expansion at an annual rate of nearly 30 per cent to the private sector (particularly to the property sector and for the purchase of stock and shares) exposed the financial system to potential risks from the price declines in property and other assets that occurred in 1997. In response to these deficiencies, the Central Bank (Bank Negara Malaysia, BNM) had earlier imposed limits on property lending – 20 per cent of total loans – and securities lending for the purchase of shares, effective on 1 April 1997. In October 1997, the authorities issued a new directive that no new loans should be approved for the property sector, except for low-income housing. Banks were asked to submit credit plans for 1998 to moderate loan growth of the banking system to 20 per cent by March 1998 and 15 per cent by end-1998.

The combination of the economic slowdown, decline in asset values, rising interest rates, and the depreciation of the ringgit severely affected the level of credit performance and bank profitability. As the regional crisis deepened, concerns about the true conditions of the financial system increased, and were related to: (1) the exceptionally fast rate of growth of credit in the banking system; (2) the exceptionally-high leverage of the private sector (163 per cent); (3) the concentration of bank loans in real estate development and in financing share purchases; and (4) the decline in asset qualities given the slowdown in economic activity.

The authorities announced several measures, effective on 1 January 1998, including a requirement for banks to classify loans as non-performing when they were three months overdue; an acceleration of the classification of doubtful loans from 12 months overdue to six months, and bad loans from 24 to 12 months; and a rise in the required general loan-loss reserves from 1 per cent to at least 1.5 per cent.

On March 25, 1998, the authorities announced a package of measures aimed at strengthening the financial system. The measures focused on:

– broad-based strengthening of the regulatory and supervisory framework requirements for increased disclosure;
– strengthening the finance company sector through consolidation into a smaller number of core companies;
– pre-emptive re-capitalisation of banks.

The measures also included initiatives to improve the framework for bank liquidity management and monetary operations.

4.1.1   The restructuring program

By April 1998 the program's improvements targeted at the loan classification and provisioning standards had been completed. In addition to a broad diagnostic review of the banking system in March 1998, the central bank grouped the banks into three categories: sound banks, those on a secondary watch list, and those on a primary watch list.

In July 1998, the Government announced a plan to bring about a consolidation of the financial industry covering 58 financial institutions (21 banks, 25 finance companies and 12 merchant banks). It was hoped that the consolidation would improve the competitiveness of the domestic banking industry, while at the same time avoiding the potentially destabilising consequences of a number of domestic banking institutions going bankrupt. During 1998, however, as the economy and loan quality deteriorated sharply, the finance company merger program was scaled back.

During summer 1998, an institutional framework was established to strengthen efforts to rehabilitate the commercial banking system by using public funds to acquire NPLs and re-capitalising commercial banks, while at the same time facilitating the restructuring of corporate debt. Danaharta, a public asset management company, was established in June 1998 to acquire NPLs, and to appoint special administrators who could take control and manage the assets of a borrower unable to pay its debts. Danamodal was established in August 1998, as a limited liability company owned by BNM, with objectives to inject new capital in undercapitalised banks and facilitate the rationalisation of the system. A Corporate Debt Restructuring Committee (CDRC) was also established to act as an informal debtor/creditor broker to achieve debt restructuring as an alternative to companies filing for bankruptcy.

The reforms described above were complicated by attempts by the authorities to stimulate credit growth in the face of the economic downturn. While the authorities wished to use interest rates to stimulate credit, they were constrained by onshore/offshore interest-rate differentials. These differentials limited the scope for reducing onshore interest rates without possibly triggering ringgit flight offshore. The authorities, therefore, introduced additional measures in September 1998 aimed at eliminating the offshore ringgit market, fixing the exchange rate, and improving the conditions for increased bank lending. The measures included:

- Exchange controls measures to restrict international capital flows, which eliminated the offshore ringgit market, and prohibited non-residents from repatriating portfolio capital held in Malaysia for a period of 12 months.[3]
- The fixing of the exchange rate at RM 3.8:US$1.
- The reduction of the statutory reserve requirements to 4 per cent of eligible liabilities (from 10 per cent in February 1998 to 8 per cent in August).

- The relaxation of existing limits on lending to the property sector and for the purchase of shares.
- The establishment, at 8 per cent, of a floor target for credit growth during 1998.
- Changes in the classification system, so that the default period for classifying loans as non-performing was increased from three to six months.

In July 1999, a central-bank decree outlined an even more radical restructuring plan designed to increase the size and competitiveness of the financial sector: to cut the number of commercial banks from 21 to 6, finance companies from 25 to 6 and merchant banks from 12 to 6, with each class of institutions built around a small number of 'anchor' institutions. The plan sought to identify merger partners by end-September 1999, and offered tax incentives to facilitate the merger process. The plan was highly directive: the bank identified the likely anchor institutions and how they would be built. As many as four of the six new banks would continue to have significant government equity, maintaining the government's presence in the financial sector, and even increasing it in relative terms.

4.1.2   Corporate sector restructuring

While the Malaysian government did establish institutions for managing bank and corporate restructuring, not all interventions took place through these institutions. In contrast to other countries in the region, a distinguishing feature of the Malaysian response to the crisis has been to extend support directly to a number of firms. Not all were straightforward bailouts; some involved indirect forms of support. Some actions could have been predicted by government efforts to use companies to fulfil social and foreign policy objectives. But others appear to stem from political and even family connections to recently privatised companies (Haggard 2000).

A common pattern in these cases has been for the government to initiate projects, either directly through state owned enterprises or through policy decisions, and then to privatise those efforts in whole or in part to favoured private partners. Not all these partners were selected on the basis of political criteria alone; all had some prior experience in business. But the discretionary and non-transparent means of allocating assets and contracts, as well as the personal connections to government officials, created risks. Because the selected government projects served some broader political and policy purposes – such as diversification of the economy (Proton); supplying credit to bumiputera borrowers (Bank Bumiputra); advancing foreign policy goals (Hottick); supplying infrastructure (Renong, Ekran) – the government had strong incentives to intervene to keep the projects afloat when they experienced distress. In all cases, the government's private partners have been shielded to some extent from losses they might have otherwise incurred.

Besides direct intervention to support some strategic firms, the Malaysian authorities also resorted to instruments and policies that were common to other crisis countries. A number of measures addressed the issues of accessibility to credit, while others aimed at stimulating output and exports, and employment.[4]

Some measures were also taken with the broader aim of promoting economic activity. Equity guidelines in the manufacturing sector were relaxed, so that all applications received between 31 July 1998 and 31 December 2000 were to be exempted from both equity and export conditions. Excise duty on some products, such as refrigerators, televisions, and air conditioners, were abolished to improve the competitiveness of local firms. A total of RM200 million has been allocated for a new micro-credit scheme to provide assistance to petty traders and hawkers in urban areas. This scheme, in particular, targets the poor and lower income group, which may have suffered a drop in real income as a result of higher prices and retrenchment.

Despite the accomplishments, some challenges remain. Low capacity utilisation rates in the manufacturing sector and rising vacancy rates in the property sector make it difficult for financial institutions to identify new safe lending opportunities. Operational restructuring of the corporate sector needs to be accelerated, while the government's objective of consolidating the financial sector still remains to be achieved. Thus far, Malaysian banks and businesses have been too slow in undertaking operational restructuring.

4.2 Financial and corporate sector reform in Thailand

In response to banking sector weaknesses in the 1980s, the Thai authorities had initiated reform measures, including the creation of the Financial Institutions Development Fund (FIDF), a separate legal entity within the Bank of Thailand (BOT) with a mandate to restructure, develop, and provide financial support to financial institutions (Lindgren et al. 1999). Notwithstanding these efforts, the authorities failed to manage the risks in the rapidly growing banking system. Among the main structural weaknesses, the quality of loan portfolios in banks and financial institutions was weak, as shown by the high and increasing rate of NPLs, while banks and finance companies had not put aside sufficient reserves for their deteriorating loan portfolios. These structural weaknesses resulted, in part, from weaknesses both in the content and the implementation of prudential regulations. The rules for loan classification, provisioning, and accounting, for example, were inadequate and were applied inconsistently. There were no prudential limits on loans concentration: banks built up excessive exposure to particular sectors such as the property market; there was also excessive lending based on collateral rather than proper credit assessment.

Finance companies had the largest exposure to the property sector and were the first institutions affected by the economic downturn. Much of the later spill-over to the banking sector was triggered by the failure of the initial measures to stabilise this sector. After the peg of the bath was abandoned on 2 July 1997, the depreciating exchange rate and falling property values led to major deterioration of banks' loan portfolios. This raised concerns about the solvency of the entire financial system. Estimates undertaken by an IMF advisory mission during summer 1997 indicate that many of Thailand's 91 finance companies were insolvent, while banks as a group were solvent, but undercapitalised.

The authorities, together with the IMF, developed a strategy to restructure the financial system based on three steps:

1. exit of all non-viable financial institutions;
2. issuance of a temporary blanket guarantee protecting all depositors and creditors in the remaining financial institutions (so as to calm the market and give the authorities sufficient time for restructuring measures);
3. restructuring and rehabilitating of the Thai financial system to raise to international standards.

A Financial Restructuring Agency (FRA) was established to replace the Bank of Thailand and the Ministry of Finance temporarily as decision-makers on all matters related to financial sector restructuring.

The program was promptly implemented. The policy framework was built on the separation of finance companies facing actual or imminent insolvency from those that were judged to be viable. Finance companies deemed to be facing actual or imminent insolvency were suspended and given 60 days to complete due diligence and present a rehabilitation plan to the Committee on Supervision of Merger or Transfer. In all, 58 finance companies out of 91 had their operation suspended. A government guarantee for depositors and creditors in all remaining finance companies and banks was announced, even if there were major uncertainties surrounding the guarantee.

However, there were delays in initiating some of the announced restructuring measures. The magnitude of the problems, along with interagency issues of co-ordination and political problems, all took time to resolve, delaying the implementation of necessary policies. An asset management company was established in October to deal with assets of the 58 finance companies that had their operations suspended. By December 1997, the permanent closure of 56 finance companies was announced; only two companies were allowed to reopen. Immediately after the closure, the focus of the FRA shifted to managing their assets, in order to prevent a further deterioration in asset quality prior to disposition.

4.2.1 Banking sector issues

Initial crisis resolution had focused on finance companies, but it soon became clear that banks also faced problems and that the public had started to loose confidence in the banks. Banks' asset quality was deteriorating, and many banks experienced deposit withdrawals and reduced rollover rates for external credit lines. Bank of Thailand data show that, as of the end of June 1997, all banks had a capital shortfall that amounted to 400 billion bath.

On 14 October 1997, the Thai authorities announced their strategy for dealing with the banking sector:

- All banks were required to write down and then increase capital in order to absorb the losses that had already occurred.
- None of the banks was allowed to pay dividends for the remaining part of 1997 or during 1998.
- Banks were required to present re-capitalisation plans to the BOT, and the requested capital would have to be injected at the latest during the first quarter of 1998.
- Banks were encouraged to try to find foreign partners since it was unlikely they could raise all the capital needed in Thailand.
- For banks that could not raise the capital, losses would be written off against capital, ensuring that existing shareholders lose their stake. The FIDF would take control of the banks, re-capitalise them and later privatise them or merge them with another bank.

The BOT was initially reluctant to intervene in banks since it feared that interventions could cause a run on the whole banking system. But with the October 1997 amendments to the Commercial Banking Act, the BOT was given specific powers to write down capital and change management on troubled commercial banks. On 31 December 1997, the BOT intervened in a medium-sized bank, Bangkok Metropolitan Bank, where management was changed. In the following month, the BOT intervened in two more banks (First Bangkok City Bank and Siam City Bank), that together with the former represented 10 per cent of the banking system's deposits. In mid-May, the BOT intervened in seven finance companies, thereby becoming the owner of six banks and nine finance companies, which accounted for one-third of total deposits.

The above measures primarily addressed the immediate liquidity and solvency problems, but there was also a need for a strategy to strengthen the remaining viable financial institutions. Focusing on the longer run, more attention was given to the prudential framework. The strategy was to maintain the capital adequacy requirement of 8.5 per cent for banks and 8 per cent for finance companies, but allow gradualism in building up loan-loss provisions. New loan classification, loss provisioning and interest suspension rules were issued on 31 March 1998.

By mid-1998, the depth of the crisis raised doubts whether the measures would be sufficient to create the necessary private sector re-capitalisation and efficient restructuring of the sector. Uncertainties about the effectiveness of the market-based and private sector-led restructuring of Thailand's financial system were rising.

On August 14, 1998 the government unveiled a new initiative for the banking sector (Haggard 2000). The centrepiece of the new strategy was a complex, and voluntary, re-capitalisation scheme, backed by only implicit threats if re-capitalisation targets were not met. But the conditions for financial support were onerous. Not only would the government have to approve the banks' restructuring plans, but banks would have to adopt end-2000 provisioning requirements immediately; given NPLs of 30–40 per cent of total portfolios, this would imply an immediate write-off of shareholder capital. Moreover, the government retained the right to displace existing management.

Banks showed little interest in the program, turning rather to a number of short-term instruments to meet capitalisation targets. By relying on these instruments, bank owners sidestepped the need to raise 'real' capital and bought time. Although the government set aside Bt 300 billion for the program, it had to be modified in June 1999 and by September only 13 per cent of the funds had been used.

4.2.2   Progress and implementation

Thailand has made greater progress in improving the supervisory and regulatory framework surrounding the financial sector (ADB 2000). The authorities are enforcing new loan classifications and provisioning requirements, and the supervisory functions of the BOT are being strengthened. All financial institutions have signed a memorandum of understanding that describes their plans to raise capital. The more stringent provisioning requirements for non-performing assets are being phased in from the second half of 1998 until the end of 2000. The BOT also began implementing a modernisation program aimed at redesigning the bank's organisational structure, streamlining work processes, and improving corporate governance.

Resolution of non-restructurable NPLs relies on efficient foreclosure and liquidation processes, both of which take years. Nonetheless, there are signs of progress. The BOT reported that NPLs of financial institutions as of March 2000 amounted to Bt 1.99 trillion (37 per cent of total loans). In the first quarter of year 2000 new NPLs continued to enter into system, but at a slower pace (1.8 per cent of total loans) than in the previous quarter (2.5 per cent of total loans).

A draft of the 'Financial Institution Law' was approved by Cabinet and the Council of State during the first quarter of year 2000. The emphasis of the draft law includes financial liberalisation, strengthened supervision, prompt corrective action, and improvement in disclosure and corporate governance.

The draft law is awaiting final cabinet endorsement, after which it will be submitted to the lower House for the first reading.

It seems that Thailand will continue with its slow 'voluntary' way for restructuring, whereby the public authority has a 'stimulus' rather than an executive role. A report of the Executive board of the IMF seems to stand by this view. It warned, however, of extra caution in order for the restructuring not to slow further down and also to press ahead with the restructuring of state owned banks, which account for more than half of the system-wide NPLs.

4.2.3 Reform measures for the corporate sector

Thailand's strategy for corporate restructuring, like that of the other countries, consisted of new institutions, better incentives, and improvements in the legal framework. In August 1998, the government created the Corporate Debt Restructuring Advisory Committee and attempted to create an effective legal framework for recovering debt through bankruptcy legislation, while providing tax and other incentives to encourage corporations and banks to restructure bad debt.

In Thailand, more than in other countries, corporate restructuring has been hindered by delays in the reform of bankruptcy laws. Such delays were often due to the fact that some political figures, particularly Senators, were closely involved in some of the failing businesses.

Reform of the bankruptcy process had been a condition of the second Letter of Intent with the IMF in November 1997, but legislation proposed by the government ran into strong objections from Senators who would be adversely affected by the legislation, including particularly the heads of two heavily indebted groups, Thai Petrochemical and NTS Steel. When bankruptcy reform was first examined in early 1998, objections centred on the relative powers granted to creditors and debtors in the new process, including the ability to appoint administrators who would influence the restructuring plan, and the absence of provisions that would allow debtors to remain in possession. Opponents feared that the lack of Thai insolvency experts would lead foreign creditors to appoint foreign insolvency professionals, who would have less of an interest in reviving the company. The changes introduced by the Senate contributed to a bill that discouraged its use; moreover, accompanying legislation governing foreclosure was not passed. Between May, when the bill was passed, and August only five business rehabilitation plans had been filed with the courts. When the amended bills were reintroduced in the fall, the criticism in the Senate widened to include a range of new issues and changes that would have weakened the legislation. In the end, the changes brought forward in the examination process were mostly pushed aside, and the bankruptcy and foreclosure laws passed with procedural concessions to the Senate. But the process had taken the government over fifteen months to complete, and even then concerns remained that the procedural concessions with respect to the appeals process made the bankruptcy process unwieldy.

Apart from reforming bankruptcy legislation, the financial crisis has highlighted the need for more clear rules and legal standards to govern the relationships among shareholders, directors, and management. These include rules and standards addressing the fiduciary duty of directors and responsibility of management, the protection of shareholder rights and most, importantly, enforcement of those rights. While substantial progress has been made in improving corporate governance, much of the reform agenda remains unfinished. The government has approved draft legislation to streamline the institutional framework for setting standards and regulating the profession. The Thailand Financial Accounting Standard Board has been established as an independent entity with authority for setting accounting standards, and the Institute of Certified Accountants and Auditors of Thailand was made an independent self-regulatory professional body consistent with international best practice.

At the same time, the Public Companies Act is being amended to improve shareholder protection: changes relate mainly to access to performance-related information and procedures for calling a shareholder meeting. But, in order to improve corporate governance practices, Thailand will need to intensify its effort to provide clear and enforceable securities and public companies laws to protect shareholder rights and to ensure an effective regulatory framework capable of enforcing such laws.

4.2.4   Progress and implementation

Overall pace of the debt restructuring completion rate has slowed down in the first quarter of year 2000.[5] At the end of March 2000, financial institutions increased the total completed debt restructuring by 52 579 cases from December 1999 to a total of 213 791 cases. The credit amount restructured over the same period increased by Bt 207 billion to a total of Bt 1.29 trillion.

As for court-supervised restructuring, 14 business re-organisation petitions (value over Bt 169 billion) were filed with the Central Bankruptcy Court between January through March 2000, a substantial increase from the total of 37 cases (Bt 363 billion) filed in 1999. Liquidation petitions have also increased during the first quarter of 2000, probably due to the fact that debtors and creditors have a better understanding of the bankruptcy law and are more confident in the legal protection under the court system. More debtors are filing petitions to protect their businesses as out-of-court direct negotiations with creditors proved futile.

Since the crisis, most sectors have experienced a reduction in the debt-to-equity ratio. For example, the debt-to-equity ratio for the construction sector fell from 7 per cent in 1997 to around 3 in 1999. Similar trends can be observed in manufacturing and commerce. But the level of debt-to-equity remains high, particularly in the construction sector.

Despite progress, some weaknesses remain, and will increasingly pose a challenge to the government if a real reform has to be achieved. Creditor-driven removal of capacity is by and large not occurring. Even where firms have negative equity and whose petitions are likely to be accepted by the bankruptcy court, creditors have in general not filed petitions and as a result assets are not clearing. Few, if any, mergers between distressed firms have occurred. The merger process in Thailand is time consuming and onerous, requiring a six-month notification period during which creditors may object to the merger or demand immediate payment. The law requires that the two merged entities lose legal status before creating a new legal entity out of the two independent units. The authorities need to consider removal of these impediments to streamline market-led mergers and acquisitions.

4.3   Malaysia and Thailand compared: a tentative assessment

By comparing both countries' restructuring efforts, a number of areas can be identified where Malaysia and Thailand showed similar features: policy and structural weaknesses, corporate debt restructuring, openness to foreign direct investment. On the other hand, there are some issues, whose analysis clearly shows the different approaches adopted by the two governments – capital control measures, financial sector restructuring, presence of political hurdles.

Policy and structural weaknesses
Before the crisis, a feature of both Malaysia and Thailand, as of most East Asian countries, was the coexistence of uninterrupted growth and both policy and structural weaknesses in the banking and corporate sectors, weaknesses that were magnified by growing capital inflows before the crisis and their subsequent massive reversal.[6] Among the structural weaknesses were ineffective bank regulation and supervision and poor accounting and disclosure, each significantly diminishing transparency. Many family-run conglomerates owned banks and exerted influence over governments, while bad laws and ineffective courts contributed to inadequate protection of minority shareholders. Well before the crisis, East Asian governments sought to influence the allocation of funds in the economy. The resulting banking system relied on tacit government approval of large loans (to sectors, if not to individual firms), and it was understood that major banks would not be allowed to fail. Furthermore, these weaknesses reinforced each other: efforts to upgrade supervision were undermined by the political connections of powerful banks. This tendency toward high corporate leverage was compounded by the controlling owners' reluctance to cede control or to disclose much information.

In addition, policy flaws made the crisis worse. Foreign exchange policies provided stable exchange rates for extended periods, reducing the perceived risks of borrowing and lending in foreign currency, thereby encouraging the growth of foreign currency debt and discouraging the use of hedging instruments. Governments also fostered foreign currency intermediation directly, through arrangements such as the Bangkok International Banking Facility (where foreign bank loans grew from $8 billion in 1993 to $50 billion in 1996), and indirectly, through higher taxation of local relative to foreign currency intermediation. More generally, the liberalisation of domestic financial systems and capital flows since the late 1980s occurred without parallel strengthening of prudential regulation and supervision, facilitating greater risk-taking by financial institutions.

Capital control measures

With a deepening economic crisis, the Malaysian authorities were hoping to lower domestic interest rates, which proved difficult with Singapore's nearby market offering ringgit transactions and trading in Malaysian shares.[7] Therefore, in September 1998, Malaysia decided to impose capital controls in an effort to weaken the link between internal and external financial markets. In February 1999 the controls were converted into taxes on repatriated short-term flows, applied at a graduated scale inverse to maturity.

Malaysia's capital controls ran counter to orthodoxy, and many observers predicted severe consequences. But the results were actually rather positive. Foreign exchange reserves increased $10 billion between September 1998 and October 1999, a rise second only to Korea's among the crisis countries and the largest in percentage terms. Offshore activities, especially in Singapore, dried up, thereby reducing the potential pressure from an organised offshore parallel market. Capital outflows were only about $330 million in the quarter after controls were lifted on 1 September 1999, far less than predicted, even if this may partly reflect the graduated tax format and partly the expectation that the Malaysian market index would be restored to the Morgan Stanley Capital International index.

The fact that the dire consequences anticipated by the critics of the selective capital controls did not materialise can be attributed to three reasons: first, the ringgit was pegged at a level where it was 'undervalued'; second, the measures made a clear distinction between short- and long-term capital; and third, they were skilfully implemented.[8]

The inflow of international capital into Asia from the end of 1998 has allowed the pegged ringgit to remain competitive as other regional currencies appreciated. The 'undervalued' ringgit gives Malaysian export a price edge, resulting in a double-digit export growth in 1999. Consequently, Malaysia recorded large trade surpluses and as the selective capital controls require export proceeds to be brought back into the country, this has increased liquidity in the economy and revived domestic consumption.

The Malaysian capital control measures restricted only short-term capital, which is normally invested in the equity market, but continued to encourage the inflow of FDI. Investment in equity market can easily leave the country if current sentiment changes but FDI are investments in the manufacturing sector, with longer gestation period and closer linkages to the domestic economy. The separation between short- and long-term capital was essential for the recovery of the Malaysian economy because the selective capital controls did not deter the inflow of long-term foreign capital.

Finally, the skilful management of the capital controls has prevented the creation of a black market for the ringgit. At the early stage of the introduction of the selective capital controls, BNM had ensured that there was adequate supply of foreign currencies to meet any increase in demand and this move has calmed the market and has created confidence among the general public.

Of course, the selective capital control measures implemented by Malaysia are not without costs. When the international capital returned to the region from the fourth quarter of 1998, Malaysia missed most of the capital inflow as reflected by the steep recovery of the equity markets of other crisis-hit countries. Another aspect of the costs concerns the issue of policy consistency – there are concerns that a similar policy can be reintroduced without prior warning. This can contribute to a higher international risk premium for Malaysia, which translate to higher funding costs. However, up to the present the benefit of the selective capital controls have out-weighed the costs.

Even if the timing and conditions of their implementation were different from Malaysia's case, Thailand too resorted to capital controls to limit growing pressures on the exchange rate. In May 1997 the authorities tried to stem capital outflows by limiting transactions with and by non-residents.[9] With the July float of the bath, a dual market in foreign exchange (onshore and offshore) was allowed to develop, and stricter conditions were later imposed on the surrender of export receipts. Largely ineffective in stemming capital outflows, the restrictions were lifted in January 1998. The ineffectiveness of the controls is not surprising: they were limited, especially in their inapplicability to residents, who could purchase foreign exchange with bath. Broad money was actually slightly less in nominal terms at the end of the second and third quarters of 1997 than in March 1997, and in real terms in the fourth quarter of 1997 as well. These declines suggest an outflow of residents' deposits, particularly taking into account the substantial increase in domestic dollar deposits (in bath terms) during this period of depreciation and the large increase in central bank credit.

Different approaches to financial restructuring
The crisis countries have taken different approaches to re-capitalising banks and resolving non-performing assets. Malaysia, for example, has injected public funds into undercapitalised banks while transferring a portion of non-performing loans to a centralised, publicly owned asset management corporation, that is responsible for recovering assets and restructuring the financial

liabilities of over-indebted debtors. Thailand, by contrast, has tied the provision of public funds to more stringent conditions imposed on bank owners. Thailand has not created a centralised asset management corporation to dispose of non-performing loans because it wants banks to re-capitalise themselves and devise their own asset disposition strategies.

Malaysia's restructuring program has been tightly orchestrated by the government, emphasising mergers and avoiding closures of financial institutions or sales to foreign institutions. Malaysia was somewhat slower than the other countries in devising an institutional structure for handling the financial and corporate restructuring process, in part because the depth of the problems in the banking sector was substantially less. It was not until mid-1998 that the government established three new institutions to deal with the problems of non-performing assets in the financial system, bank re-capitalisation and corporate debt restructuring. But the operation of the formal institutions did not constitute the full scope of the government's approach to financial and corporate distress; the government also engaged in a number of bank and corporate bailouts.

Thailand, on the other hand, closed two-thirds of its finance companies, with the FRA auctioning off most of the assets acquired from them. The establishment of bank-owned asset management corporations was then encouraged by the removal of tax disincentives and by a regulation allowing private banks to transfer loans to their majority-owned asset management corporations at book value, less provisioning required under a phased-in forbearance program. This strategy clearly differentiates Thailand's reform program from other programs in the region. In Malaysia, the government vested new public institutions to resolve corporate debts and restructure banks. Thailand did the same for the finance companies, which were the first hit by the crisis, but which represented a small part of the overall losses in the system. However, for banks, which went into crisis later, the Thai Government has followed a market-led, decentralised approach to reform.

Corporate debt restructuring

Both in Malaysia and Thailand, the government's initial strategy did not directly address the question of corporate debt restructuring. Institutional efforts where finally implemented during Summer 1998, when a corporate debt restructuring committee was established in both countries, with the aim of facilitating debtors-creditors relations.

Malaysia and Thailand, like other crisis countries, relied heavily on voluntary, out-of-court settlements for corporate restructuring, the hallmark of the London approach.[10] Given the absence of well-functioning bankruptcy courts, this was perhaps inevitable. Within this framework, however, the government was expected to play the role of mediator, facilitating an orderly resolution, while banks, as creditors, managed the workout. Given their under-capitalisation and

Table 4.8 Summary of measures directed at financial sector restructuring

Measure	Malaysia	Thailand
Emergency measures		
Liquidity support	yes	yes
Introduction of a blanket guarantee	yes	yes
Institutional measures		
Establishment of an overarching restructuring authority	yes[1]	no
Establishment of a separate bank restructuring authority	yes	no
Establishment of a centralised asset management corp.	yes	no[2]
Adoption of a special corporate debt restruct. framework	yes	yes
Operational autonomy of restructuring agencies	yes	n.a.
Restructuring Measures		
Intervention in weak or insolvent financial institutions	yes	yes
Use of public funds to purchase non-performing assets	yes	no
Use of public funds to re-capitalise institutions	yes	yes
Elimination or dilution of current shareholder stakes of insolvent banks	yes	yes
New direct foreign investment	limited[3]	yes
Other measures		
Measures to encourage corporate restructuring	yes	yes
Steps to improve prudential supervision and regulation	yes	yes

1. steering committee chaired by the central bank; 2. the FRA was established to liquidate 56 closed finance companies, and the asset management company to deal with residual FRA assets; 3. foreign banks are allowed to purchase up to a 30 per cent stake.

Source: Lindgren et al. 1999.

the heavy burden of NPLs, banks did not play their part, particularly in Thailand. The large role played by foreign-based accounting firms, consulting agencies, and investment banks also complicated matters. These firms followed international standards for accountancy and due diligence, which were often more stringent than traditional local standards. The new and tougher criteria made it difficult for the lead banks and corporations to reach agreement on debt workouts. As a result, the London approach had only mixed success, and corporate reform has been slow.

Openness to foreign investment

It is important to consider the longer-term consequences of legal and regulatory changes spawned by the crisis which will take some time, perhaps a decade, to have effects at the level of the firm and particular markets. Two important examples are the development of bankruptcy and foreclosure laws and reforms of corporate governance. A third reform, born of financial constraint and pushed by the IMF but also championed by reformers, were the rules governing foreign direct investment.

Well before the crisis, all countries had already begun to liberalise the rules governing foreign direct investment. This was particularly true in Malaysia and Thailand which took advantage of the sharp appreciation of the yen in the mid-1980s to position themselves as major sites for manufacturing investment not only from Japan, but from the other newly industrialising countries, the United States and Europe as well. However, the rules governing foreign direct investment were often ringed with exceptions, for example emphasising export-oriented industries, shielding the non-tradable goods sector, and particularly finance, from foreign entry, and continuing to impose equity requirements.

In all countries, the crisis accelerated the liberalisation of foreign investment, often with the explicit objective of facilitating the restructuring process. In Thailand, the government eased restrictions governing land ownership and replaced the Alien Business Law of 1972 with a new Foreign Investment Law in October 1999. The new law retains a restrictive negative-list system and still requires firms to seek approval for investment in a number of sensitive sectors, but it opens domestic transport, retail trade, and legal services to foreign ownership. In the manufacturing sector, the Board of Investment substantially liberalised the criteria required for firms to receive investment incentives, particularly with respect to equity requirements, and even set up a mergers and acquisitions unit. Foreign firms responded quickly by expanding their stake in joint ventures or buying out partners entirely. Finance Minister Tarrin was also explicit in his desire to use foreign investors to facilitate the financial restructuring process. Foreign parties were major bidders in the asset sales organised by the FRA, and the government encouraged Thai banks to seek foreign equity partners and approved foreign take-overs of four failed banks in 1998.

Of the ASEAN countries, Malaysia was the most aggressive in courting export-oriented foreign investment prior to the crisis, but a number of domestically-oriented and import-substituting industries, such as autos, were restricted. Following the crisis, the government eliminated sectoral restrictions on new manufacturing projects, allowed foreign joint-venture partners serving the domestic market to increase their shareholdings, and permitted wholly-owned foreign firms to expand their local sales. The imposition of the capital controls in September 1998 explicitly guaranteed convertibility on current account transactions and free flows of direct foreign investment and repatriation of interest, profits, and dividends and capital, thereby trying to minimise disruption to ongoing foreign operations. In one respect, however, Malaysia did take a more restrictive stance than the other most seriously affected countries. Wholly foreign-owned banks licensed in the past continue to occupy an important position in the financial system, but the government has retained the 30 per cent equity cap on new investment in the financial sector. Nor was foreign purchase of assets seen as a central component of the restructuring process.

4.3.1 Assessment of reforms

Almost three years after the onset of the Asian crisis, financial and corporate restructuring can be seen as a work in progress. All the crisis countries have begun to lay the foundations for stronger financial and corporate sectors. Throughout the region, new accounting standards, improved disclosure requirements, and better rules for corporate governance were introduced. However, effective implementation and enforcement of these rules are still lacking (ADB 2000).

Similarly, all the crisis countries have made progress in the task of financial and corporate restructuring, but much remains to be done. Banks remain undercapitalised and still hold large amounts of NPLs on their balance sheets. Public sector involvement has been much higher than anticipated: while restructuring, governments nationalised many weak financial institutions. Although all the region's governments have placed a high priority on divesting state owned banks and assets, willing and qualified buyers have been scarce. Consequently, the restructuring process will likely require a further infusion of public money.

The strength of the crisis countries' public commitment to structural, financial, and corporate reform may have contributed to their economic recovery. Market confidence – and hence the return of foreign direct and portfolio investment – has been boosted by the expectation that Asia will emerge from the crisis with more stable and efficient financial sectors than before. But it is too early to be certain of such success. Moreover, it is an open question whether some crisis countries have sufficient political leadership and institutional capacity to implement such massive and complex structural reforms within a short time. Institutional weaknesses, for instance, have been the main obstacle to rapid and efficient implementation of reform programs in Thailand.

Table 4.9 Fiscal costs of re-capitalisation (mid-October 1999) (per cent of 1998 GDP)

Cost	Malaysia	Thailand
Estimated re-capitalisation cost	10.0	31.9
Funds disbursed	4.2	23.9
Expected additional costs	5.8	8.0

Source: Asian Development Outlook 2000, Asian Development Bank.

Though much remains to be done, it is not too early for a critical appraisal of the region's reform efforts. With hindsight, the crisis countries did not have a well-designed plan to guide their financial and corporate restructuring. With the crisis deepening daily, these countries could not spend months designing an optimal reform program. Nonetheless, there are several lessons to be learned.

First, a comprehensive plan for the financial and corporate sector would have required more synchronised restructuring efforts. In every crisis country, the restructuring process began with financial institutions: balance sheets were cleaned up and capital bases strengthened so that these institutions could take charge of restructuring ailing firms. This strategy did not work, as financial institutions were ill-prepared to lead the corporate restructuring efforts. Their main priority was to avoid a further deterioration of their assets by becoming more conservative in lending and asset management and sharply scaling back normal intermediary operations. This retrenchment created a vicious circle in which heavily indebted but viable firms could not get credit. This, in turn, led to still more NPLs. In some countries stricter regulatory and supervisory standards made matters worse. In Thailand, for instance, banks became even more reluctant to lend as regulatory standards were tightened. This exacerbated the credit crunch, creating more business failures and deepening the recession. Although identifying all troubled firms and accurately forecasting how many will be able to survive the crisis are difficult, a comprehensive restructuring strategy based on a clear assessment of the corporate and financial sectors would avoid the costs of repeated bank restructuring.

Second, more attention should have been paid to minimising the damage to the credit system. A properly functioning credit system contains the most important financial and industrial information of the private sector. Similarly, corporations embody organisational and social capital that is difficult to recreate quickly. Thus, it is important to avoid damage to the credit system during bank restructuring and to minimise the erosion of social capital during corporate restructuring. Mergers and acquisitions are preferable to outright bank closure, and workouts are better than outright insolvency. Most of the crisis countries, among them Thailand, did not adhere to these principles. Many financial institutions were closed in the early months of the crisis without adequate thought about how this would affect the credit system. Similarly, institutional and supervisory improvements, although well intentioned, further endangered the credit system by making it more difficult for banks to function. Most countries did not, for instance, follow reform policies that would encourage mergers by liberalising domestic laws to make foreign take-overs easier.

Finally, the crisis countries had few intermediary institutions, such as investment banks, to facilitate mergers and acquisitions. Instead commercial banks, which specialised in providing short-term working capital, led the corporate restructuring effort, with disappointing results. Instead of evaluating project viability and debt-service capability, commercial banks were more inclined to recover as much of their loans as possible. If they could not recover collateral, the commercial banks kept the NPLs on their books and continued to provide short-term emergency financing to avoid further losses.

5. CONCLUSION

In this paper, we noted that convergence can take place at a number of different levels. We endeavoured, therefore, to separate out the 'real' convergence factors from the 'policy convergence' issues. We then used the case of Thailand and Malaysia as our 'case study'. Our main conclusion on the real side is that, in fact, there is evidence that Thailand and Malaysia, and indeed all of Southeast Asia, have been 'converging'. We showed this trend using both trade-related (less convincing) and structural change/'real' business cycle (more convincing) approaches.

However, the main debate with respect to whether or not Malaysia and Thailand may be 'diverging' centres on what we have called 'policy convergence'. Hence, we have focused most of the paper on this area.

When analysing financial and corporate restructuring efforts of the crisis countries in a comparative perspective, the cases of Malaysia and Thailand appear as particularly interesting. Malaysia declined an IMF rescue plan, opting for capital controls, and closed no financial institutions; Thailand, on the other hand, turned to the IMF for financial support, closed virtually all its finance companies, and subsequently adopted a more gradual, market-based approach to restructuring, with banks allowed to raise equity capital over a long period. But, even if the details have varied among crisis countries, the broad principles of financial and corporate restructuring have been similar.

While designing a reform program for the financial sector, all crisis countries adopted policies that were inspired by three broad principles: ensuring that government ownership would increase commensurately with the infusion of bank re-capitalisation; maximising the participation of the private sector by providing fiscal and administrative incentives; ensuring that the restructuring process was comprehensive and covered the institutional, legal and regulatory aspects of the banking sector as well as its financial health. A similar approach was also adopted for the restructuring of the corporate sector: new systems were adopted to restructure the debt of large firms, corporate debt restructuring committees were set up by many governments, domestic bankruptcy laws were strengthened to accelerate resolving bankruptcy cases, protect creditors' rights, and discipline managers. Policies to improve corporate governance were also embraced, so as to reduce ownership concentration, increase market competition, reduce government monopolies, strengthen the rights of minority shareholders and increase the transparency of financial reports and transactions.

Malaysia and Thailand, as in the case of most of the crisis countries, have made progress toward financial and corporate reform. However, there is much more to be done. The biggest risk facing the region is complacency. As markets recover and foreign investors return, the momentum for further reform is weakened. With the growing opposition from vested interests, the risks of backtracking are high. Slowing or halting the reform process would have serious consequences: it would erode investor confidence, waste the resources already expended, lose an opportunity to modernise Asia's financial and corporate sectors, and reduce the region's growth potential. The region has much to do, both in the short term, such as strengthening ongoing reforms and improving the governance process, and in the longer term, as reducing fiscal imbalances and developing financial markets (ADB 2000).

NOTES

*   This paper is the result of joint work. Michael Plummer wrote the introduction and paragraphs 2 and 3; Benedetta Trivellato wrote paragraph 4 and the conclusion.
1. For details on methodology, see Kim, Kose, and Plummer (2000).
2. Data included in this paragraph are taken from ADB (2000).
3. In view of concerns about the possibility of a massive capital outflow upon the expiration of the 12-month period in September 1999, the authorities in February 1999 replaced the 12-month rule with a declining scale of exit levies.
4. World Bank and Economic Planning Unit, Prime Minister's Office, Malaysia; 'The Asian Financial Crisis: Impact at the Firm Level - The Malaysian case' (1999).
5. World Bank - Thailand Economic Monitor, June 2000.
6. World Bank, East Asia - Recovery and Beyond (2000).
7. World Bank, East Asia - Recovery and Beyond (2000).
8. Mahani Zainal-Abidin, 'Malaysian Economic Recovery Measures: A response to Crisis Management and for Long-Term Economic Sustainability', Paper presented at the ASEAN University Network's Conference on Economic Crisis in Southeast Asia: Its Social, Political and Cultural Impacts, February 17–19, 2000, Bangkok, Thailand.
9. World Bank, East Asia - Recovery and Beyond (2000).
10. The London approach evolved in the UK when numerous firms faced bankruptcy in the recession of the early 1990s. During this period, more than 160 British companies used the London approach, in which creditor financial institutions and indebted firms work under the close co-ordination of a government institution (in the British case, the Bank of England), but outside the judiciary process.

REFERENCES

Asian Development Bank (2000), *Asian Development Outlook 2000*, Manila.
Corsetti, G., P. Pesenti and N. Roubini (1998), *What caused the Asian currency and financial crisis?*, mimeo.
Ding, W., I. Domac and G. Ferri (1998), *Is There a Credit Crunch in East Asia? World Bank Policy*, Washington D.C.: Research Working Paper No. 1959.

Ghosh, S.R. and A.R. Ghosh (1999), *East Asia in the Aftermath: Was there a Crunch?*, Washington D.C.: IMF Working Paper 99/38.

Goldstein, M. (1998), *The Asian Financial Crisis: Causes, Cures and Systemic Implications*, Washington D.C.: Institute for International Economics.

Haggard S. (2000), *The Political Economy of the Asian Financial Crisis*, Washington D.C.: Institute for International Economics.

Hardy, D. (1998), *Leading Indicators of Banking Crises: Was Asia Different?*, Washington D.C.: IMF Working Paper 98/91.

International Centre for the Study of East Asian Development (ICSEAD) (2000), *East Asian Economic Perspectives*, Vol. 11, February, pp. 105–106 and 147–148.

Kose, M., H. Kim A. and M.G. Plummer (2000), *Dynamics of Business Cycles in Asia: Evidence and Similarities*, mimeo, March.

Lane, T., A. Ghosh, J. Hamann, S. Phillips, M. Shulze-Ghattas and T. Tsikata (1999), *IMF-Supported Programs in Indonesia, Korea, and Thailand: A Preliminary Assessment*, Washington D.C.: IMF Occasional Paper No. 178.

Lindgren, C., T.J.T. Balino, C. Enoch, A. Gulde, M. Quintyn and L. Teo (1999), *Financial Sector Crisis and Restructuring - Lessons from Asia*, Washington D.C.: IMF Occasional Paper No. 188.

Mahani Z. (2000), 'Malaysian Economic Recovery Measures: A response to Crisis Management and for Long-Term Economic Sustainability', Paper presented at the ASEAN University Network's Conference on Economic Crisis in Southeast Asia: Its Social, Political and Cultural Impacts, February 17–19, Bangkok, Thailand.

Petri, P.A. (1993), 'An Analytical History of East Asian Integration', Ch. 1 in M. Kahler and J. Frenkel (eds), *Regionalism and Rivalry*, Cambridge: MIT Press.

Radelet, S. and J. Sachs (1998), *The Onset of the East Asian Financial Crisis*, Cambridge, Massachussets: National Bureau of Economic Research.

World Bank (1998), *East Asia: The Road to Recovery*, Washington D.C.

World Bank (1999a), Fiscal Policy Office and the Office of Industrial Economics, Bangkok, Thailand, *Thailand: The Road to Recovery*, Paper presented at the Conference 'Asian Corporate Recovery: Corporate Governance, Government Policy' - Bangkok, March 31-April 2.

World Bank (1999b), Economic Planning Unit, Prime Minister's Office, Malaysia, *The Asian Financial Crisis: Impact at the Firm Level - The Malaysian case*, Paper presented at the Conference 'Asian Corporate Recovery: Corporate Governance, Government Policy' - Bangkok, March 31-April 2.

World Bank (2000), *East Asia: Recovery and Beyond*, Washington D.C.

– (2000), *Malaysia - Corporate Sector Update*, March 20.

– (2000), *Thailand Economic Monitor*, June.

5. New Impulses Towards Economic Integration in East Asia: Prospects and Issues

Robert Scollay

1. INTRODUCTION

In the aftermath of the East Asian economic crisis, the East Asian economies are facing crucial choices not only in relation to internal economic reforms but also in relation to the future configuration of their international economic relations. While East Asia has long been recognised as one of the three major centres of global economic activity, it has not hitherto sought to establish itself as a formal economic bloc. In committing themselves to APEC, the East Asian economies had earlier chosen to emphasise trans-Pacific rather than intra-East Asian regional economic integration, based around non-discriminatory 'open regionalism' rather than the traditional preferential approach to regional integration.[1] Monetary integration had likewise not been a serious item on East Asia's economic agenda.[2]

A willingness to re-evaluate these choices has however become increasingly evident since the East Asian economic crisis. Recent commentators, for example Bergsten (2000)[3], have noted an increased interest among East Asian policymakers in the possible establishment of an East Asian economic bloc. A potential vehicle for the development of such a bloc was created in the late 1990s with the rapid formalisation of the 'ASEAN 7 plus three' group, comprising seven members of ASEAN[4] together with China, Japan and Korea. This group has now held summits for three successive years, and has moved quickly from exploratory talks to concrete initiatives on monetary co-ordination and co-operation. At the most recent summit a study was also commissioned on the possible establishment of an East Asian Free Trade Area.

Bergsten also reports that the upsurge of interest in East Asia in the possible creation of its own economic bloc has to an important degree represented a reaction to the experience of East Asia during the economic crisis of 1997–98 and its aftermath. At that time the United States was able to quickly squash embryonic proposals for the establishment of an Asian Monetary Fund (AMF), leaving the three most deeply-affected crisis economies with little option but to allow the response to the crisis to be led by the IMF and the United States. As the condition for IMF rescue packages, the three economies (Indonesia, Thailand and South Korea) had to accept the imposition of policy packages whose appropriateness has subsequently been questioned by economists not only in East Asia but also in the West. As Bergsten notes, East Asian policymakers have found it instructive to compare and contrast their own experience during the East Asian crisis with the achievement of the European Union in forging monetary arrangements of its own which have allowed it, first, to handle monetary and financial crises largely within its own institutional framework, and subsequently to underline its economic independence by launching its own single currency, the euro, as a potential rival to the dollar. There appears to be a growing determination on the part of East Asians to strike out for a greater degree of economic autonomy of their own, with the aim of ensuring that the degree of subservience to Western institutions and policy prescriptions experienced during the 1997–98 crisis and its aftermath cannot be repeated.

Establishment of an East Asian economic bloc would bring to fruition a concept first floated at the beginning of the 1990s by Malaysian Prime Minister Dr Mahathir Mohammed, with his stillborn proposal for establishment of an East Asian Economic Group (EAEG).[5] An East Asian bloc could also signal the emergence of a tripartite, or 'three-bloc' world, a possible development which was the subject of much discussion and considerable apprehension[6] in the early 1990s. The first of the three blocs, based on the European Union, already exists. NAFTA forms a substantial bloc in North America, which will be expanded into a Western Hemisphere bloc if the countries of the Western Hemisphere follow through on their 1998 decision[7] to establish the Free Trade Area of the Americas (FTAA) by 2005. An East Asian bloc would thus be the final step in the development of a 'three-bloc' global economic architecture.

The recent quickening of interest in the European experience among East Asian policy thinkers contrasts with earlier attitudes which tended to dismiss the European model of economic integration as inappropriate to East Asian conditions. In part the increased attention being paid to the European experience is a natural consequence of a willingness to contemplate deeper and more formal economic linkages among the East Asian economies. This inevitably raises a series of political questions regarding the conditions for successful integration. These include the degree to which successful trade integration needs to be accompanied by financial and monetary integration, and the extent in turn to which successful financial and monetary integration demands the co-ordination of macroeconomic and other economic policies as well as deeper market integration.

The evolution of the European Union represents one set of answers to these questions, developed within a particular economic, political and institutional context. As momentum begins to gather for deeper economic integration in East Asia a comparative analysis is of interest for two reasons. On the one hand it can indicate how far the objective conditions that favoured deeper integration in Europe are replicated in East Asia and how far East Asia is likely to be driven to find similar solutions to the issues raised by a move to deeper integration. On the other hand it may also indicate ways in which different conditions in East Asia may result in differences in the trajectory and final outcome of the integration process.

This chapter endeavours to provide a preliminary comparative analysis of this nature. The discussion focuses first on trade integration, and then widens to consider the financial and monetary aspects of economic integration. As a preliminary to the comparative discussion, the outline of a possible East Asian economic bloc and its place in the global economic architecture are briefly sketched in the next section.

2. A POSSIBLE EAST ASIAN BLOC IN GLOBAL PERSPECTIVE

Tables 5.1 and 5.2 provide a summary indication of the significance in global terms of the possible emergence of both an East Asian economic bloc and a 'three-bloc world'. Table 5.1 shows that an East Asian bloc comprised of the economies of Northeast and Southeast Asia[8] would account for just over 21 per cent[9] of world GNP as measured by official statistics. This compares with just under 31 per cent of world GNP for the three NAFTA economies, or just over 36 per cent of world GNP for the 34 prospective members of the FTAA. The European Union's share in official world GNP is almost 29 per cent, potentially rising to almost 31 per cent if all 13 candidate members are successful in gaining entry to the European Union as part of the latter's 'eastern enlargement'.

An East Asian economic bloc would thus represent a very significant part of the world economy as measured by official statistics, albeit accounting for a substantially smaller share than either the European Union or the Western Hemisphere economies. If GNP is measured in purchasing power parity terms the relativity in economic size between East Asia and the other two 'blocs' alters significantly. Even without Taiwan[10], the East Asian bloc is comparable in size to NAFTA, and substantially larger than the European Union.

Table 5.1 also indicates how far the world economy could be dominated by three large blocs in Europe, the Western Hemisphere and East Asia. These three blocs together would account for 88 per cent of world GNP as measured by official statistics. The countries excluded from the three blocs on the other

Table 5.1 Comparative GNP data for selected economic groupings

	GNP (US$b)	Population	GNP per capita	% of world GNP	ppp GNP US$b	% of world ppp GNP*
Japan-Korea	4 460	172	25 929	15.45	3 498	9.57
Japan-Korea-China	5 547	1 418	3 912	19.22	7 628	20.87
Northeast Asia	5 830	1 440	4 050	20.20		
AFTA (Southast Asia)	575	507	1 133	1.99	1 588	4.34
East Asia	6 122	1 925	3 180	21.21		
CER	436	23	18 974	1.51	438	1.20
East Asia = CER	6 558	1 948	3 366	22.72	9 654	26.41
NAFTA	8 914	397	22 454	30.89	9 444	25.83
Mercosur	1 112	210	5 293	3.85	1 440	3.94
FTAA	10 463	789	13 262	36.25	11 866	32.46
EU-15	8 280	375	21 420	28.69	7 564	20.69
EU-28	8 837	543	16 273	30.62		
East Asia + FTAA + EU-28	25 421	3 257		88.08		
WORLD	28 862	5 897	4 894	100.00	36 557	100.00

* *following excluded from group figures: APEC: Brunei, Peru, Taiwan; Andean Community: Peru; AFTA: Myanmar; Caricom: Monserrat, Surinam.*

Source: World Bank, World Development Report 1999/2000.

hand would account for not far short of 50 per cent of the world's population as well as a very substantial share of the world's land area.

Table 5.2 narrows the focus to East Asia, and shows that Northeast Asia accounts for over 90 per cent of total East Asian GNP, again as measured by official statistics. On this basis Japan, China and Korea are respectively the second-, seventh-, and fifteenth-largest economies in the world. On a per capita basis Japan and Hong Kong SAR have vastly higher incomes than any of the Southeast Asian economies except Singapore, and Korean per capita GNP is also roughly double the per capita GNP any Southeast Asian economy other than Singapore.

Thus despite the leading role taken by the ASEAN countries in promoting East Asian economic integration, it is clear that Northeast Asia would have to comprise the core of any East Asian bloc. The economies of Northeast Asia accordingly hold the key to any possibility that such a bloc might emerge. Dr Mahathir's earlier proposal for an East Asian Economic Grouping foundered in part on the unwillingness at that time of Japan and Korea in particular to support the establishment of an East-Asia wide preferential trading arrangement. This stance was consistent with the longstanding policy of those two countries of favouring rigid adherence to the GATT's (now WTO) non-discrimination and consequently avoiding involvement in preferential trading arrangements. This policy stance had led to Japan and Korea, along with Hong Kong SAR, being numbered among the last remaining 'friends of

Table 5.2 Shares in East Asian GNP and population

	% of East Asian GNP	% of East Asian Population
Japan	63.85	6.47
Korea	5.77	2.36
China P.R.	14.50	63.64
Hong Kong SAR	2.47	0.36
Taiwan	4.42	1.11
NORTHEAST ASIA	91.02	73.94
Brunei Darussalam	0.08	0.02
Cambodia	0.05	0.56
Indonesia	2.16	10.48
Laos	0.02	0.26
Malaysia	1.25	1.13
Myanmar	0.20	2.47
Philippines	1.23	3.85
Singapore	1.48	0.15
Thailand	2.10	3.13
Vietnam	0.40	4.01
SOUTHEAST ASIA (ASEAN)	8.98	26.06
EAST ASIA	100.00	100.00

Source: World Bank, World Development Report 1999/2000.

GATT Article I'.[11] At the same time, well-known political sensitivities and tensions have long been an important factor inhibiting any move towards closer economic integration among the Northeast Asian economies themselves.

Signs that Japan and Korea are willing to consider abandoning their respective policies of non-involvement in preferential trading arrangements have thus always been a crucial prerequisite for any credible discussion of a possible East Asian economic bloc. Evidence that the political obstacles to any such arrangement might be surmountable has been another prerequisite. The announcement by Japan and Korea that they were willing to consider the establishment of a free trade area, discussed in more detail below, was therefore an enormously significant development in this context.

3.   POTENTIAL FOR AN EAST ASIAN TRADE BLOC

The degree of trade integration between the economies of East Asia is already substantial, as can be clearly seen from Tables 5.3 and 5.4. From Table 5.3 it

Reforming Economic Systems in Asia

Table 5.3 Shares of East Asian/APEC economies in trade of Northeast Asian economies (%)

	Japan		Korea		China		Hong Kong SAR		Taiwan	
	Imports 1996–99	Exports 1996–99	Imports 1996–99	Exports 1996–99	Imports 1996–99	Exports 1996–99	Imports 1996–99	Exports 1996–99	Imports 1996–99	Exports 1996–99
WORLD	100.00	100.00	100.00	100.00	100.00	100.00	100.00	100.00	100.00	100.00
Japan			19.74	10.85	20.48	17.51	12.94	5.84	27.01	9.58
Korea	4.60	5.73			10.15	4.31	4.70	1.43	4.70	1.73
China	12.68	5.32	6.69	9.34			39.62	34.28	3.44	12.55
Hong Kong	0.65	5.93	0.68	7.60	4.83	21.38			4.58	11.57
Taiwan	3.94	6.60	1.93	3.71	11.72	1.97	7.57	2.47		
Northeast Asia	21.88	23.58	29.04	31.51	47.19	45.17	64.84	44.02	39.72	35.43
Brunei Darussalam	0.38	0.02	0.22	0.01	0.00	0.01	0.00	0.02	0.09	0.03
Cambodia	0.01	0.01	0.00	0.04	0.03	0.05	0.01	0.06	0.02	0.07
Indonesia	4.16	1.74	2.98	2.04	1.78	0.87	0.86	0.45	1.79	1.15
Laos	0.04	0.01	0.00	0.00	0.01	0.01	0.00	0.00	0.00	0.00
Malaysia	3.34	3.07	2.29	2.94	1.88	0.92	2.25	0.87	3.31	2.71
Myanmar	0.03	0.05	0.01	0.09	0.06	0.28	0.03	0.04	0.05	0.06
Philippines	1.50	2.02	0.64	1.93	0.36	0.73	0.67	1.09	1.22	1.27
Singapore	1.82	4.40	1.77	3.92	2.77	2.31	4.73	2.52	5.20	3.74
Thailand	2.88	3.27	0.86	1.49	1.55	0.75	1.59	0.94	1.61	2.05
Vietnam	0.62	0.33	0.14	1.11	0.21	0.55	0.12	0.31	0.33	1.03
Southeast Asia (ASEAN)	14.78	14.92	8.91	13.57	8.65	6.50	10.25	6.28	13.61	12.11
East Asia	36.66	38.50	37.96	45.07	55.83	51.67	75.08	50.30	53.33	47.54

Australia	4.26	1.94	4.23	1.70	2.21	1.23	0.99	1.34	2.84	1.48
New Zealand	0.67	0.35	0.52	0.13	0.28	0.15	0.22	0.18	0.39	0.07
CER	**4.93**	**2.29**	**4.75**	**1.84**	**2.49**	**1.38**	**1.21**	**1.52**	**3.24**	**1.55**
Western Pacific	**41.59**	**40.79**	**42.70**	**46.91**	**58.32**	**53.05**	**76.30**	**51.81**	**56.56**	**49.10**
USA	22.72	29.37	21.42	17.74	11.74	19.57	7.56	22.56	19.44	25.21
Canada	2.77	1.49	1.79	1.09	1.56	1.13	0.61	1.51	0.98	1.86
Mexico	0.50	0.98	0.22	1.12	0.13	0.30	0.10	0.30	0.05	0.90
NAFTA	**25.99**	**31.85**	**23.43**	**19.95**	**13.43**	**21.00**	**8.28**	**24.38**	**20.46**	**27.97**
Chile	0.84	0.20	0.75	0.31	0.33	0.32	0.11	0.31	0.67	0.18
APEC	**69.75**	**73.09**	**68.19**	**68.18**	**75.25**	**75.09**	**84.96**	**76.64**	**77.63**	**77.12**

Source: IMF Direction of Trade Statistics.

Table 5.4 Shares of East Asian/APEC economies in trade of principal Southeast Asian economies (%)

	Brunei Darussalam		Indonesia		Malaysia		Philippines		Singapore		Thailand		Vietnam	
	Imports 1996–99	Exports 1996–99	Imports 1996–99	Exports 1996–99	Imports 1996–99	Exports 1996–99	Imports 1996–99	Exports 1996–99	Imports 1996–99	Exports 1996–99	Imports 1996–99	Exports 1996–99	Imports 1996–99	Exports 1996–99
WORLD	100.00	100.00	100.00	100.00	100.00	100.00	100.00	100.00	100.00	100.00	100.00	100.00	100.00	100.00
Japan	8.08	49.83	18.86	21.63	21.94	12.07	20.49	15.13	16.29	7.05	25.80	15.03	10.70	20.31
Korea	1.40	16.39	6.86	6.16	5.30	2.88	6.70	2.12	3.19	2.94	3.57	1.62	11.94	1.15
China	1.91	0.09	4.51	4.40	2.88	2.55	2.99	1.35	4.07	3.12	3.63	3.31	7.76	3.18
Hong Kong	3.07	0.07	1.46	3.07	2.46	5.12	4.16	4.80	2.79	8.15	1.57	5.44	4.36	2.30
Taiwan	1.15	2.05	4.14	3.40	5.03	4.30	4.95	5.94	3.78	4.22	4.53	3.05	9.99	3.69
Northeast Asia	15.63	68.43	35.82	38.68	37.60	26.93	39.28	29.34	30.11	25.49	39.10	28.45	44.76	30.63
Brunei Darussalam			0.06	0.08	0.02	0.33	0.00	0.01	0.15	0.85	0.24	0.10	0.00	0.01
Cambodia	0.00	0.00	0.00	0.10	0.02	0.07	0.00	0.00	0.06	0.32	0.07	0.59	1.22	2.49
Indonesia	2.19	0.70			2.18	1.49	1.60	0.40	4.35	2.56	1.64	1.93	2.96	2.45
Laos	0.00	0.00	0.00	0.00	0.00	0.00	0.00	0.03	0.00	0.03	0.09	0.65	0.43	0.31
Malaysia	12.85	2.36	2.96	2.63			2.82	3.57	14.32	16.22	4.93	3.72	2.79	1.79
Myanmar	0.05	0.00	0.06	0.27	0.07	0.35	0.01	0.01	0.12	0.47	0.00	0.00	0.00	0.00
Philippines	0.37	0.04	0.33	1.32	1.68	1.44			1.72	2.13	1.10	1.35	0.75	0.00
Singapore	26.58	7.28	8.81	10.26	13.50	18.50	5.64	6.45			5.75	10.23	12.70	2.79
Thailand	3.24	9.66	3.11	1.63	3.70	3.54	2.33	2.81	4.77	4.48			4.44	4.94
Vietnam	0.05	0.01	0.66	0.70	0.25	0.45	0.67	0.23	0.38	1.29	0.32	0.97		
Southeast Asia (ASEAN)	45.32	20.04	16.00	16.98	21.42	26.17	13.07	13.53	25.85	28.36	14.15	19.56	25.29	16.71
East Asia	60.95	88.47	51.82	55.66	59.02	53.10	52.35	42.87	55.97	53.85	53.24	48.01	70.05	47.33

Australia	2.41	0.80	5.44	3.03	2.47	1.99	2.55	0.69	1.29	2.47	1.98	1.80	1.56	5.86
New Zealand	0.39	0.56	0.47	0.20	0.45	0.30	0.52	0.07	0.16	0.31	0.35	0.22	0.35	0.24
CER	2.80	1.35	5.91	3.23	2.92	2.30	3.07	0.76	1.45	2.78	2.32	2.02	1.92	6.09
Western Pacific	63.75	89.83	57.73	58.89	61.94	55.40	55.42	43.63	57.42	56.63	55.56	50.02	71.96	53.42
USA	11.92	6.31	10.69	14.81	17.15	20.05	20.29	32.93	16.11	18.24	12.95	20.32	2.91	5.14
Canada	1.11	0.02	1.52	0.90	0.66	0.73	0.77	0.90	0.42	0.36	0.67	1.12	0.27	1.22
Mexico	0.00	0.00	0.13	0.42	0.10	0.33	0.08	0.20	0.38	0.42	0.26	0.33	0.00	0.00
NAFTA	13.03	6.32	12.33	16.13	17.90	21.12	21.14	34.03	16.91	19.02	13.87	21.78	3.17	6.36
Chile	0.00	0.00	0.46	0.16	0.24	0.09	0.09	0.07	0.16	0.05	0.20	0.08	0.01	0.03
APEC	76.73	96.15	70.63	74.95	80.40	76.33	76.87	77.70	74.42	75.45	69.82	70.76	75.28	57.42

Source: IMF Direction of Trade Statistics.

can be seen that the share of intra-East Asian trade for the Northeast Asian economies ranges in the case of imports from 36 per cent for Japan to 75 per cent for Hong Kong SAR, and in the case of exports from 38 per cent for Japan to 51 per cent for China. The trade of China, Hong Kong and Taiwan is particularly heavily concentrated within Northeast Asia itself. By contrast Japan trades less intensively with its Northeast Asian neighbours, but conducts a larger share of its trade with Southeast Asia than any of the other Northeast Asian economies.

Table 5.4 shows that the trade of the Southeast Asian economies is even more concentrated within East Asia than that of Northeast Asia. The share of East Asia in Southeast Asian trade ranges from 52 per cent for Indonesia to 70 per cent for Vietnam (imports) and from 43 per cent for the Philippines to 88 per cent for Brunei (exports). It is also noticeable that most Southeast Asian economies conduct a much larger share of their trade with Northeast Asia than within Southeast Asia itself.[12] Northeast Asia generally accounts for between 25 per cent and 45 per cent of the trade of the Southeast Asian economies, whereas the share of intra-Southeast Asian trade typically lies within a range of 12 per cent to 25 per cent. Furthermore, a large part of this intra-Southeast Asian trade consists of trade between other Southeast Asian economies and Singapore, which typically accounts for over half of the intra-Southeast Asian trade of its ASEAN neighbours. Trade among the other Southeast Asian economies in generally much less intense.

Although Northeast Asia has traditionally been much more important as an import source than an export destination for Southeast Asian economies, Table 5.3 shows that it has become a very important export market for Southeast Asia as well, even if import shares still for the most part exceed export shares. Northeast Asia now accounts for a larger share than North America of the exports of every Southeast Asian economy except the Philippines.

Although these intra-East Asian trade shares are impressive, they are however significantly lower than the shares of intra-EU trade in the trade of the members of the European Union, which invariably exceed 50 per cent, and in 1996 averaged 64 per cent for imports and 63 per cent for exports.

Furthermore, the two most industrialised economies of East Asia, Japan and Korea, lie conspicuously at the bottom of the ranges of intra-East Asian trade for both imports and exports. The share of intra-East Asian trade for Japan in particular is the lowest for any of the economies shown in the two tables, at 36 per cent for imports and 38 per cent for exports. The relatively low share of intra-East Asian share for Japan is matched by a relatively large share for trade with North America, particularly the United States. The three NAFTA economies in total account for 26 per cent of Japan's imports and 32 per cent of its exports, with the United States accounting for by far the largest part of this trade. In fact, North America accounts for a larger share of both the exports and imports of Japan than either Northeast Asia or Southeast Asia.

Although Japan is unique among the East Asian economies in this respect, it is in general true however that North America continues to account for a significant share of the trade of most East Asian economies, as can also be clearly seen in Tables 5.3 and 5.4. It is also very noticeable that in almost all cases[13] North America is more important, often much more important to the East Asian economies as an export market than as a source of imports. For all East Asian economies, therefore, and especially for Japan, the ongoing importance of their trade links with North America, and the potential impact on those trade links, are likely to be factors given considerable weight in any assessment of the benefits and costs of forming an East Asian trade bloc.

The current level of trade integration in East Asia has been achieved despite the absence to date of any preferential trade arrangements either within Northeast Asia or linking Northeast and Southeast Asia. The region's only significant preferential trading arrangement to date has been the ASEAN Free Trade Area (AFTA), launched in 1992 to succeed a number of limited and largely unsuccessful preferential trading initiatives. AFTA established a framework for the timetabled elimination of tariffs in trade among the ASEAN members, subject to initially substantial lists of exceptions. Subsequent revisions to AFTA accelerated the timetable and narrowed the lists of exceptions, to the point where by the turn of the century agreement existed for the elimination by specified dates of tariffs on virtually all products. Lengthier timetables were allowed for the phasing out of tariffs on a relatively small number of 'sensitive' products, and the recently admitted members of ASEAN[14] – Vietnam, Laos, Myanmar and Cambodia – were also allowed longer periods to phase out their tariffs. For a very small number of 'highly sensitive' products[15] the agreement specified a target tariff level rather than complete elimination of tariffs as the end-point of the process. Subsequently, the insistence by Malaysia on excluding its sensitive auto and auto parts industries from the tariff elimination programmes has re-opened the issue of 'sensitive' products and possibly opened the way to the exclusion of further products from the agreement. Although AFTA has led to increasing trade integration within Southeast Asia, as noted earlier intra-Southeast trade generally remains less intense than intra-Northeast Asian trade or trade between Southeast and Northeast Asia.

There have been ongoing efforts over a number of years to establish closer linkages between AFTA and the CER agreement between Australia and New Zealand, principally through harmonisation of standards and other trade facilitation measures. More recently, a high-level task force presented a report[16] entitled the 'Angkor Agenda' to the 2000 meeting of ASEAN and CER economic ministers, in which they recommended the establishment of a new free trade arrangement encompassing the members of AFTA and CER. The Ministers adopted a work program to match designed to enhance the AFTA-CER linkage, but stopped short of adopting the task force's recommendations on free trade.

It is very clear however that it is Northeast Asia which holds the key to any credible proposal for an East Asian economic bloc. Here a dramatic development was the decision in 1999 by Japan and Korea to launch a study of the implications of an FTA between the two countries, as part of a wider programme of deepening economic ties. This initiative resulted from meetings during the October 1998 visit to Japan of Korean President Kim Dae Jung, and received further impetus from the March 1999 visit to Korea by then Prime Minister Obuchi of Japan. The results of the study were published in May 2000 (IDE 2000). The Korean side has suggested that it might be preferable to include China in any such arrangement (Yamazawa 2000), and there have been unconfirmed reports that less formal studies are also under way on this possibility.

As noted above, the apparent willingness of Japan and Korea to consider participation in preferential trading arrangements represents a fundamental change in the strategic direction of the trade policies of those two countries. An FTA between Japan and Korea would also be a major step in the traditionally difficult political relationship between the two countries, and would signal an intention to reverse previous tendencies in their trade policies which have more often seemed directed towards discouraging rather than encouraging bilateral trade between them, despite their close geographic proximity to each other.[17] Less promisingly, the FTA would bring together two countries known for their fierce resistance to agricultural liberalisation within the WTO, fuelling suspicions that they may see a bilateral FTA as a way to pursue the benefits of trade liberalisation in a framework which would allow the exclusion of all sensitive agricultural and other natural resource-based products.

A proposal to extend the prospective FTA to include China would multiply the political difficulties already inherent in the proposed Japan-Korea FTA. The sense of rivalry and grievance that would have to be overcome in order for Japan and China to agree to participate together in the arrangement is perhaps even more deep-seated and complex than in the case of Japan and Korea. If these obstacles were to be overcome, however, the negotiation of an FTA linking Japan, Korea and China would transform the political and security equation associated with regional trade liberalisation in Northeast Asia, and would likely represent a decisive and defining step in the development of the configuration of trade arrangements in the entire East Asian region. Such an FTA would bring together the three economic superpowers of East Asia, accounting for over 20 per cent of world GNP, and almost 85 per cent of the combined GNP of the East Asian region as a whole, as can be seen from Tables 5.1 and 5.2. This FTA would represent the essential 'core' of any East Asian trade entity.

The proposal for a Japan-Korea FTA is perhaps the most significant development in what has become a veritable explosion since early 1999 of new proposals for bilateral and plurilateral preferential trading arrangements in the APEC region.[18] The majority of these proposals in fact involve proposed trans-Pacific linkages, clearly indicating the continued importance that many East Asian economies place on their trade links with North America in particular, and suggesting some of the tensions these economies are likely to feel between the desire to preserve these trans-Pacific links on the one hand, and the ambition to create a strong East Asian economic entity on the other. New preferential trade proposals have however also emerged within East Asia itself. The proposal to have reached the most advanced stage of discussion is one between Japan and Singapore, initially foreshadowed in an announcement at the time of the 1999 APEC Economic Leaders' meeting in Auckland, and subsequently the subject of a detailed study.[19] Negotiations have now commenced on this proposal, with the intention of the parties being to conclude an agreement by the end of 2001. Subsequently there have been reports of a proposal for a Korea-Singapore FTA, and in late 2000 came the indication that China is willing to consider an FTA with ASEAN. It was following this indication that the 'ASEAN 7 plus three' summit decided to commission a study on a possible East Asia Free Trade Area.

The results of computable general equilibrium simulations reported in Scollay and Gilbert (2000) indicate that if a move towards preferential trade arrangements becomes established in Northeast Asia a strong economic logic will operate in favour of the emergence of an East Asia-wide preferential arrangement rather than an arrangement based on some more limited grouping. This is both because the broader arrangements will deliver greater economic benefits to the participants, and because smaller preferential groupings will cause significant damage to the trade interests of East Asian economies excluded from the agreement(s). Thus widening the proposed Japan-Korea arrangement to include China is to the economic advantage of all three countries, especially China and Korea, but would have a strong negative effect on ASEAN, whose exports compete directly with those of China in many areas, and would consequently suffer badly from the resulting discrimination. Broadening the arrangement further to include ASEAN would remove these negative effects, and produce a more satisfactory outcome for all participants. It will thus appears likely that a kind of 'domino effect' will operate, of the kind proposed in Baldwin (1999), whereby the establishment of closer integration among a regionally dominant group of economies sets up almost irresistible pressures for smaller peripheral economies in the region to seek inclusion of the arrangements.

The fact that economic logic favours a broader rather than some narrower East Asian trade grouping does not however mean that the broader grouping will necessarily be the one to emerge. It could be that the broader grouping is also the one which faces the greatest political obstacles, suggesting the worrying possibility that economic and political pressures may point in opposite directions. If political considerations point to the formation of narrower preferential trade groupings the outlook is likely to be for a period of heightened trade tensions and conflict among the East Asian economies.

There are also further potential clashes of political and economic considerations relating to the possible inclusion or exclusion of Taiwan and Australia and New Zealand. The simulations by Scollay and Gilbert (2000) suggest that Taiwan would be badly hurt by exclusion from an East Asian trade bloc. This however also suggests the potential for China to use inclusion or exclusion as an economic lever against Taiwan. Australia and Zealand will also be hurt by exclusion from an East Asian trade bloc, while conversely their inclusion promises economic benefits both to them and to the East Asian economies. The benefits to East Asia would however depend to a significant extent on adoption within the arrangement of measures to liberalise agricultural trade, something which has consistently been resisted by all Northeast Asian economies (except Hong Kong SAR), and by some Southeast Asian economies as well.

Political and economic considerations will also inevitably be important in considering the implications of a possible East Asian trade arrangement for trans-Pacific relations. The Northeast Asian powers in particular are unlikely to launch a major new joint economic initiative without careful consideration of the implications for their economic, political and security relationships with the United States. A further implication of the importance of trade links with North America for virtually all East Asian economies is that, while the economic logic favouring an East Asian trade grouping may be strong, the logic in favour of APEC-wide liberalisation is even stronger, if only the process of trade liberalisation within APEC could be made more effective. Realisation of the additional benefits potentially available from APEC liberalisation depends crucially however on the full participation of the United States. East Asian assessments of the likely attitude of the United States towards APEC under a new Administration are thus likely to be an important factor in determining whether the possibility of APEC-wide liberalisation continues to hold attention, or whether the East Asian trade bloc appears increasingly attractive as a viable alternative.

One further potential difficulty facing a possible East Asian trade bloc is very familiar from the European experience. This is the question of the treatment of agriculture. As in Europe earlier, the process of industrialisation in Northeast Asia has been accompanied by a strong tendency to provide increased trade protection for agriculture, a process well documented in Anderson and Hayami (1986). Japan and Korea in particular are now among the world's fiercest opponents of agricultural trade liberalisation. Japanese officials have openly stated that their selection of Singapore as Japan's likely first preferential trading partner was heavily based on the consideration that the potential for agricultural trade between Japan and Singapore is minimal.

Even in this case Japan has apparently insisted on excluding from consideration those few agricultural and fisheries products in which there exists even a slight potential for increased trade, such as goldfish and cut flowers.

The report of IDE (2000) on a possible Japan FTA was perhaps predictably non-specific on the subject of agriculture. After noting the 'sensitivity' of agriculture in both countries, the report went on to say that:

> it is important that these sensitive items be handled in ways that comply with the GATT-WTO provisions and that are agreeable to relevant parties in both countries, bearing in mind their common goal of developing and maintaining the agriculture, forestry and fisheries industries in industrialised countries. It is essential that, to conclude a Japan-Korea FTA, both countries adjust their border protection policies to enable their agriculture, forestry and fisheries businesses to co-exist and co-prosper. To do this, both countries must, for the time being, co-operate in the study of crucial agricultural policies that are common to them both, such as food security, maintenance and conservation of national land and natural resources, and promotion of agricultural areas.

It seems very likely that Japan and Korea will seek the partial or full exclusion of agriculture from any East Asian trade arrangement. This approach is also likely to be congenial to other Northeast Asian economies. On the other hand Southeast Asia is divided between members of the Cairns Group (Malaysia and Thailand) and other economies which have traditionally been more protectionist towards agriculture (Indonesia and the Philippines). It seems unlikely however that pro-liberalisation forces in Southeast Asia will have the strength to resist the very strong pressure for exclusion of agriculture likely to be applied from Northeast Asia.

It is also unlikely that the approach adopted within East Asia will follow the model of the European Union's Common Agricultural Policy (CAP), since introduction of new support measures along the lines of the CAP is now largely precluded by the disciplines of the WTO Agreement on Agriculture. The approach is more likely to follow that of the European Union in its agreements with central and Eastern Europe and the Mediterranean countries, from which agriculture is generally excluded to a greater or lesser extent. This approach is potentially in conflict with the provisions of GATT Article XXIV setting out the conditions under which preferential trading arrangements will be considered consistent with GATT/WTO obligations. Under these provisions preferential trade agreements must cover 'substantially all trade' between the parties, and it has often been argued by agricultural exporting countries that this requirement precludes the complete or substantial exclusion of agriculture from any agreement. The terms of Article XXIV are however notoriously imprecise and the members of the WTO have never been able to reach consensus on how to interpret the requirement for coverage of 'substantially all trade'. As a result the provisions of Article XXIV remain to a large effect ineffective as disciplines on the design of new preferential trade agreements.

The European experience also highlighted the additional economic benefits to be gained from moving beyond conventional trade barrier reduction or elimination to implement also the type of 'trade facilitation' measures that comprised the European Union's 'single market' programme, included harmonisation or mutual recognition of standards and technical regulations, streamlining or removal of border controls, liberalisation of government procurement, and harmonisation of indirect tax rates. The famous though controversial Cecchini report purported to show that the economic gains from these measures exceeded the gains from removal of conventional trade barriers such as tariffs and quantitative restrictions.

Some progress in trade facilitation has been made within AFTA and also in the context of the AFTA-CER dialogue, and APEC also has some significant achievements in this field, particularly in the areas of custom procedures and standards and conformance. All this progress has been made without the need for guidance and supervision from a centralised bureaucracy such as the European Commission. It is unclear however how far a prospective East Asian trade bloc would be willing to follow the European Union towards instituting a 'single market' programme. The fact that all preferential trade proposals currently emerging in the region are for free trade areas rather than customs unions suggests that if an East Asia-wide arrangement emerges it also will be in the nature of a free trade area, implying in turn that it is envisaged that some degree of market segmentation will remain within such an arrangement.[20] Furthermore, if trade facilitation issue is in fact pursued more vigorously within an embryonic East Asian bloc, questions would inevitably arise as to how those efforts should be related to existing trade facilitation initiatives within both APEC and AFTA. It is not clear at this stage how those questions would be answered.

4.   MONETARY INTEGRATION: PARALLELS AND CONTRASTS WITH EUROPE

The move towards economic integration in East Asia is unusual in that faster progress is initially being made on the financial front than the trade front. This reflects recent East Asian experience of the economic crisis of 1997–8, and the lessons drawn from the response to that crisis. The 'contagion effect' that operated during the crisis, as capital flight spread rapidly from one East Asian economy to another, clearly demonstrated the interest that East Asian economies have in the soundness of each other's monetary and macroeconomic policies, and in developing mechanisms to protect themselves against destabilising capital movements and exchange rate fluctuations. Thus steps have been taken, first within ASEAN and subsequently within the 'ASEAN 7 plus three' grouping to establish 'early warning systems' to provide early identification of potential sources of future economic crises. More recently the 'ASEAN 7 plus three' announced in 2000 the establishment of a Network of Bilateral Swap Arrangements, designed to provide the financial support necessary for members to defend themselves against destabilising capital movements and to protect the region against the destabilising exchange rate fluctuations that would otherwise be likely to follow. The Swap Arrangements will initially provide mutual currency supports up to US$50 billion, and this figure could eventually increase to US$100 billion. These figures amount to only a small fraction of the combined monetary reserves of the East Asian economies, estimated by Bergsten (2000) to total US$668 billion.

As noted in the introduction to this chapter, an important motivation for these developments is the determination by East Asia to achieve a greater degree of economic autonomy. A second key consideration is the degree of economic interdependence which now exists among the East Asian economies, as indicated among other things by the level of intra-East Asian trade. Avoiding the disruptions to regional trade and production patterns which follow from large and sudden exchange rate movements has clearly become a high priority. In addition to the establishment of the Swap Arrangements attention is also being given to the possibility of increased co-ordination in the establishment and management of appropriate exchange rate mechanisms in the region. Proposals have been floated for establishment of currency pegs based on the Japanese yen[21] or on a currency basket comprising the Japanese yen, Korean won, and Chinese yuan. Each of these proposals however faces very significant economic and political obstacles.

The situation in East Asia has some parallels to the situation faced by Europe in the late 1960s and early 1970s, when increasing exchange rate instability emerged as a threat to progressive economic integration in Europe. Unlike the 'ASEAN 7 plus three' group, the then European Community already had formal arrangements in place establishing free trade among its members, together with common policies, especially the Common Agricultural Policy, whose smooth operation was threatened by exchange rate instability among the membership. The conclusion reached in Europe was that achievement of exchange rate stability among the members was an essential prerequisite for continuing progress towards further economic integration. This led first to establishment of the ill-starred 'snake' system of currency bands, replaced in 1979 by the more durable European Monetary System (EMS). The EMS in turn was the precursor of the single currency or Euro, seen by many as the logical conclusion of the European process of monetary integration.

It can be inferred that if the 'ASEAN 7 plus three' group, or any similarly East Asia-wide group, decides to move towards the establishment of a free trade arrangement, it will face the same question as to the degree of monetary integration needed to support the degree of market integration being introduced through the free trade arrangements. It does not however follow that the same answer will be given to the question in East Asia as was earlier given in Europe. The establishment of the Swap Arrangements does put in place a likely prerequisite for the establishment of arrangements aimed at greater currency stability, but different conditions in East Asia may lead to different conclusions as to the balance between costs and benefits of a move towards a system of fixed exchange rates or a single currency on the European model, and even about the feasibility of such a move.

For one thing, East Asia may be contemplating a much lower level of market integration. Europe from the outset set itself a goal of creating a common market, and eventually began to realise this goal with the establishment of the 'single market', entailing free trade in goods and services and free movement of capital and labour. Within East Asia however there is no consensus on the desirability of free movement of capital, and the issue of labour mobility remains highly sensitive. It seems likely therefore that at least in the short term East Asia's market integration ambitions may be limited to the achievement of free trade in goods and possibly services. Under these conditions the cost-benefit analysis of a move to a system of fixed exchange rates along the lines of the EMS, or ultimately to a single currency such as the Euro, may produce rather different results. Benefits may be lower and costs may be higher.

The benefits of moving towards a system of fixed exchange arrangements among the members of an economic integration arrangement include enhanced trade and investment flows and the consequent improved allocation of resources resulting from reductions in uncertainty associated with unpredictable exchange rate fluctuations, lower levels and greater convergence of interest rates leading to higher levels of investment, and perhaps most importantly the avoidance of the potential disruption of free trade arrangements arising from the temptation to engage in competitive devaluation. Mercosur provides a recent example of the importance of the latter consideration.[22] A single currency also confers the additional benefits of elimination of transaction costs associated with currency exchange, increased efficiency of money as a unit of account and store of value, the ability to economise on international reserve holdings, and the enhancement of market integration and competition that follows from increased price transparency across borders. Most if not all of these benefits are likely to increase as the level of intra-bloc trade increases among the members, and may thus well be substantial for a free trade area among a group of economies that trade intensively with each other, such as East Asia. The benefits are likely to be significantly higher however for the members of a 'single market' along the lines of the European model.

The costs of adopting a system of fixed exchange rates or a common currency are principally those associated with the loss of independence in the conduct of monetary and exchange rate policies. The well-established economic literature on optimal currency areas highlights that these costs are likely to be lower for groups of countries that trade intensively with each other and which tend to face symmetric external shocks, since they are less likely to experience a need for divergent monetary and exchange rate policies. While the East Asian economies have developed intensive trade relations with each other, as noted above, the structures of their economies remain quite diverse, and it would be difficult to argue that they are not subject to· asymmetric external shocks to a significant extent.

The costs of losing monetary and exchange rate policy autonomy are also likely to be less if wages and prices are flexible within the individual members of the arrangement, if labour is mobile between the members, and if the possibility exists for fiscal redistribution among the members. If monetary policy and exchange rate policies are not available as policy instruments, the impact of a country-specific external shock on an individual economy may nevertheless be cushioned if its wage and price structures adjust quickly to the changed external situation, if labour can move freely to more buoyant sections of the regional economy, or if the members of the arrangement operate a centralised budget from which resources can be transferred to afflicted members. In the case of the European Union the implementation of the 'single market' has increased price and wage flexibility and also increased the potential for labour mobility, while the 'structural funds' offer the possibility of transfers to depressed regions. None of these factors however operate among the economies of Asia, and there is little sign that a 'single market' or the introduction of redistributive mechanisms are being contemplated there in the near future.

It is therefore relatively straightforward to conclude that in comparison with the European Union, East Asia may expect that both smaller benefits and larger costs are likely to be associated with moves to closer monetary integration, and accordingly will have less incentive to move along this path.

More fundamentally, the world has greatly changed since the inauguration of the EMS, and the possibilities that were open to Europe then may no longer be open to East Asia now. Under the EMS, Europe was able to move gradually towards the achievement of irrevocably fixed exchange rates through several distinct phases involving management of exchange rates within progressively tighter bands. Under today's conditions of dramatically accelerated capital flows however exchange rate pegs of all types have become increasingly difficult to operate. There is a growing body of opinion among economists that the realistic choice of exchange rate regimes may in future be restricted for many countries to the polar extremes of free floating on the one hand and full currency convertibility or a single currency on the other. Even the European

Union found in the mid-1990s that the final phase of its EMS was unstable, and that it had to quickly choose between reversion to increased exchange rate flexibility or pressing forward to the establishment of the single currency.

Furthermore there were political and institutional factors favouring monetary integration in Europe which are not present in East Asia. Even if the economic arguments in favour of monetary integration had been unconvincing, there was nevertheless a substantial body of opinion in Europe inclined to support it on the grounds that it was a useful tool for furthering an ultimate objective of political integration. Institutionally, the strength and credibility of the German Bundesbank provided an important anchor for the process of monetary integration in Europe. It is difficult to see any parallel in East Asia, especially given the recent decline in the reputation of the Bank of Japan.

The European experience has also demonstrated the need for monetary integration to be accompanied by co-ordination of fiscal policies and possibly other economic policies as well. The requirement for policy convergence under the Maastricht treaty arrangements often created political strains within Europe. Political support for the integration process has been difficult to maintain in a number of European countries, even though the political leadership has more often than not been strongly committed to the process. Political obstacles to closer economic integration are likely to be still greater in East Asia, where a comparable level of commitment on the part of political leadership has yet to emerge.

5.   CONCLUDING REMARKS

The growing momentum in favour of increasing trade and monetary integration in East Asia is beginning to attract widespread attention. If an East Asian economic bloc does emerge this will be an event of great significance both for the economies involved and for the world economy as a whole. The economic logic supporting closer trade integration is reasonably strong, although initial activity appears to be more focused on monetary co-operation.

The political obstacles to the establishment of formal arrangements for trade or monetary integration are however formidable. Furthermore East Asia has yet to face crucial questions regarding the relation between trade and monetary integration, which have been highlighted by the earlier European experience. Although increased monetary integration is essential for the realisation of East Asian aspirations for greater economic autonomy, a clear path to monetary integration in East Asia has yet to emerge, and the form of any monetary integration that might emerge in East Asia also remains far from clear.

NOTE

1. APEC consciously embraced 'open regionalism' as an alternative to the expansion of preferential trading arrangements in the Asia-Pacific region. APEC's interpretation of 'open regionalism' envisages a concerted regional approach to achieving free trade and investment, but on the basis of non-discriminatory rather than preferential liberalisation.
2. APEC has never embraced an objective of monetary integration to complement its trade and investment objectives, nor has monetary integration been an objective of ASEAN. Both in ASEAN and East Asia generally, discussion on closer monetary links has largely been a post-crisis phenomenon, and has so far typically focused largely on less ambitious forms of monetary co-ordination.
3. Bergsten, C.F. (2000), 'Towards a Tripartite World', *Economist*, 15th July.
4. Brunei Darussalam, Indonesia, Malaysia, Philippines, Singapore, Thailand and Vietnam. The remaining members of ASEAN are Cambodia, Laos and Myanmar.
5. The EAEG was proposed by Dr Mahathir as an alternative to APEC. His proposed EAEG would have excluded both North America and Australia and New Zealand. East Asian economies however remained committed to the more inclusive APEC process, and the EAEG proposal was subsequently watered down to a proposal for an East Asian Economic Caucus (EAEC) to operate informally within APEC.
6. In the early 1990s there were fears that the GATT Uruguay Round would fail and that the multilateral trading system would be replaced by a global economic architecture based around three economic 'mega-blocs', located in Europe, North America (or the Western Hemisphere), and East Asia. Krugman (1991) argued that a 'three bloc' world could be the worst possible outcome for the world as a whole, because of the strength of the incentive each bloc would have to use its very considerable economic power to pursue its own interests at the expense of the other two blocs, potentially leading to destructive trade wars. A desire to avert the threat of a 'three-bloc world' was an important motivating factor behind the development of APEC as a trans-Pacific entity embracing both North America and East Asia, and for the emphasis given within APEC to non-discriminatory liberalisation and support for the WTO-based multilateral system, as opposed to the preferential approach to trade liberalisation.
7. The FTAA concept was first taken up at the first Summit of the Americas at Miami in 1994. At the second Summit, in Santiago in 1998, the leaders decided that negotiations should be launched for establishment of the FTAA by 2005.
8. Northeast Asia is defined here to include China, Japan, Korea, Hong Kong SAR and Taiwan. Southeast Asia comprises the ten members of ASEAN (Association of Southeast Asian Nations): Brunei Darussalam, Cambodia, Indonesia, Laos, Malaysia, Myanmar, Philippines, Singapore, Thailand and Vietnam. The inclusion of the CER economies (Australia and New Zealand) in East Asian economic arrangements has been a sensitive issue. Dr Mahathir's proposal for an East Asian Economic Grouping specifically excluded Australia and New Zealand as well as the North American economies, and Dr Mahathir has typically also sought to veto the participation of Australia and New Zealand in other East Asian economic initiatives. On the other hand, Australia and New Zealand are included in the recently-launched East Asia Latin America Forum (EALAF).
9. As Table 5.2 makes clear, the inclusion of Australia and New Zealand would not significantly change the relativities in economic size discussed here.
10. Purchasing power parity data for Taiwan is not available on a comparable basis.
11. GATT Article I establishes non-discrimination as the fundamental principle of the multilateral trading system. Exceptions provided under GATT Article XXIV allow for the establishment of free trade areas and customs union, subject to certain conditions being met.
12. The exceptions being Brunei and Singapore.
13. The exceptions are Brunei and Korea.
14. These new members have much lower levels of per capita income and industrialisation compared to the longer-established ASEAN.
15. Principally rice and sugar.
16. Available at http://www.aseansec.org/aem/angkor_agenda.pdf.

17. IDE (2000) catalogues a number of elements in each country's trade policy which have tended to discourage bilateral trade, of which the best-known is perhaps Korea's Import Sources Diversification Program, finally eliminated in June 1999.
18. By early 2001 there were well over 20 such proposals at various stages of discussion, study and negotiations. See Findlay (2001) and Scollay and Gilbert (2000) for surveys and discussions of these developments.
19. See http://www.mofa.go.jp/region/asia-paci/singapore/index.html.
20. Interestingly the FTAA is also conceived as a free trade area rather than a customs unions, although some existing arrangements among the prospective members of the FTAA do take the form of customs unions, for example Mercosur, the Andean Community, the Central American Common Market and Caricom.
21. See for example Kwan (2001).
22. The substantial devaluation by Brazil in 1998 placed enormous pressure on the Argentinian economy, which was constrained from matching Brazil's devaluation by its 'currency board' arrangement requiring strict convertibility between its own currency and the US dollar. This situation has led to considerable friction among the members of Mercosur.

REFERENCES

Anderson, K. and Y. Hayami (1986), *The Political Economy of Agricultural Protection: East Asia in International Perspective*, Sydney: Allen & Unwin.
Baldwin, R.E. (1999), 'A Domino Theory of Regionalism', in Bhagwati, J., P. Krishna and A. Panagariya (eds) (1999), *Trading Blocs: Alternative Approaches to Analyzing Preferential Trade Agreements*, Cambridge Mass.: MIT Press.
Bergsten, C.F. (2000), 'Towards a Tripartite World', *Economist*, 15th July.
Bergsten, C.F. (2001), 'America's Two-Front Economic Conflict', *Foreign Affairs*, March/April, pp. 16–27.
Findlay, C. (2001), 'Old Issues in New Regionalism', paper presented at the International Conference on 'The Trade and Monetary System in the Asia-Pacific Region', 3–4 February.
Hitiris, T. (1998), *European Union Economics*, 4th edition, London: Prentice Hall.
Institute of Developing Economies (2000), *Towards Closer Japan-Korea Economic Relations in the 21st Century: Summary Report*, Tokyo, May.
Krugman, P. (1991), 'Is Bilateralism Bad?', In Helpman, E. and A. Razin (eds), *International Trade and Trade Policy*, Cambridge, MA, MIT Press.
Kwan, C.H. (2001), *Yen Bloc: Towards Economic Integration in Asia*, Washington DC: Brookings Institute.
Scollay, R. and J. Gilbert (2000), 'Measuring the Gains from APEC Trade Liberalization: An Overview of CGE Assessments', *World Economy*, Vol. 23, No. 2, pp. 175–197.
Yamazawa, I. (2000), 'Towards Closer Japan-Korea Economic Relations: A Supplementary Note', mimeo, July.

6. APEC and Trade Liberalisation after Seattle: Transregionalism without a Cause?*

Vinod Aggarwal

1. INTRODUCTION

The eruption of protests in the streets of Seattle in November 1999 against the Millennium Round of the World Trade Organisation (WTO) marked the peak of anti-globalisation fervour. Protesters claimed the WTO is insensitive to the negative externalities produced by free trade on the environment and US labour, and criticised its lack of transparency. While there is considerable debate about the root of the WTO's problems in Seattle (Aggarwal, Ravenhill 2001), there is no doubt that the multilateral trading system faces severe challenges. Meanwhile, across the globe in Asia, the Asia-Pacific Economic Co-operation forum (APEC) was still picking up the pieces left from the Asian crisis of 1997–8. Because APEC and the WTO both pursue free trade, among other goals, and are seen by their members to be inextricably and purposefully linked, we might have expected to see APEC respond to some of the criticisms levelled at the WTO. Indeed, in 1993, APEC proved to be the beneficiary of the impasse in the GATT Uruguay Round, and was invigorated with the creation of annual leaders' meeting.

How has APEC responded to the pressures felt in Seattle? What progress, if any, has it made toward its trade goals in the wake of the Asian crisis, the Seattle debacle, and anti-globalisation sentiments? Has APEC benefited from the WTO's problems or has it been unable to step into the vacuum of trade liberalisation at the multilateral level? Finally, has APEC continued to prove its usefulness as a transregional trade organisation, or is it being institutionally squeezed, both from above and below? It is worth noting that although APEC has purported to be a forum for discussion on a host of issues, including finance, investment, the environment, women's rights, security, and the like, its original impetus has come from a desire to move forward with trade liberalisation. APEC's role in these other areas is an important topic,[1] but my focus in this chapter is on an examination of APEC in the trading system.

Hence, I consider APEC's work in other areas only insofar as it bears directly on trade issues.

This chapter is organised as follows. Section 2 provides a conceptual analytical framework on modes of trade liberalisation, focusing on alternative paths that might be pursued in the Asia-Pacific, including unilateral liberalisation, bilateral accords, minilateralism, and multilateralism, and also considering the dimensions of geographical propinquity and sectoralism vs. multiproduct coverage. Next, section 3 briefly examines APEC's role in trade liberalisation and then considers how APEC has fared over the past year. Section 4 then turns to consideration of APEC's role in other areas that might affect its role as a trade forum, focusing on finance, technology, and the environment. Section 5 then considers how APEC has addressed the issue of nesting, both with respect to APEC within the WTO and for arrangements within APEC such as the North American Free Trade Agreement (NAFTA), ASEAN Free Trade Agreement (AFTA), and Closer Economic Relations (CER) between Australia and New Zealand. In this context, a key question concerns the evolution of other approaches to trade liberalisation in the Asia-Pacific as possible complements or alternatives to APEC. In concluding, the chapter assesses APEC's current status, evaluates some scenarios, and then proposes some ideas to strengthen its role and contribution to the international trading system.

2. MODES OF TRADE MANAGEMENT: AN ANALYTICAL CONSTRUCT

Over the last fifty years, states have utilised a host of measures to regulate trade flows. In terms of bargaining approaches, these include unilateral, bilateral, minilateral, and multilateral strategies; in terms of product coverage, the range has been narrow in scope (a few products), or quite broad (multiproduct). In addition, some arrangements tend to be focused geographically, while others bind states across long distances. It is worth noting that this category is quite subjective, since simple distance is hardly the only relevant factor in defining a 'geographic region.' But despite conceptual difficulties, this would appear to be a useful category. Finally, these measures have been either market closing or market opening. One can array the resulting options in the following table, focusing only on the first three dimensions of bargaining approaches, products, and geography to simplify our presentation.[2] The cells include generic types or specific examples of modes of governance.

In brief, the top row (cells 1–6) refer to different forms of sectoralism. Cell 1 includes such important measures as US use of Super 301 against various countries, as well as specific market opening or restrictions in particular products. In cell 2, we have agreements in specific products such as the US-

Table 6.1 Trading arrangements

Product Scope		Actor Scope					
			Bilateral		Minilateral		Multilateral
		Unilateral	Geographically concentrated	Geographically dispersed	Geographically concentrated	Geographically dispersed	
Few products *(sectoralism)*		(1) Specific quotas or tariffs or Super 301	(2) U.S.-Canada auto agreement	(3) U.S.-Japan Voluntary export restraints	(4) European Coal and Steel Community	(5) Early Voluntary Sectoral Liberalization (EVSL)	(6) Information Technology Agreement or Multifiber Arrangement
			(regionalism)		*(regionalism)*		
Many products		(7) APEC individual action plans	(8) Australia-New Zealand CER	(9) Mexico-Chile free trade agreement	(10) AFTA, NAFTA, EU	(11) APEC, ASEM, EU-Mercosur	(12) GATT and WTO
			(regionalism)		*(regionalism)*	*(transregionalism)*	*(globalism)*

Adapted from: Vinod K. Aggarwal, 'Governance in International Trade: Changing Patterns of Sectoralism, Regionalism, and Globalism', P.J. Simmons and Chantal de Jonge Oudraat (eds), *Managing a Globalizing World: Lessons Learned Across Sectors* (Washington, D.C.: The Carnegie Endowment for International Peace), in press.

Canada auto agreement. Cell 3 refers to bilateral agreements that are geographically dispersed, which could include Voluntary Export Restraints or bilateral market opening agreements such as the U.S.-Japan semiconductor agreement. In cells 4 and 5, we have product specific sectoral agreements, with the first of these being geographically concentrated and focus on only a few products. There are few examples of arrangements such as the European Coal and Steel Community as in cell 4 because such agreements are inconsistent with Article 24 of the GATT, which calls for liberalisation on a multiproduct basis, rather than only a few products. Cell 5 provides an example of dispersed sectoral minilateralism, as in the case of the Early Voluntary Sectoral Liberalisation (EVSL) effort that did not pan out among APEC members. Finally, cell 6 provides an example of multilateral accords such as the Information Technology Agreement (pushed forward actively in APEC before it made its way into the WTO), Basic Telecom Agreement, or recent Financial Services Agreement.

The next row focuses on multiproduct efforts. Cell 7 is an example of unilateral liberalisation or restriction, and could include such APEC encouraged efforts as Individual Action Plans (IAPs). In cell 8, the Australia-New Zealand agreement fits the category of geographically concentrated accords. In cell 9, we have cases of geographically dispersed bilateral agreements. Examples within the Asia-Pacific include the Mexico-Chile accord, as well as current discussions between Japan and Singapore. Cell 10 focuses on geographically focused minilateral agreements, accords that have traditionally been referred to as 'regionalism'. As should be clear from the table, however, Cells 2, 4, and 8 (and even cell 11) are also forms of 'regionalism', although theoretically they may have quite different political-economic implications. On a minilateral basis, for example, cell 11 points to such accords as APEC or the EU-Mercosur accord, which span regions. These accords, which I have referred to as 'Transregional agreements' (Aggarwal 2000a) or what others have called 'Interregional agreements' are of key theoretical importance in understanding the likely evolution of trading arrangements in the Asia-Pacific. Finally, cell 12 refers to the case of global trading arrangements, namely multilateral, multiproduct arrangements such as the GATT and its successor organisation, the WTO.

This chart provides a categorisation of modes of trade governance that allows us to capture the vast array of methods used to promote trade opening or closure. The next step, of course, would be to develop hypotheses about the implications of various types of arrangements, for member states, the interaction of different types of arrangements, and the like. To take a couple of examples, what are the effects of sectoralism, say of a minilateral or multilateral type on globalism such as the WTO? As I have argued elsewhere,[3] sectoralism, particularly of the 'open type' may ironically be detrimental to the WTO, and may help account for the some of the problems we have seen in

Seattle. The logic of this counter-intuitive view is that as firms receive benefits from such arrangements, they no longer have an interest in pressing for broad scale trade liberalisation, but only for extensions or modifications of their sectoral specific arrangements. Other examples of relationships among forms of trading arrangements include claims about how unilateralism might promote liberalisation (or the counter argument, that such measures undermine the WTO).[4] Similarly, there is an ongoing debate about whether regional accords serve as 'building or stumbling blocks' for the global trading system.[5]

In the Asia-Pacific context, such questions on the relationship among different modes of trade organisation are central to assessing the future of APEC, efforts to develop bilateral or regional accords and the implications of these arrangements for the WTO. For example, the recent Japanese turn toward consideration of bilateral agreements with Singapore and Korea, particularly in the aftermath of the problems in APEC and the WTO, are now hotly debated by analysts and policymakers. While space limitations preclude a comprehensive discussion of every combination of trade accords in the Asia-Pacific, this analytical approach provides a basis for exploring our questions on the future of APEC and scenarios for trade arrangements in the Asia-Pacific.

3.   APEC'S ROLE IN TRADE

How is APEC faring in trade liberalisation in a post-Asian Crisis world and post-Seattle debacle world? Before examining these issues directly in the context of APEC's effort to promote widening and deepening, while maintaining consistency (nested) with the WTO, it is useful to briefly survey some key developments in APEC's history.

3.1   The development of APEC

Created in 1989, APEC currently groups 21 economies in the region with the professed aim of liberalising trade and investment in the region.[6] As a trade liberalisation forum, APEC began to take on a significant role in 1993 when heads of states met in Seattle, giving the Uruguay Round of negotiations a strong boost. By indicating that the United States was willing to move forward with trade liberalisation in what was then the most dynamic region of the global economy, the United States was able to encourage the European Union to be more forthcoming and willing to conclude the long-delayed trade negotiations. At least in the minds of some observers, then, APEC had proved its benefit in serving as a building block for trade liberalisation on a global level.

In November 1994, the members of APEC, following the advice of an APEC-sponsored Eminent Persons Group, issued the Bogor declaration at their annual meeting in Indonesia. This agreement set APEC members on the road to trade liberalisation with a target for achieving open trade for developed nations by the year 2010 and developing nations by 2020. APEC leaders then met in November 1995 in Osaka, Japan to hammer out the details of how to reach the free-trade goal. APEC members continued to espouse the principle of 'open regionalism', arguing for the nesting of APEC within the WTO, but without the creation of a formal free trade area or customs union as permitted under Article 24 of the GATT.

This notion of 'open regionalism' was not one on which members had or have achieved a stable cognitive consensus.[7] We can identify at least four schools of thought with respect to institutions in the Asia-Pacific area: (1) pure GATTists; (2) the currently dominant PECC (Pacific Economic Co-operation Council)-led GATT-consistent school of open regionalism; (3) sceptics of open regionalism; and (4) advocates of an Asian bloc. The pure GATTists/WTO proponents argued that the GATT would be undermined by APEC, and that such arrangements would only foster a break-up of the world economy into competing economic blocs. With the successful conclusion of the Uruguay Round in 1993, these advocates began to argue that regionally based efforts were superfluous and could be highly detrimental to efforts to promote global trade liberalisation. From their perspective, such movements posed a threat to non-Asia-Pacific states as well as being an obstacle to the liberalisation process for countries in the region. In addition, they argued that the Asia-Pacific region has done quite well without having formal institutional arrangements. Thus, from this perspective, institutionalisation is a dangerous recipe for impeding the dynamic growth of the region. More recently, with the Asian crisis and subsequent slowdown in the region, such analysts have not advocated stronger institutions in the region, but rather have criticised domestic policy mistakes in the affected countries.

The second group, led primarily by academics and business groups in PECC, has advanced several mutually compatible arguments in promoting open regionalism. First, some argue that APEC-type arrangements will help WTO's cause by providing impetus from a committed group of countries to advance liberalisation. This 'building block' approach can be seen as encouraging liberally-oriented states in different regions to use their political pull to come together into a larger pro-WTO coalition.[8] A second perspective suggests that WTO inconsistency can be avoided by simply dealing with issues that are *not* on its agenda, thus preventing conflict with other non-participating WTO members. Thus, issues such as investment, environmental concerns, technology transfer, and standards in communications would be fair game in a forum such as APEC. A third perspective calls for liberalising on a non-discriminatory basis, rather than seeking concessions from trading partners who are not party to an agreement. The economic logic underlying this approach is that APEC members can tolerate free riding because the benefits of trade barrier reductions will most probably accrue to the participants in the region. While such liberalisation has not come to pass, such ideas have continued to gain currency among these analysts, even during and after the Asian crisis. Fourth, support for an Asian-Pacific regime also draws on the popular notion of 'natural' blocs, which argues that arrangements based on regional trading patterns do little to harm the multilateral economic system.[9]

The proponents of the open regional concept have not been without their critics. In this group, several scholars have argued that permitting diffuse instead of specific reciprocity allows potential free-riders to benefit from APEC liberalisation, and reflects a politically naive perspective.[10] Even the most ardent proponents of open regionalism, Peter Drysdale and Ross Garnaut, have admitted that 'The building of support for non-discriminatory APEC-based liberalisation may make it necessary to limit European free riding on multilateral liberalisation in some commodities – perhaps agriculture'.[11]

Finally, a fifth view has found expression in Malaysia's 1990 proposal to create an East Asian Economic Group that would include ASEAN, Burma, Hong Kong, China, Taiwan, South Korea, and Japan, and exclude Australia, New Zealand, and the North American countries. In essence, this view reflects the concern that the world is splitting up into regional blocs as the United States presses ahead with NAFTA and the European Union admits new members. Thus, proponents argued that the time had come for Asians to develop their own grouping.[12] In practice, however, this approach failed to garner much support from Asian states, and was sharply criticised by the United States. Although Malaysia did not attend the 1993 Seattle summit to demonstrate its displeasure with lack of support for some type of Asian caucus group, it was not joined in this boycott by other states. If successful, an Asian-only approach could have undermined the principle of open regionalism and would have threatened the interests of many Asian countries that are highly reliant on the US market. With the recent 1998 Kuala Lumpur meeting, Malaysia appears to have boarded the APEC wagon, but as we shall see below, calls for Asians to go it alone have now found their way into suggestions for an Asian Monetary Fund.

In 1996 in Manila, APEC steered onto a new tack, this time emphasising the possible benefits not of regionalism in building and reinforcing globalism, but that of sectoralism. The US, supported by other countries, pressed to use APEC to leverage trade liberalisation in the WTO. Specifically, in an effort to push negotiations forward in information technology, APEC members agreed to an APEC-wide liberalisation program in this sector. This minilateral, geographically dispersed, sectoral approach to market opening appeared to bear significant fruit with an agreement on a liberalisation schedule in products in this area, they then successfully multilateralised this agreement at the WTO's December 1996 Singapore Ministerial meeting. The agreement calls for the phasing out of tariffs on several categories of equipment by the year 2000, including computers, selected telecommunications equipment, software, semiconductors, and printed circuit boards. This effort can be seen as using sectoralism regionally to pursue sectoral liberalisation globally.

With this success, the US began to pursue a minilateral sectoral path with enthusiasm, employing this model to promote liberalisation in a variety of other sectors. In Vancouver in 1997, Ministers agreed to consider nine additional sectors for fast track liberalisation: chemicals, energy-related equipment and services, environmental goods and services, forest products, medical equipment, telecommunications equipment, fish and fish products, toys, and gems and jewellery. In addition, they called for discussion of liberalisation in six other sectors: oilseeds and oilseed products, food, natural and synthetic rubber, fertilisers, automobiles, and civil aircraft. The US led a movement to make the nine-sector liberalisation a package in order to discourage countries from picking and choosing sectors based on domestic concerns.

This strategy initially appeared to be viable, but quickly ran into difficulties. In Kuala Lumpur at the 6th Leaders' Summit in November 1998, Japan – supported by other Asian countries who were concerned about moving forward with liberalisation in their weakened economic state – refused to liberalise trade in fishing and forestry products. With an economy that is still moribund, the government was unwilling to take the political heat from interest groups who strongly opposed liberalisation in this area. With lack of movement by the Japanese, the position of interest groups opposed to tariff cutting in other sectors was strengthened. Instead, the ministers agreed to shift the negotiations in these sectors to the World Trade Organisation.

The abandonment of further negotiations on Early Voluntary Sectoral Liberalisation (EVSL) with the package being sent to the WTO for further debate can be viewed in one of two ways: first, that APEC wishes to become the springboard for new WTO initiatives, thereby making the decision to transfer EVSL to the WTO a predetermined plan. Second, one could argue that APEC has conceded defeat in further trade reductions via EVSL, and the decision to transfer the EVSL to WTO was an act of desperation after it failed to make any progress in terms of trade liberalisation. Given Japanese opposition to the tariff reductions, the evidence would support the latter conclusion. Thus, what seemed in the mid-1990s to be a promising avenue to pursue trade liberalisation (at least from the American perspective) in the world's most dynamic region began to look more like a dead end, or at the very least, a very bumpy road.

3.2   APEC and trade liberalisation after the Asian crisis

APEC has played two principal roles in trade liberalisation. It has pursued liberalisation on a transregional basis, which serves as a potential positive building block toward globalism. APEC has also promoted multilateral sectoralism as a step toward liberalisation. We take up the question of APEC's own liberalisation in this subsection, and then turn to links with other issues in section 4. Following that discussion, we will then examine how APEC's problems in moving forward and the Millennium Round's aborted start have stimulated other forms of trade organisation in the Asia-Pacific.

We can consider APEC's development with respect to trade from both a deepening and a widening perspective. The first notion refers to additional commitments in existing issues, while the latter refers to an expansion in either issue scope or membership. We begin with the question of deepening. APEC members have shown a significant degree of deepening of commitment within the last year under the trade regime. Thanks to a few notable innovations that have surfaced under the APEC regime such as electronic IAPs (Individual Action Plan reports that monitor progress toward the Bogor goals of free trade), restrictions against E-commerce tariffs and a new BizAPEC website, members have created the potential for a more efficient APEC. There has not, however, been across-the-board success with trade liberalisation as the case of Japan has shown.

At APEC's First Senior Officials Meeting in early 2000 (SOM I) APEC set in motion several steps to promote better understanding of the benefits of trade liberalisation. The officials also agreed to launch, pending budget approval, a redesign of the Individual Action Plans. These electronic IAPs would be more transparent and user-friendly, allowing comparison between years. At their second meeting, senior officials monitored the development of this new system.[13]

As would be expected, APEC officials have responded to criticism levelled at the WTO. Members have undertaken to provide transparency and a friendlier interface to track their progress toward free trade. Efforts to disseminate information about the uses of free trade have also been an obvious response to the crisis in Seattle. While advocating education does not mark a greater depth of commitment by member economies, providing a transparent window to look in upon their progress toward free trade obviously is such a deepening mechanism. Allowing other states to easily access progress toward the Bogor goals will lead to a dialogue between states regarding their compliance with APEC's goals. APEC does operate on a voluntary basis, but this form of dialogue may take on a sharp edge if one state appears to be lagging far behind others. Reputation costs for future interactions among these states may grow if transparency is increased because other states will have a tool with which they may hold states to their commitments, however informally. Seattle demands for more transparency within the WTO have clearly reverberated in the Asia-Pacific.

During the 1999 Auckland Leaders' Meeting, ABAC (APEC Business Advisory Council) members called upon economies to avoid imposing tariffs on E-commerce. At a two-day meeting last June in Darwin, APEC agreed to an extension of the moratorium on the imposition of customs duties on E-commerce until the next WTO ministerial conference.[14] This agreement appears to be a successful deepening of members' commitment to APEC. Because the moratorium had lapsed after the Seattle meeting fell apart, APEC's reaffirmation of the principal shows APEC's continued support for free-trade and a deepening of commitment. APEC had the opportunity to let the agreement lapse, but members chose to extend it.

During the Darwin Meeting, APEC Ministers Responsible for Trade inaugurated a new APEC web site to facilitate trade liberalisation. BizAPEC.com is aimed at making APEC services and information more readily available to businesses.[15] While this web site does not mark any sacrifice of member economies to mark a deepening of commitment, it will allow businesses to utilise the APEC mechanism and may also allow another avenue of critique toward the APEC members. It certainly promises to help APEC along in its free trade aspirations.

In its key recommendations for 2000, ABAC has requested to tackle the growing issue of non-tariff barriers within IAPs; to remove impediments associated with standards and conformance; and to support sectoral government-business dialogue to promote APEC's facilitation agenda.[16] These measures do indeed remain at the verbal level for the time being, and thus, remain aspirations.

Turning to widening, the moratorium on membership continues. Although, President Kim of South Korea has advocated North Korea's membership as a way of integrating this isolated nuclear power, membership will most likely wait until 2008 – the end of a ten-year moratorium on APEC expansion. Similarly, Vietnam has recently backed India's admission as a necessity to successful trade in APEC. Both states will be able to participate in certain sectors, such as human resources and food security of the forum.[17] With respect to issue scope in trade specifically, there have been calls for work on related issues such as trade competition and regulatory reform.

In short, APEC has undertaken some steps toward deepening its commitment to trade liberalisation, but these are very small steps indeed. As the APIAN group (APEC International Assessment Network) notes with respect to trade, APEC must 'clarify and prioritise some of its trade policy initiatives', have IAP commitments which are 'specific, measurable and accompanied with a time line' and promote the 'establishment of effective and transparent systems to monitor the implementation of APEC's voluntary, non-binding commitments...'.[18]

4. APEC'S ROLE IN RELATED ISSUE AREAS

With significant problems in moving forward in trade liberalisation over the last few years, many had hoped that APEC would play a dynamic role in other areas. Yet for the most part, APEC has found it difficult to advance in other issue areas, facing many of the same problems it has faced in developing a consensus on trade liberalisation. To keep our analysis manageable, we focus on three issues that directly impact trade: finance, technology, and the environment.

4.1 Finance

The 1997–8 financial crises in Asia provided an opportunity for APEC to play a pivotal role. Yet, the organisation's ability to deal with the financial crisis has been disappointing, to say the least. In fact, since the start of the Asian financial crisis in the summer of 1997, APEC has been very slow to react. In part, this slow reaction can be attributed to the loose structure of APEC. As a forum for discussion rather than a formal organisation where states make binding commitments, APEC has been unable to cope with short-term problems. With varied preferences based on sharply differing economic problems, the result has been a lack of any consensus at APEC summit meetings. So many differences existed that even agreements on the causes of the crisis were hard to find.

Given the structural difficulties in dealing with the financial crisis, APEC continued to work to provide a forum for discussions on the crisis. Indeed, in Vancouver at the 1997 meeting of APEC members, the financial crisis overshadowed trade liberalisation efforts. But the possibility of an active role by APEC or other Asia-Pacific regional organisations in resolving the financial crisis came to naught. In fact, other institutions in the Asia-Pacific have also attempted to play an active role, but the IMF, supported by the United States and European countries have resisted this effort. Beginning with its first key Asian program after the crisis began (a total package of $17 billion to Thailand in August 1997), the IMF, supported by the United States, attempted to deter any rival institutions from taking a significant role. With the United States failing to financially participate in the Thai rescue package, the Japanese took the lead in September 1997 with a proposal for an Asian Monetary Fund (AMF), to be backed by $100 billion that they had lined up in commitments in the region. But the IMF, the United States, and most other G-7 countries attempted almost immediately to quash this initiative, with the US Treasury leading the charge. The United States viewed such a fund as undercutting its preferred approach of IMF loans accompanied by conditionality. In addition, it expressed concern about the relationship that any such fund would have to the IMF.

Three positions quickly emerged: The Japanese argued for some division of labour and parallel linkage between the two funds, with an AMF playing a role in the crisis prevention as well. A second view, expressed by Malaysian Prime Minister Mahathir, was to have an AMF that would be independent of the IMF, thus creating a clear institutional rivalry. The third view, the IMF and American position, was that any Asian fund should be fully nested within the purview of the IMF. As Michel Camdessus put it, 'There is unanimity... to avoid creating whatever facility which would not be triggered by a programme with the IMF'.[19]

The success of the United States and the IMF in forestalling creation of a rival financial institution was embodied in the November 1997 Vancouver APEC summit meeting leaders' endorsement of the so-called Manila framework, agreed to by the APEC financial ministers shortly before the start of the summit. The Manila framework called for the International Monetary Fund to take the lead in providing emergency loans to Thailand, Indonesia, and South Korea, with APEC member nations taking only a secondary role, if necessary, to supplement IMF resources on a standby basis without any formal commitment of funds. Thus, with the APEC action providing a seal of approval for the U.S.-IMF backed plan, the AMF idea was put on hold.

More recently, several groups under the APEC umbrella have played a prominent role in APEC's financial development over the past year. APEC finance ministers have taken the lead in forging visions for APEC as well as reviewing its progress. APEC Finance Ministers met in Brunei from 9–10 September 2000 to assess APEC's progress over the past year. Finance ministers applauded progress made in the dissemination of best practices among member states as well as international standards and codes. These improvements fell into a broad array of issue areas including regulation and supervision of banking, securities and insurance. APEC tasked international financial institutions, such as the International Monetary Fund (IMF) with improving transparency;[20] this increasing disclosure would mirror efforts by Asian states to increase transparency following the Asian Crisis as part of IMF conditions to receive loans. Furthermore, this thrust for transparency seems to be a vivid response to some of the criticisms levelled at the WTO in Seattle.

Finance ministers also noted that private sector participation in the prevention and resolution of crises remains a major challenge to APEC. In response to this challenge, finance ministers have sought to increase collaboration with the APEC Financiers Group (AFG), ABAC and the Pacific Economic Co-operation Council to craft novel responses to future crises that will better employ the private sector.[21] Finance ministers have agreed to undertake an investigative study of APEC economies' experience in managing bank failures with the goal of establishing a set of guidelines to help avert future failures. The ministers also noted progress made in establishing training programs for banking supervisors and securities regulators.[22] These training programs, in the finance ministers' view, have helped to strengthen financial systems. Criticisms have emerged, however, about the efficacy of these APEC training programs. They are seen to be insufficient to meet the demand of the emerging market economies and these training programs have also been seen as lacking clarity of purpose and exhibiting a general lack of co-ordination.[23]

Advisory groups for these training programs met in November 2000 to discuss broadening the scope of the training initiative in order to amplify and deepen its effect.[24] These courses will be prepared in light of international best practices for the region and will be assisted, initially, by testing programs in the Philippines, the People's Republic of China and Indonesia. The finance ministers have also formed a taskforce on accounting to improve the quality of financial disclosure in APEC economies.[25]

The action taken thus far by the finance ministers serves as a case in point to show that APEC member economies are not making significant sacrifices to carry APEC's work forward. The training groups, private sector collaboration, and dissemination of best practices do not require much commitment by member economies.

Deepening activity in the financial sphere has also proven to be very limited. The APEC Forum on Shared Prosperity and Harmony in Seoul succeeded in bringing together government officials, financiers and scholars for the first time in APEC's history. This conference also produced a proposal, advocated by Japan, Thailand and New Zealand, to monitor and check hedge funds.[26] Recognising the role of hedge funds in disrupting Asian economies during the Crisis, this pact could be a tool to prevent another crises. This forum did, therefore, establish one important proposal; how and if this proposal is established, however, is the important question. If it were to be implemented by member economies, the program would indeed involve a deepening of commitment.

For its part, ABAC set in motion a financial task force that will build stronger financial systems through benchmarking and promoting best practices, much like the finance ministers have sought to accomplish.[27] Furthermore, at the finance meeting in September, the APEC Secretariat affirmed the importance of encouraging participation in both the IMF/World Bank Financial Sector Assessment Program (FSAP) and Reports on Observance of Standards and Codes (ROSC) in order to strengthen the financial systems in each APEC member economy. APEC members would provide implementation status of the key financial and economic policy recommendations of both FSAP and ROSC regulations.[28] If member economies were to follow these recommendations, members would clearly be deepening their commitment to APEC institutions. Again, progress remains at the level of a recommendation without consequences for non-compliance; therefore, deepening of commitment is difficult to assess.

At the September 1999 Auckland Leader's Meeting, ABAC members examined economic recovery and sustainability. The finding of this group was that economic recovery was indeed underway in the region, albeit weak in some areas. ABAC sought to ensure continued recovery by three main measures. First, greater transparency and predictability in the corporate and public sector governance would help increase dialogue regarding best practices. Second, the group recommended that improving both the quality and capacity of regulation would help to sustain growth. Finally, the group sought to reduce compliance costs (reducing depth of commitment) to help business growth.

In short, with regard to APEC members deepening their commitment on finance, it appears that most members have been acting with less commitment in mind. Programs such as training sessions and benchmarking do not require much change on the part of APEC member economies and, therefore, do not stand out as compelling evidence of continued deepening of commitment.

There has also been very little evidence of widening of the scope of APEC's financial regime. At the seventh APEC Finance Ministers' Meeting from 9 to 10 September 2000, APEC members agreed to several new initiatives to fall under APEC's financial regime. These initiatives include: social safety nets, managing regulatory change in life insurance and pensions, company accounting and financial reporting, paperless trading, strategic objectives for the APEC Finance Ministers process, and an enhanced role in the fight against the abuse of the financial systems.[29] These initiatives do indeed represent a significant increase in the scope of APEC's financial regime; however, they stand out as the only examples of widening in 2000.

4.2 Technology

With the development of the new economy, APEC's work on technology directly affects trade issues. ABAC's technology task force will work on broadening access to technology through E-commerce readiness assessment and will look at ways of reducing the 'digital divide' among APEC member economies.[30] APEC telecommunications ministers met in Cancun on 22–26 May 2000. They discussed the challenges and opportunities presented by the convergence of telecommunications broadcasting, and information technology. The 'Cancun Declaration', adopted by these Ministers, addressed issues such as bridging the digital divide, enhancing access to telecommunication services by APEC communities, strengthening human resources and skills development and continuing work on ensuring that policy and regulatory environments promote the uptake of E-commerce in the APEC region.[31]

Furthermore, ABAC recommended the following key initiatives in 2000: to develop action plans for E-commerce; to implement 'Government Online' as a catalyst for E-commerce; adopt regulatory framework conducive to E-commerce development; and to harness the Internet for Human Resources Development.[32]

At the 9–10 September 2000 meeting in Brunei, finance ministers strove to create new opportunities for information technology. Ministers called on economies to formulate and implement appropriate policies and arrangements to facilitate electronic financial transactions and supported efforts by APEC member economies and international financial institutions to ensure that the benefits of information technology are as widely shared as possible. Ministers also agreed to establish a working group on electronic financial transactions systems to develop and implement programs to foster paperless trading in collaboration with the E-Commerce Steering Group.[33]

APEC has spent an inordinate amount of its time dealing with issues relating to E-commerce. This may be a function of two factors. First, APEC may view E-commerce as the link needed to expedite free trade within the APEC community in the New Economy. E-commerce is obviously a powerful tool for overcoming boundaries and borders and as such, may prove to be a powerful tool for the APEC group. Second, a null hypothesis to this focus on E-commerce is simply that it is a growing part of the global economy and has therefore taken more of APEC's attention than in the past. Wherever the truth lies between these two hypotheses, the fact remains that APEC is turning more of its attention to dealing with this emerging giant of international trade.

4.3   Labour and the environment

While it is evident that APEC has attempted to address a host of issues, two areas that have escaped APEC action are the environment and labour. This might be seen as a surprise to any student of the Seattle protests because one might have anticipated some of the protests to lead to changes in APEC's scope. After Seattle, APEC might have been expected to push harder for these issues; yet, there is no such evidence. For example, APEC could have presented its model as a viable alternative to that of the WTO if it could produce some of the same results the WTO has, as well as covering better the areas in which the WTO is weak, e.g., labour and the environment. However, we will see that in both areas, private interests in developing and developed states have divided APEC.

We turn first to labour issues in APEC. Since its inception in 1989, most of APEC's efforts to deal with labour have fallen under the scope of human resource development, labour market development and human resource management (Feinberg 2000, p. 28). The 1996 Subic Declaration incorporated these ideas by advocating liberalisation efforts that contribute to 'sustainable growth and equitable development and to a reduction in economic disparities'.[34] While projects have inspected workplace safety and health contribution to productivity and comparative advantage, APEC has avoided dealing with the relationship between trade and labour comprehensively (Feinberg 2000, p. 28).

The impasse reached at Seattle over labour, in part because of the binding nature of WTO regulations, might have suggested that APEC would be a better forum to move closer to international core labour rights; yet, APEC members have been very reluctant to discuss labour issues in this setting. Even the United States, which has consistently advocated binding international labour regulations, chose not to press labour issues in APEC, but instead focused its efforts on the WTO and through a unilateral change in GSP that incorporates workers' rights provisions in US trade law (Harcourt 2000). Little has changed in the aftermath of Seattle. Furthermore, wide resistance among developing members of APEC is inevitable. States such as Malaysia have argued that labour standards would be used as a pretext for protectionist measures and seek to undermine competitive advantage derived from low-waged labour. Both at the June Darwin meeting and the 2000 November meeting, this ongoing dispute between developing and developed states dominated with respect to APEC's stance on the next round of WTO talks. While Malaysia leads developing countries with support from China and Australia, the US trade representative pointed out that the next US Congress would be unlikely to ratify any trade agreement that excludes either labour or environment.[35]

There are two primary positions regarding labour in APEC. In the past, the Human Resources Development group of APEC has encouraged the efforts of the International Labour Organisation (ILO) to create standardised labour practices, although several ASEAN states remain sensitive to ILO involvement on trade-related issues.[36] However, members debate whether APEC should take a more active role to nest itself within the ILO protocol in order to help that organisation to achieve its goals (Feinberg, in press). A large group in APEC believes that in order for APEC to proceed with liberalisation, labour should be simply left to other NGOs to deal with. Whether or not members support dealing with this issue in APEC, the organisation is probably not in a position to deal with hotly debated issues because both the Asian Crisis and US failure to lead have left APEC weakened (Petri 2000, p. 30). At the same time, without resolving these issues it seems that trade liberalisation has reached a deadlock. What the Seattle WTO meeting and the last two major APEC meetings have shown is developing economies' unwillingness to continue with trade liberalisation without more concessions in response to the needs of their underdeveloped status.

APEC remains a leader in rhetoric and failure in action concerning the environment. Waving the flag of sustainable growth, APEC states still account for over half of the world's production of pollutants.[37] The Environmental Vision Statement, adopted by the Ministers of Environment in March 1994, set up a framework of principles that linked economic development and environmental stability. In 1996 the Manila Action Plan addressed environment as one of six areas of focus. It called for APEC members to emphasise three priorities: clean technologies, sustainable cities and sustainable marine environment.[38] The 1997 Toronto conference on environment and sustainable development made recommendations in each of these areas for the goal of sustainable development. For example, to improve the quality of urban environments, APEC ministers responsible for environment and sustainable development implemented a plan of action that would 'bridge the knowledge gap, integrate the agenda of the public and private sectors, enhance human well-being and quality of life'.[39] This plan of action, while identifying areas of weakness, seems consistent with APEC's inability to act. Looking at the exact recommendations for implementation of these goals through conferences, training programs and best practices,[40] we find that, because of the voluntarism principle, projects are largely educational rather than definitive actions that would set limits on pollutants or erect standards for infrastructure (Feinberg 2000, p. 28). Under these initiatives APEC launched some sixty projects, the effectiveness of which many question (Feinberg 2000, p. 28). Workshops accompanied these statements achieving little if any substantive reform of environmental degradation. However, it must be recognised that in contrast to the labour issue, APEC countries have validated the link between environment and trade although they are reluctant to act on that reality.

APEC's involvement with the environment remains at the level of rhetoric. APEC's difficulty in dealing with environmental issues is tied to APEC's economic model of export-oriented industrialisation (EOI) in Southeast Asia: as with labour, developing states in these regions have little choice than to keep costs of raw materials down to achieve international competitive advantage.[41] In the face of private interests of multinational corporations that bring investments into these states, governments lack incentive to maintain sustainable development or to stop using low cost labour. While special interests agitate in LDCs, NGOs like Human Rights Watch act to influence the policies of developed countries, most prominently the United States. As with regime formation, it could be argued that the need for the provision of regional public goods should give rise to concerted government action with regard to environment – in this case through monitors on trans-border environmental issues (Lee 2000, p. 17). However, this transaction cost motive to co-operate is unlikely to compete with the special interests mentioned above in the near future; particularly since countries, who suffer from negative trans-border externalities, are unwilling to disengage from the same practices that would eliminate the pollution.

Why would APEC members not have used this opportunity to strengthen the regime? The most significant reason would appear to be fears that developed countries would use the environment issue to institute new forms of trade protection. Thus, raising an environment-trade link in APEC would be almost as controversial as such a link in the WTO. Another reason may be that APEC leaders, remembering the collapse of talks over EVSL, feared that the institution could not risk handling such a wide scope of issues.

5.   APEC, NESTING AND ALTERNATIVE TRADING ARRANGEMENTS

APEC has long claimed to and has succeeded in making an effort to be consistent with the GATT (and now the WTO). As we have seen, how this consistency might be achieved and what proper meaning should be attributed to the concept of 'open regionalism' remains an issue of contention. After considering the effort to nest from a theoretical perspective, we will turn to APEC's more recent efforts to maintain WTO consistency after the problems with the Millennium Round. We will then turn to the reactions that we have seen in the region in terms of the pursuit of alternatives to APEC-based liberalisation, guided by the theoretical framework presented in section 2.

5.1   Nesting APEC in the WTO: the theory[42]

With respect to nesting APEC in the WTO, we can consider four options for APEC members: First, one could pursue a free trade agreement or customs union under Article 24, the strategy pursued by NAFTA members and other regional groupings. Second, only non-WTO issues might be discussed in a particular forum, thus also ensuring consistency. Third, states could freely extend any concessions within a grouping to all WTO members – the APEC idea of open regionalism. And fourth, and most controversially, APEC could engage in conditional liberalisation along the lines of the Tokyo Round codes.

   The first notion, of pursuing a free trade agreement in APEC, was raised at the Seattle meetings by the Group of Eminent Persons' report. Yet most APEC states were reluctant to commit themselves to forming a free trade arrangement, despite apparent US backing for the idea. Given the difficulty that the Clinton administration had in passing NAFTA, it would also appear that US support for this idea is more rhetorical than real.

   The second approach – dealing exclusively with non-GATT issues – is considerably less likely under the WTO than the GATT. The WTO's scope has continued to expand, leaving little that is not a part of this organisation's mandate – even as the organisation itself faces grave challenges. What appears to remain is limited to co-operation on business visas.

   The third approach, of extending APEC concessions freely to other states, does not appear to be likely from either an international or domestic political standpoint. While several APEC members are pushing for just such an approach, the US remains strongly opposed, and the prospects of outsider free riding continues to be a daunting challenge.

   Finally, the notion of pressing forward with some type of conditional liberalisation has also proved to be contentious, and despite some calls for such an approach from American quarters, has met with opposition from Asians. Moreover, in light of the elimination of Tokyo Round forms of conditionality as a result of the incorporation of codes from this round as part of the WTO, such conditionality would appear to be clearly WTO-inconsistent.

5.2   Recent efforts to maintain consistency with the WTO

APEC has continued to profess WTO consistency. At the September 1999 Leaders Meeting, ABAC members strongly supported continued trade liberalisation both under the APEC and the WTO.[43] Members also spoke in favour of not only supporting the existing WTO regime, but also strengthening it through a new round of WTO negotiations that would include the following three goals: covering industrial tariffs in addition to services and agriculture; improving market access for all economies, including developing ones; and a balanced and broad-based agenda to be concluded within three years.[44] Officials have also supported the abolition of agricultural export subsidies and unjustifiable export prohibitions and restrictions and they also have called on WTO members to not impose new restrictive trade measures for the duration of the negotiations.[45] ABAC's interest in supporting the launch of another WTO round is a clear example of that group's interest in ensuring that APEC nests its trade liberalisation regime within the WTO.

5.3   Multilateral alternatives

As noted, during the 1999 APEC Ministerial meeting in New Zealand, the APEC ministers agreed to refer current negotiations on tariff elimination in six specific trade sectors – oilseeds, food, rubber, fertiliser, civil aircraft, and car industries – to the WTO. This effort signals a significant shift in attitudes of countries such as Japan and South Korea that had previously resisted such a move.[46] While APEC countries, therefore, have now in principle agreed on including industrial tariff negotiations at the WTO, developing countries including China, India, Indonesia, and Brazil continue to disagree with the United States, the EU, and Japan on including subjects like government procurement and investment policy.[47]

APEC members have failed to show unity on a new WTO round largely because Japan and the US failed to narrow the gap between their approaches during the APEC meetings: Japan wanted a 'single-undertaking' approach (supported by South Korea), while the US wanted to allow participating economies to implement accords as soon as they are reached.[48] Following the Auckland APEC meeting, the US won out and it was decided that tariff reductions would be delivered sector by sector according to each economy.

Also, Japan preferred to take up a variety of issues at the WTO round, but the US wanted a limited agenda. A senior Japanese official correctly predicted that the Seattle WTO meeting would not succeed if the US stuck to its stance. Japan and the US are likely to continue their long-running battle of wills over fish, timber products and agriculture. At the same time, many developing nations, particularly Malaysia, are cautious of moves to widen the scope of WTO negotiations to include non-trade issues. Malaysian ministers were glad that APEC did not set a decisive time for new trade negotiations in the Millennium Round, against US pressures to do so.[49] Early on Malaysia had refused to dispatch its trade minister to Auckland's APEC meeting because it opposes the 'extraneous' new issues such as the linkage of trade with environment protection and labour standards, both topics supported by US representatives.[50]

5.4   Transregional alternatives

Problems in APEC and the WTO have set off alternative efforts to organise trade in the Asia-Pacific. Referring to Table 6.1, we can divide these efforts along several dimensions, but the most useful approach would appear to be a consideration of transregional, minilateral regional, and bilateral alternatives to the WTO and APEC.

The Asia-Europe Meeting (ASEM), founded in 1996 symbolises the most ambitious effort toward free trade between Europe and Asia. ASEM includes all ASEAN plus three member states (with the exception of Myanmar) and primarily strives to establish an Asian-Europe free trade area by 2020. The European Union (EU) ranks as either the second or third most important trading partner to ASEAN countries (Dosch 2000b, p. 2). Given the highly critical trade relations between the two regions, it is hardly surprising that free trade talks have begun to solidify between the two economic powerhouses.

Jörn Dosch has noted that official and institutionalised relations between Europe and Asia regarding free trade areas remain at a historic low. Dosch attributes this deficiency to three primary factors: that Europeans have considered Asians incapable of 'keeping up' economically with Europe after the Asian Crisis; a conflict of norms and values between the two regions, especially human rights and; questions raised about global governance resulting from the war in Kosovo (Dosch 2000b, p. 3). Thus, with these constraints in mind, ASEM's prospects for passing up gains made by APEC seem limited.

Turning next to free trade aspirations in Latin America: the Free Trade Area of the Americas (FTAA) was launched at the Miami Summit in 1994, and calls for completion of negotiations by 2005. On paper, FTAA is currently the most ambitious trade initiative in the world, building on the trend of regional trading blocs in the past five years. However, in reality efforts toward substantive negotiation have been slow and face formidable challenges arising from regional diversities, conflicting strategic interests, and global economic conditions.

At this time, the FTAA does not appear to be a viable alternative for the United States to pursue at the expense of APEC because the FTAA has still not been granted US fast-track' status.[51] The Republican denial of fast-track status to President Clinton for FTAA negotiations shows a marked lack of support for this route to free trade agreements. Whether the new Bush administration does indeed pursue a Latin American strategy remains to be seen, and problems in obtaining fast track are likely to remain for the near future.

5.5   Regional alternatives

The Association of Southeast Asian Nations (ASEAN), consisting of ten member states,[52] presents an example of the kind of regional organisation competition this paper has presented as a potential challenge to APEC. ASEAN, however, like APEC, has struggled in the wake of the Asian Crisis. Faith in ASEAN continues to be weak regardless of the economic recovery in Asia since 1997. ASEAN members continually face difficulties in implementing their free trade agreement, the ASEAN Free Trade Area (AFTA). For example, instead of crafting a new, speedier approach to free trade, the Foreign Ministers at the annual AFTA meeting in 2000, merely recalled an earlier proposal to dissolve all import duties on intra-ASEAN trade by 2010 for the six original signatories and by 2015 for Vietnam, Laos, Myanmar, and Cambodia (Dosch 2000a, p. 3).

ASEAN's uphill struggle to invigorate AFTA, however, has witnessed some progress during the past year. At the 25 November 2000 ASEAN summit, members explored the possibility of expanding the existing the AFTA to include the ASEAN plus three states: China, Japan and South Korea.[53] If instituted, this new ASEAN plus three free trade area could exert more pressure on the existing free trade aspirations of APEC by the entry of economic behemoths, Japan, China and South Korea. ASEAN has also floated ideas of permanently incorporating these 'plus three' nations into a formalised 'East Asian' summit to increase the scope and puissance of the organisation. However, both of these ambitious plans remain aspirations.

ASEAN has also succeeded in making progress toward free trade via its Closer Economic Relations (CER) accord with Australia and New Zealand. The AFTA-CER agreement, entered into force in 1983, has sought to facilitate trade and investment flows between the ASEAN region and CER countries (New Zealand and Australia). At present, all tariffs and quantitative restrictions on trade in goods between New Zealand and Australia have been eliminated via the CER. The CER states estimate a gain of US$48.1 billion if a similar free-trade area were to be constructed between the ASEAN and CER regions.[54] AFTA-CER also seeks to harmonise a range of non-tariff measures that affect the flow of goods and services between the two regions. Again, if these hopes were to reach fruition, APEC may be quickly replaced as APEC member economies gravitate toward ASEAN's momentum. However, the AFTA-CER free trade area has not yet materialised.

The ASEAN group also signed an AFTA protocol governing the relaxation of tariff reduction. The protocol was first announced at the ASEAN Economic Ministers meeting in early October, and was adopted following Malaysia's decision to delay tariff reductions on automobiles and CKD kits. Senior Malaysian officials will meet with their counterparts from Thailand, the country most directly affected, to negotiate compensatory measures. The protocol contains the following four provisions: that compensation will be provided to ASEAN members by the party wishing to modify its concessions; the scope refers to products in the temporary exclusion list as of 31 December 2000; relevant states must consult with each other to come up with a resolution 180 days after submission of a formal notifications, and finally; countries can impose unilateral retaliatory actions if there was no such agreement.[55]

This mechanism serves to strengthen AFTA provisions because it makes existing provisions more difficult to alter. In a very concrete sense, ASEAN members have deepened their commitment to pursuing free trade within their own region as well as with other regions. As an alternative to APEC, ASEAN has displayed mixed results. At present, ASEAN's challenge to APEC as a potential alternative seems to be climbing yet has not yet made APEC insignificant in the Asia-Pacific.

5.6   Bilateral alternatives to APEC

East Asian countries have shown a growing appetite for bilateral trade during the post-Seattle WTO standstill. Led by Japan and Singapore – two countries that had previously negotiated trade deals exclusively through multilateral and regional/transregional (or 'minilateral') means – many countries in East Asia seem to have wholeheartedly embraced the new bilateralism. Much of the activity is concentrated within the East Asia region itself. For example, Japan and Singapore are pursuing a bilateral agreement with each other, and each is separately negotiating similar measures with South Korea. However, these countries are not limiting their vision to the immediate region. Indeed, both Japan and Singapore are considering free trade agreements (FTAs) with Mexico, and Singapore is also engaged in talks with Canada, Chile, and New Zealand, among others. While Japan and Singapore remain in the vanguard of this new trend, other East Asian countries – such as Vietnam and South Korea – seem to be similarly well-disposed toward cementing trade relationships through bilateral measures.

Let us consider some specific country cases to examine the motivation behind these trends.

Japan. Since the end of World War II, multilateralism has consistently been the basis of Japan's trade policy. Since the WTO setback in Seattle, however,

Japan has been actively pursuing bilateral FTAs, particularly with South Korea and Singapore. To date, negotiations with Singapore have been moving faster than with South Korea. In October 2000, after a one-year feasibility study Japanese Prime Minister Yoshiro Mori and Singaporean Prime Minister Goh Chok Tong agreed that the two countries would enter into negotiations for a bilateral FTA in January 2001 and aim to conclude a deal by the end of the year. With the momentum gained from this process, Japan is now trying to speed up negotiations with South Korea.

What might be driving Japan toward bilateralism? First, the Japanese government likely anticipates various positive economic effects from FTAs. For example, if a bilateral FTA is concluded with South Korea, the Japanese trade surplus with South Korea is expected to expand by 34.5 per cent (Yamazawa 2000, p. 27). Other more general benefits might include a reduction in domestic prices of imported items, increases in productivity and employment, and attraction of foreign corporations.

Second, Japan's emphasis on bilateralism may be connected to the surge in FTAs in other parts of the world. While an increasing number of countries have joined FTAs in the 1990s (currently there are more than 120 FTAs), among the advanced industrial countries only Japan has yet to sign such an agreement (Kojima 2001). Thus, concern grew in both government and the private sector that Japan might fall behind in the new trend toward bilateralism. In particular, Japan's export-oriented industries called for the government to change its position: in July 2000 the Japan Federation of Economic Organisations (Keidanren) warned that if Japan failed to conclude any FTAs it would suffer an erosion of its position in international competition.

Third, Japan's increased interest in bilateral FTAs may have been prompted by a reconfiguration of internal bureaucratic influence. In the past, institutional opponents of FTAs such as the Ministry of Foreign Affairs argued that they would create trade diversion, reducing overall gains in global trade. Moreover, the Foreign Ministry lacked jurisdictional authority to hold negotiations with foreign countries on specific economic issues, cementing its preference for a multilateral approach. However, the pro-FTA view has in recent years gained ground among other government ministries such as the Ministry of Economy, Trade, and Industry (METI, formerly MITI), and the Ministry of Finance. These ministries have accepted the logic that FTAs do not run counter to the basic direction of multilateralism, but rather serve as an interim process that actually sustains multilateralism by accelerating the liberalisation measures intended to be pursued by the WTO. This new perception of FTAs drastically changed the power configuration among government ministries in Japan. As an exclusive focus on multilateralism lost ground within the Japanese government, the Foreign Ministry had to shift its policy focus, paving the way for METI, a vocal champion of bilateralism, to seek bilateral FTAs without serious opposition.

Japan has clearly started to explore its options by means of bilateral deals. Though MITI professes WTO consistency, Japan may ultimately abandon its commitments to APEC and the WTO if bilateral deals become ubiquitous and effective.

South Korea. In the wake of the WTO breakdown in Seattle and the Asian financial crisis, South Korea has become concerned about the lack of institutional trade frameworks in which to anchor its economy. In response, Seoul is energetically pursuing FTAs with some strategic countries – in particular, Chile and Japan.

South Korea likely sees Chile as an ideal trading partner with which to pursue an FTA due to the broad compatibility of their two economies. Chilean exports of primary goods would be highly complementary to South Korea's exports of manufactured products. In addition, any adjustment costs for South Korea are likely to be relatively low, as the size of Chilean economy is relatively small and the trade volume between the two countries amounts to a small percentage of South Korea's total trade. Indeed, Seoul likely sees an FTA with Chile as a stepping-stone to greater things: with the successful launch of an FTA with Chile, South Korea may be in a better position to pursue FTAs with Japan and other major economies.

As to a South Korea-Japan FTA, Japan would probably benefit more than South Korea – at least in the short run – as South Korea's trade structure depends heavily upon Japanese parts, intermediate goods, and equipment in various industries. Furthermore, a South Korea-Japan FTA might exacerbate South Korea's chronic trade deficit with Japan, as South Korea's tariff rates on Japanese goods are generally higher than those of Japan on its products (7.9 per cent vs. 2.9 per cent as of 1995). Still, the South Korean government may be willing to engage in a bilateral FTA with Japan because of the potentially huge gains from reliable Japanese capital inflows in terms of foreign direct investment (FDI) and portfolio investment. As such, South Korea wants an FTA with Japan to cover not only the elimination of tariff barriers but also comprehensive areas such as investment liberalisation, establishment of effective dispute settlement mechanisms, and regulatory reforms on import restrictive measures.

Singapore. As a highly trade-dependent nation with the highest trade-to-GDP ratio in the world, Singapore has sought to sustain the momentum of global free trade. Singapore has thus placed the highest priority on the multilateral trading system embodied by the WTO. However, since 1999 Singapore has pursued bilateral FTAs as well. In November 2000, Singapore concluded an FTA with New Zealand that came into effect in January 2001; it is also negotiating FTAs with Mexico, Japan, Canada, Chile, Australia, and the United States.

Do these forays into bilateralism signify that Singapore has abandoned its long-standing multilateralist approach? First, Singapore appears to regard this as a false choice, viewing multilateralism and bilteralism as fundamentally complementary. As momentum for trade liberalisation at the multilateral level dissipated, Singapore turned to bilateralism not to abandon multilateralism but to accelerate it, committing itself to FTAs to move forward the global free trade agenda in the belief that FTAs could strengthen the multilateral trading system. The Singaporean government thinks that this approach will be particularly effective in setting out new trade rules in such sectors as telecommunications, finance, and e-commerce. In these areas, trade rules are still being discussed or have not yet been raised at APEC and the WTO. Thus, any moves toward further liberalisation would be properly nested within the confines of the WTO. In addition, the Singaporean government expects that after observing the benefits of Singapore's FTAs, other APEC countries may seek similar FTAs that could ultimately form an APEC-wide FTA.

Second, since Southeast Asian countries suffered through the financial crisis in 1997–98, Singapore found it necessary to diversify its trading partners to maintain its economic vitality in the face of regional uncertainty. As such, Singapore is eager to sign FTAs with non-ASEAN countries so that these countries can serve as an alternative outlet in the event of another crisis in the region.

APEC has not ignored the looming bilateralism trend. At APEC's Second and Third Senior Officials Meeting (SOM II and SOM III), officials recommended that they adopt a strategic APEC plan on Capacity Building, designed to develop capacity building programs by both member economies and related international organisations within the APEC region. SOM also agreed that free-trade agreements could serve as building blocks for wider multilateral liberalisation provided that they are consistent with WTO rules.[56] The senior officials basically gave the green light to FTAs such as the Japan-Singapore accord, but attached the crucial caveat that these must be consistent with WTO rules, in other words, properly nested.

Recent bilateral moves toward free trade were placed high on the 15–17 November 2000 APEC Economic Leaders Meeting in Brunei. Leaders again emphasised the importance of keeping these accords 'open' and maintaining consistency with APEC rules on comprehensive coverage.[57] The proliferation of these free trade agreements may mark the growing trend toward disenchantment with APEC's progress toward free trade in the Asia-Pacific. Sub-regional bilateral agreements are certainly another avenue in which free trade may take shape. This has several implications for the APEC regime. If APEC fails to address the growing importance of these accords, the regime may be quickly replaced by them. If, on the other hand, APEC chooses to embrace these FTAs as building blocks toward the Bogar goals of trade liberalisation, APEC may find itself in a revitalised position able to lead the Asia-Pacific toward free trade in 2010.

6. CONCLUSION AND PROSPECTS

The break-up of WTO talks opened a window of opportunity for APEC to establish itself as a pioneer and leader in trade liberalisation. In the wake of the Seattle debacle, however, the past year has demonstrated that APEC has been unable to assume a role at the forefront of continuing liberalisation measures; instead, it has chosen, for the most part, to advocate and reinforce the pre-eminence of the WTO. We have looked at trade and a wide array of other issues that APEC attempts to address and we have found that the most progress and fervour surrounds new issues that had considerable room to move forward. APEC remains at almost the same place it stood a year ago in attaining the goals of the Bogor Declaration as the reality of free trade by 2020 dissipates.

Trade has made little headway in the months following Seattle. Trade took a step closer to developing more compliance of members by advancing aspects of IAPs – the key to APEC liberalisation. While electronic IAPs and proposed improvement of non-tariff barriers within IAPs do not demonstrate tremendous improvements, these initiatives may lead toward more stringent rules regarding conformance. The move by Japan among others to arrange bilateral Fats proves to be an area of concern. Though Fats may be stumbling blocks toward regional and global trade, APEC has condoned them as individual initiative to achieve trade. Furthermore, the real relevance of such Fats must address the percentage of trade conducted between states. For example, if Japan's major trading partners are the United States and Europe, an FTA with Singapore is not going to produce a significant impact in trade.

Finally, myriad issues have found their way to the top of APEC agendas generating the most advancement for APEC this year, yet these results have neither moved forward with issues that disrupted the WTO nor brought member states closer to Bogor aspirations. Under this area, APEC's most significant action was attempting to keep E-commerce duty- and barrier-free. While all issues here are relevant to member states, it will be important that these issues, such as tourism, remain periphery to the core objectives of APEC.

The basic question of where APEC will fit in an increasingly crowded world of varying forms of trade arrangements has not been suitably settled. While the stand-off in the Uruguay Round propelled APEC forward and raised hopes of a co-operative integrated set of trade institutions, the conflict over the Millennium Round in Seattle has failed to generate a similar salutary effect on APEC's prospects. Instead, with both global and transregional trade liberalisation efforts stalled, the way now appears to be paved for both bilateral and regional minilateral approaches – neither of which bode well for the long term health of the international trading system.

NOTES

*   The author would like to thank Justin Kolbeck for his extensive research assistance. Lily Bradley, Min Gyo Koo, and Seungjoo Lee also provided research assistance and comments on this chapter.
1.   See Aggarwal (2000a) and Aggarwal and Lin (in press) for a discussion of APEC's efforts in other issue areas.
2.   This table has been developed and discussed at length in Aggarwal (in press).
3.   See, for example, Aggarwal (in press) and Aggarwal and Ravenhill (2001) on the role of piecemeal sectoral liberalisation in undermining the coalition for free trade.
4.   Jagdish Bhagwati has used this phrase. For a discussion, see Lawrence (1991).
5.   See Bhagwati and Patrick (1990), and Aggarwal and Morrison (1998), among others.
6.   Australia, New Zealand, United States, Canada, Japan, Republic of Korea, Thailand, Malaysia, Republic of the Philippines, Singapore, Brunei Darussalam, People's Republic of China, Chinese Taipei, Hong Kong, Mexico, Papua New Guinea, Chile, Peru, Russia, and Vietnam.
7.   See Aggarwal (1994) for a discussion. This section draws on this chapter.
8.   This perspective views smaller coalitions of states as a potential replacement for the lack of a hegemonic power in the international system to drive negotiations in the WTO forward. For a discussion of this idea, see Snidal (1985).
9.   See Lawrence (1991) and Krugman (1991).
10. Ravenhill (1992) makes this point and also attacks the notion of unilateral liberalisation in the Australian context in a co-authored work (Matthews and Ravenhill, 1991).
11. 1992. They do, however, go on to note that only measures aimed at export subsidies in the form of some anti-dumping tools would be appropriate as a response.
12. Additional arguments include the need for a forum for interest aggregation, the inability of the GATT/WTO to address issues of specific concern to Asia-Pacific countries, and the more complex idea of strategic trade policy as a rationale for bloc formation.
13. *What's happening in APEC?* Business Briefing, Vol. 8, March 2000.
14. *The Financial Times*, p. 12. June 8, 2000.
15. *What's happening in APEC?* Business Briefing, Vol. 9, July 2000.
16. *What's happening in APEC?* Business Briefing, Vol. 10, October 2000.
17. *Agence France Press*, Section: International News, March 31, 2000.
18. Feinberg (in press).
19. *Financial Times*, November 14, 1997.
20. *What's Happening in APEC*, Business Briefing, Vol. 10, October 2000.
21. *What's Happening in APEC*, Business Briefing, Vol. 10, October 2000.
22. *What's Happening in APEC*, Business Briefing, Vol. 10, October 2000.
23. *Agence France Presse*, financial pages, 9 September 2000.
24. 'APEC Secretariat Media Advisory 34/2000'. Brunei Darussalem, 9–10 September.
25. *What's happening in APEC?* Business Briefing, Vol. 10, October 2000.
26. *Korea Times,* 2 April 2000.
27. *What's happening in APEC?* Business Briefing, Vol. 8, March 2000.
28. 'APEC Secretariat Media Advisory 34/2000'. Brunei Darussalam, 9–10 September.
29. *The Straits Times,* 1 April 2000.
30. *What's happening in APEC?* Business Briefing, Vol. 8, March 2000.
31. *What's happening in APEC?* Business Briefing, Vol. 9, July 2000.
32. *What's happening in APEC?* Business Briefing, Vol. 10, October 2000.
33. *What's happening in APEC?* Business Briefing, Vol. 10, October 2000.
34. 'APEC Economic Leaders' Declaration From Vision to Action'. Available on: http://www.apecsec.org.sg/.
35. *The Associated Press*, 14 November 2000.
36. Harcourt (2000). Australia APEC Study Centre Issues Paper No. 9.
37. APEC environment ministerial meeting on sustainable development. Available on: http://www.iisd.ca/linkages/sd/sd0603.html.

38. APEC environment ministerial meeting on sustainable development. Available on: http://www.iisd.ca/linkages/sd/sd0603.html.
39. 'APEC – 2nd Environment Ministers Meeting', Available on: http://www.apecsec.org/.
40. APEC environment ministerial meeting on sustainable development. Available on: http://www.iisd.ca/linkages/sd/sd0603.html.
41. 'What does APEC say about the environment?', Available on http://www.apec.gen.nz/facts6.html.
42. See Aggarwal (1994) for a discussion of these issues.
43. *What's happening in APEC?* Business Briefing, Vol. 8, March 2000.
44. *What's happening in APEC?* Business Briefing, Vol. 8, March 2000.
45. *What's happening in APEC?* Business Briefing, Vol. 8, March 2000.
46. *Financial Times*, p. 4, June 30, 1999.
47. *Japan Economic Newswire*, June 26, 1999.
48. *Japan Economic Newswire*, September 8, 1999.
49. *Bernama: The Malaysian National News Agency*, September 19, 1999.
50. *Japan Economic Newswire*, June 26, 1999.
51. *Agence France Presse*, 1 September 2000.
52. Brunei Darussalam, Cambodia, Indonesia, Laos, Malaysia, Myanmar, Philippines, Singapore, Thailand, and Vietnam. The ASEAN plus three nations are those mentioned above with the addition of China, Japan and South Korea.
53. *US-ASEAN Business Report*, First Quarter, 2001, Vol. 12, No. 1.
54. Media Release: 11 July 2000. Australian Department of Foreign Affairs and Trade.
55. *US-ASEAN Business Council* prepared by PricewaterhouseCoopers, November, 2000.
56. *What's happening in APEC?* Business Briefing, Vol. 10, October 2000.
57. *Agence France Presse*, November 15, 2000.

REFERENCES

Agence France Presse, Various.
Aggarwal, Vinod K. (1994), 'Comparing Regional Cooperation Efforts in Asia-Pacific and North America', in Andrew Mack and John Ravenhil (eds), *Pacific Cooperation: Building Economic and Security Regimes in the Asia Pacific Region*. Sydney: Allen and Unwin, pp. 40–65.
– (2000a), 'The Wobbly Triangle: Economic Relationships among Europe, Asia, and the US after the Asian Crisis', in Maria Weber (ed), *After the Asian Crises: Implications for Global Politics and Economics*, London: MacMillan.
– (2000b), 'Withering APEC? The Search for an Institutional Role', in Jörn Dosch and Manfred Mols (eds), *International Relations in the Asia-Pacific: New Patterns of Power, Interest, and Cooperation*, Muenster: Lit-Verlag and New York: St. Martin's Press.
– (in press), 'Governance in International Trade: Changing Patterns of Sectoralism, Regionalism, and Globalism', in P.J. Simmons and Chantal de Jonge Oudraat (eds), *Managing a Globalizing World: Lessons Learned Across Sectors*, Washington, D.C.: The Carnegie Endowment for International Peace.
Aggarwal, Vinod K. and Kun-Chin Lin (in press), 'Strategy Without Vision: The US and Asia-Pacific Economic Cooperation', in Jürgen Rüland, Eva Manske and Werner Draguhn (eds), *APEC: The First Decade*, London: Curzon Press.
Aggarwal, Vinod K. and Charles Morrison (eds) (1998), *Asia-Pacific Crossroads: Regime Creation and the Future of APEC*, New York: St. Martin's Press.
– (2000), 'APEC as an International Institution', in Ippei Yamazawa (ed), *APEC: Its Challenges and Tasks in the 21st Century*, London and New York: Routledge.

Aggarwal, Vinod K. and John Ravenhill (2001), 'How "Open Sectoralism" Undermines the WTO', *Asia Pacific Issues*, No. 48, Honolulu: East-West Center.

Allison, Tony (2000), 'APEC: Trade saviors or talking heads?' Available on: http://www.atimes.com/se-asia/BH19Ae01.html#summary. August 19.

'APEC – 2nd Environment Ministers Meeting', Available on : http://www.apecsec.org/

'APEC "Economic Leaders" Declaration From Vision to Action', Available on: http://www.apecsec.org.sg/.

'APEC Environment Ministerial Meeting on Sustainable Development', Available on: http://www.iisd.ca/linkages/sd/sd0603.html.

'APEC Secretariat Media Advisory 34/2000', Joint Ministerial Statement from the Seventh APEC Finance Ministers Meeting at Bandar Seri Begawan, Brunei Darussalam 9–10 September 2000. Available on: http://www.apecsec.org.sg/whatsnew/press/rel34_2000.html.

'ASEAN to sign AFTA deferral mechanism at the Summit', *US-ASEAN Business Council* prepared by PricewaterhouseCoopers, November, 2000.

'ASEAN plus three to Study Free Trade Zone', *US-ASEAN Business Report*, First Quarter, 2001, Vol. 12, No. 1.

Asia Pulse Pte Limited, Various.

BBC Monitoring Asia Pacific, Various.

Bergsten, Fred C. (ed) (1997), *Whither APEC? The Progress to Date and Agenda for the Future*. Washington, D.C.: Institute for International Economics.

Bernama: The Malaysian National News Agency, Various.

Beveridge, Dirk, 'Environment, labor issues strangle trade talks at APEC summit', The Associated Press, November 14, 2000.

Bhagwati, Jagdish and Hugh Patrick (eds) (1990), *Aggressive Unilateralism*, Ann Arbor, MI: University of Michigan Press.

Borneo Bulletin, Various.

Cameron, Maxwell A. (1998), 'Nesting NAFTA in APEC: The Political Economy of Open Subregionalism', in Vinod K. Aggarwal and Charles Morrison (eds), *Asia-Pacific Crossroads: Regime Creation and the Future of APEC*, New York: St. Martin's Press.

Croner, Donald (1993), 'Does Hegemony Matter? The Re-organisation of the Pacific Political Economy', *World Politics*, 45.

Dosch, Jörn (2000a), 'ASEAN 2000: Institutionalization or Marginalization', *BASC News*, Fall 2000, Vol. 3, No. 2.

Dosch, Jörn (2000b), 'European-East Asian Relations: More Conflict than Cooperation?', Asia/Pacific Research Center, Stanford University, Manuscript.

Drysdale, Peter and Ross Garnaut (1992), 'The Pacific: An Application of a General Theory of Economic Integration', Twentieth Pacific Trade and Development Conference, Institute of International Economics, Washington, D.C. 10–12 September.

Feinberg, Richard (2000), 'Comparative Regional Integration: APEC and the FTAA', UC San Diego: Unpublished ms..

– (in press), *APEC's Progress: APIAN Evaluates Trade, Ecotech and Institutions*, Singapore: ISEAS.

– (2001), 'Free Trade Agreements as Constructive Regionalism', Akira, Kojima. *Journal of Japanese Trade and Industry*, Jan/Feb. Website: http://www.jef.jp/en/jti/200101_016.html.

Harcourt, Tim (2000), Australia APEC Study Centre Issues Paper No. 9.

Japan Economic Newswire, Various.

Kojima, Akira (2001), 'Free Trade Agreements as Constructive Regionalism', *Journal of Japanese Trade and Industry*, January/February.

Korea Times, Various.

Krugman, P. (1991), 'Regional Trade Blocs: the Good, the Bad and the Ugly', *The International Economy*, November/December, pp. 54–56.

Lawrence, R.Z. (1991), 'Emerging Regional Arrangements: Building Blocks or Stumbling Blocks?', in R. O'Brien (ed), *Finance and the International Economy*, Vol. 5, Oxford: Oxford University Press.

Lee, Chung H. (2000), *Toward Economic Cooperation in East Asia*, EWC/KDI Conference on *A Vision for Economic Cooperation in East Asia: China, Japan and Korea*, p. 17.

Lloyd, P.J. (1999), 'Towards APEC's Second Decade: Challenges, Opportunities and Priorities'. Paper presented at the APEC Study Centre Consortium Conference 1999, 31 May–2 June, Auckland, New Zealand.

Matthews, Trevor and John Ravenhill (1991), 'The Economic Challenge: Is Unilateral Free Trade the Correct Response?', in J.L. Richardson (ed), *Northeast Asian Challenge: Debating the Garnaut Report*, Canberra: Canberra Studies in World Affairs, No. 27, Department of International Relations, Australian National University, pp. 68–94.

– 'New Study Shows Big Gains From AFTA-CER Free Trade Area', Media Release: 11 July 2000. Australian Department of Foreign Affairs and Trade: http://www.dfat.gov.au/media/releases/trade/2000/mvt072a_00.html

Ostry, Sylvia (1998), 'APEC and Regime Creation in the Asia-Pacific: The OECD Model?', in Vinod K. Aggarwal and Charles Morrison (eds), *Asia-Pacific Crossroads: Regime Creation and the Future of APEC*, edited by Vinod K. Aggarwal and Charles Morrison, New York: St. Martin's Press.

Petri, Peter (June 14–16, 2000), 'New trade and investment policy priorities in face of globalization'. The 26th Pacific Trade and Development Conference, Seoul, Korea.

Plummer, Michael G. (1998), 'ASEAN and Institutional Nesting in the Asia-Pacific: Leading from Behind in APEC', in Vinod K. Aggarwal and Charles Morrison (eds), *Asia-Pacific Crossroads: Regime Creation and the Future of APEC*, New York: St. Martin's Press.

Ravenhill, John (1992), 'Discussion Paper for Workshop on Pacific Economic Cooperation'. Paper presented at a conference entitled, 'The Politics of Regional Trade Agreements', East-West Center, Honolulu, October 29–30.

Singapore Press Holdings Limited, Various.

The Associated Press, Various.

The Economist, Various.

The Financial Times, Various.

The Nikkei Weekly, Various.

The Straits Times, Various.

'What does APEC say about the environment?'. Available on http://www.apec.gen.nz/facts6.html

What's Happening in APEC? Business Briefing Vol. 8 - March 2000 - http://www.apecsec.org.sg/whatsnew/announce/prev_busbrief7.html.

What's Happening in APEC? Business Briefing Vol. 9 - July 2000 - http://www.apecsec.org.sg/whatsnew/announce/prev_busbrief8.html.

What's Happening in APEC? Business Briefing Vol. 10 - October 2000 - http://www.apecsec.org.sg/whatsnew/announce/busbrief.html.

Yamazawa, Ippei (2000), 'Toward Closer Japan-Korea Economic Relations in the 21st Century', *Institute of Developing Economies*, Tokyo: JETRO.

7.   Shifts in East Asia Regional Security: Old Issues and New Events Amidst Multilateral-Bilateral Tensions

Maria Julia Trombetta and Maria Weber

1.   INTRODUCTION

The geopolitical and security scenario in East Asia has changed deeply during the last year, largely as a result of two landmark events. First, the election of Chen Shui-bian, the first non-Guomintang leader and a member of the pro independence Taiwan's Democratic Progressive Party, has determined a fundamental change in the cross strait relations. Second, the historical summit between South Korean President Kim Dae-jung and North Korean leader Kim Jong-il, and the symbolic march of the two countries under a unified flag at Sydney Olympics, necessitate a rethinking of the future of the peninsula (Cossa 2000). Both the events have had a profound impact on stability and security strategies in East Asia.

Nevertheless these historic events have obscured the recent outcomes in a slow and difficult process of multilateral security co-operation – encompassing the Asia-Pacific region – which has progressively emerged during the last decade, in a region characterised, first and foremost, by bilateral security strategies. In this context, the 27 July 2000 ASEAN regional Forum[1] (ARF) meeting in Bangkok was most notable for the presence, for the first time, of North Korea and the gathering of all key North East Asia players in the Forum could provide the opportunity for multilateral discussions on regional security. Accordingly, the first meeting of the foreign ministers of the ASEAN plus three showed a shift in emphasis from the original focus on economic co-operation to a broader regional political security agenda (Cossa 2000, p. 12). Analogously the G8 summit in Okinawa, in July 2000, created the opportunity to discuss the US military presence in a multilateral context. Nevertheless, bilateral relations, which have long been important to regional peace and stability, are still critical and more relevant. In the post-Cold War environment these relations have taken on new forms since the states are involved in multiple ties and the strategic environment is more fluid and complex.

The aftermath of Cold War saw an enthusiastic attempt to create regional security institutions but, after a decade, they are still embryonic and they proved themselves unable to cope with crises as the East Timor tragedy clearly demonstrates. This situation has determined a de-legitimisation of the existing institution and has renewed the debate on regional security, its subject, content and meaning. The concept of 'comprehensive security', coined by Japan in the 1980s, has re-emerged in the debate. After a decade, the basic question is still how to define security strategies for a region that in its recent history, has not produced security strategies of its own. In this perspective we will try to give an account of the paradox of the co-existence of an emerging regional security narrative, which considers new threats and multilateral security institutions, and the still dominant realistic strategies based on bilateral accords and balance of power among the main players of the region. The regional equilibrium dominated, after the decline of the ex-Soviet Union, by the relative weights of the United States-Japan-China, remains absolutely crucial.

In the first part, we will analyse the recent development in the Korea peninsula and in the Cross Strait relations which are key events for the regional security strategies and we briefly consider their effects on regional equilibrium, amidst growing internal tensions. We will then consider the outcome of the recent multilateral meetings in the context of multilateral institution development.

Finally we will evaluate these events in a theoretical framework to outline whether and how the dominant understanding of the concept of security can change the practice and the discourse of security in the regional context.

2. THE REGIONAL SCENARIO AND THE MAIN ACTORS

East Asia is – and in the decades ahead will be more and more – a critical region on the global stage. 'It is here that the major powers of the present and future come into closest contact with each other. It is here that the crucial issues of population, resources, and environmental conditions will be most challenging. And it is here that the interaction between internationalism, nationalism, and communalism will unfold with greatest intensity' (Scalapino 1998). The end of the Cold War brought political uncertainties to the Asia-Pacific as well as the necessity to define security strategies for a region that in its recent history has not produced security strategies of its own (Weber 2000).

Concerns include tensions in the Taiwan Straits, persistent uncertainty on the Korean peninsula in spite of the recent developments, confrontations in the South China Sea, and hostility in South Asia, as well as ongoing territorial and maritime disputes, ethnic strife, and internal turmoils. The situation is complicated by historical animosities, economic inequality, competition for a power vacuum and dispute among the regional actors. In the short term, territorial problems may prove to be the most delicate, but the rise of new powers with clashing interests will likely become the greater concern of the future.

During the Cold War the regional security strategy was largely based on bilateral agreements. In the aftermath, the very complexity and seriousness of these problems claim for intra-regional institutions to deal with security matters. On the one hand proponents of multilateral institutions argued that Asia-Pacific nations share common interests, particularly the pursuit of economic development, which could be major incentives for co-operation. The rationale was that, as economic interdependence grew, webs of overlapping institutions would gradually emerge, motivating nations to maintain peace and stability and generating shared security concerns. For this approach, regional security institutions would help confidence building by promoting greater transparency, thus deterring states from resorting to force.

On the other hand, the realist approach pointed out that the deterrence and balance of power approach had a relatively good track record of maintaining peace and stability. In this view, since there was no evidence to suggest that regional institutions could either stop conflicts from breaking out or resolve them, the key determinant of regional security would be the balance of power. So far bilateral accords have proved absolutely crucial to guarantee regional stability and security.

The equilibrium appears dominated by the relative weights of the United States, Japan, China and Russia. Even if Russia lacks the influence the Soviet Union once wielded in world affairs, due to its internal problems, Moscow's diplomacy towards Asia has been extremely active. Throughout the 1990s, it has expressed itself mainly in a rapprochement with Beijing.[2] A broad and comprehensive friendship treaty is in progress[3] and Russia openly supports Chinese position on the Taiwan question. What prevails today is a 'realpolitik' vision of the common interests. Thus, while the 'strategic partnership' with China anchors Russian policy in Asia, this relationship does not rule out ties with other states (Dassù, Silvestri 2000). Nevertheless, since the mid 1990s, Moscow has also begun to diversify its contacts across Asia, giving real meaning to the Russian official declarations regarding the 'multipolar' post-Cold War world (Dassù, Silvestri 2000).

One of the consequences of the end of the Cold War was the growing importance of Beijing's regional foreign policy. Nevertheless this policy is characterised by a marked ambiguity. On the one hand China allowed more weight to regional integration, multilateral dialogue, and confidence building initiatives, on the other hand it restated national claims, in the South Chinese Sea even with military initiatives (Dassù, Silvestri 2000).

The second major shift is the change in the perception of China, from a potential threat to regional security to an essential pillar to Asian stability.

Nevertheless the ambiguity of Chinese policy poses the question whether emerging China is a status quo power or a revisionist state.[4] Different schools of thought have promoted a compelling debate. Pessimists predict that a rising China, with rapid economic growth and revived nationalistic aspirations, will be confrontational.[5] The optimists suggest that China is not likely to challenge the regional stability, due to its growing interdependence with the international community.[6] A more pragmatic approach suggests that China's power projection capabilities remain limited since the country still faces both internal problems and external constraints.[7]

Japan was considered the major player in Asia for its economic performance and its regional influence, backed by the strong security commitment of the United States. This role has, progressively, begun to shift towards Beijing both for China's economic and strategic rise; and Tokyo's own internal weaknesses. This shift has caused a growing interest and involvement of Japan in multilateral security institutions. Finally, even if their role is diminished, the US remains the principal guarantor of regional security. Basic aspects of the Cold War security framework remain in place and the US plays a major role in all the security questions in the region.

3.   THE CHANGING LANDSCAPE

3.1   The Korean peninsula

The year 2000 was, by any standard, a landmark in the history of the peninsula. The historic 13–15 June inter-Korean summit in Pyongyang between South Korean President Kim Dae-jung and North Korean Leader Kim Jong-il and the wholly new phase of substantive inter-Korean dialogues that it had provided calls for a rethink of what is and is not possible on the peninsula as South Korea forges a post economic crisis identity (Cossa 2000) and North Korea rushes for gaining economic viability. The unexpected, symbolic meeting took place in the 50th anniversary of the outbreak of Korean War. The conflict, brought up in 1950, lasted three years and the parties have not yet signed a Peace Treaty. The war failed to resolve the political division of the country but had a great impact on the global politics, determined a deep transformation of the balance of power in the region, changed the fortune of Japan and Taiwan, left the peninsula devastated and locked in a seemingly perpetual hostility, even after the end of the Cold War.

The origins of the conflict are rooted in the division of the peninsula into an American and a Soviet occupation zone in 1945 and the perpetuation of this division is the result of the creation of two hostile regimes and two different states. The North Korean Leader Kim Il-sung , with Soviet approval and aid, invaded on Sunday 25 June 1950 the South in an attempt to unite the peninsula under his control. The US moved quickly to prevent South Korea's extinction. The involvement of the UN magnified the international aspect of the conflict. The UN had played a central role in Korea, since 1947, even sponsoring the Republic of Korea in the South. The US tried to perpetuate that role so as to depict their effort against North Korea in a framework of collective security. On 27 June 1950 the Security Council (in the absense of the Soviet delegate[8]) passed a resolution which called on 'members of the UN to furnish such assistance to the Republic of Korea as may be necessary to repel the armed attack and to restore international pace and security in the area'.[9] October 1950 was a critical month in the war. Despite Chinese warnings, UN ground forces crossed the 38th parallel, the former border, and pushed their way toward Manchuria. China responded by sending troops to the peninsula and launching massive counterattacks. They rapidly faced a choice: whether to cross the 38th parallel and along with their North Korean allies attempt to unify the peninsula by military means or to halt at the old dividing line. They proceeded southward. The situation was critical. Finally the UN forces regrouped and slowly came back to the original border. During the summer of 1951 the war reached a stalemate at the point where it had begun and both sides abandoned hope of total victory. The long and costly stalemate was to last for another two years. After an armistice North and South remained at war. For decades the peninsula has seen a South and North intent on the ultimate collapse of their rival.

Nevertheless, since 1988 South Korea has been orchestrating a heady diplomatic action and a steady internationalisation campaign to engage the North (Noerper 2000). The process included establishing relations with the former Soviet Union and China. Meanwhile North Korea, with the consolidation of the Kim Jong-il regime in 1994, has tentatively embraced South Korea's approach, seeking better ties abroad, both reviving old alliances and embarking on new ones. The year 2000, in this respect, was impressive for North Korea, which started with the establishing of diplomatic relations with Italy and ended with that with Britain. Kim Jong-il personally embarked on this opening, first visiting China, then welcoming Kim Dae-jung in June, Putin in July and Albright in October.

The commitment of the South Korean President and the North Korean Leader to economic co-operation and eventual unification demonstrated a marked victory for Seoul and Kim Dae-jung engagement strategy (Noerper 2000). A risky strategy since South Korea's opposition (the Grand National Party,[10] that in two years could return to power) has criticised the Sunshine policy as appeasement (Foster-Carter 2001, p. 104), arguing that it had accomplished little, giving aid to the North and getting only continued hostility in return.

The greatest effort, pushed strongly by Seoul, was the attempt to normalise North Korea relations with the US. It took a while to get started. The Joint

Declaration's commitment 'to resolve the question of reunification independently' and the June summit worried the US that better North-South relations meant sidelining the US (Foster-Carter 2001, p. 104) and the incident at Frankfurt Airport[11] which caused the North Korean delegation's withdrawal from the Millennium Summit, was a clear demonstration of these tensions. More generally the US is sceptical toward regular, senior-level dialogue with North Korea. Nevertheless new heights of protocol between US and North Korea started during the last months. In July, Albright met North Korean foreign minister Peak Nam-sum at the ARF in Bangkok, and in October, she went to Pyongyang. In spite of this Clinton suspended the expected visit to Pyongyang. In this ambiguous scenario main uncertainty is the approach of the Bush administration, especially to the sensitive missile issues. The problem is not only the Korean disarmament but the broader issue of American theatre missile defence and its implication for the regional stability.

Russia has recently accelerated its contact with both North and South Korea to reintroduce itself into the peninsula equation. Russia resumed supplying the North Korea with crude oil in 1999 and in 2000 Putin's visit to Pyongyang undid a decade of distrust under Gorbachev and Yeltsin following the recognition of South Korea in 1990. The visit resulted in a renewal of friendship arrangements, although not in a security guarantee since the new post Soviet treaty, signed and ratified after years of negotiations excluded the old pledges of mutual military support (Foster-Carter 2001, p. 107). The most immediate interest of Russia is in transport. A rail link across the Demilitarised Zone could represent a new Trans-Siberian freight route linking South Korea to Europe (Foster-Carter 2001, p. 107).

China has been consistent in its call for peaceful transition on the Korean peninsula. Since 1992 it has succeeded, with great skill, in building new ties with Seoul, without alienating Pyongyang and it has been an effective facilitator and interlocutor between the two Koreas, in the attempt to resume its historical role as peninsular hegemon and consolidate itself as an essential pillar of Asian stability. In the short term it fared best as a result of the summit. However if China's long-range goal is to replace the US as the security guarantor on the peninsula and displace the US and its troops, the summit was not all good news for Beijing due to South Korean comments on the continued need for a US military presence not only during the peace process but also afterwards (Cossa 2000).

Japan-Korea normalisation accords are weakened by old problems. North Korea insists on apology and compensation for Japanese aggression as the precondition for any further discussion; Japan is concerned about the missile threat in light of the August 1998 Teapedong launch. Anyway Tokyo has committed significant food assistance (after several years of refusing food aid) in line with Seoul's and Washington's experiences. In addition Japan's establishment, in 1965, of diplomatic ties with South Korea, accompanied by an aid and loan package, is a promising precedent (Foster-Carter 2001, p. 107) in spite of the persistent diffidence. In this context the emergence of new narratives on security might contribute to dialogue and confidence building.

Other states both in and outside of the region have established contacts with North Korea in response to its overtures. Italy was the first European state to establish ties with North Korea[12] while the comment of the other European countries was that full relations would be held in reserve as a reward for substantial progress on various issues, ranging from missiles to human rights (Foster-Carter 2001, p. 107). Nevertheless at the ASEM[13] meeting in October the UK, Germany and others announced their intention to move to full diplomatic relations.[14] This European position will make it harder for the new US administration to move in the opposite direction and seek to isolate North Korea.[15] Also Australia, the Philippines, Canada and others have initiated discussions with North Korea.

The magnitude of the June 2000 inter-Korean summit and the degree of progress obtained were hardly predictable; however, it is useful to carefully consider that North and South Korea still remain at war and the process of normalisation and cross diplomatic recognition will probably be a very long one. North and South Korea are two of the most heavily fortified nations in the world and at present are unlikely to discuss military confidence building measures or balanced force reductions. Nevertheless a start was made when a North Korean minister visited Seoul in September even if a subsequent working level meeting found the North reluctant to widen the agenda beyond mine-cleaning the DMZ and rebuilding road and rail links across it (Foster-Carter 2001, p. 103).

The vast changes under way raise questions on the future of the US military presence on the peninsula. The US continues to argue for an indefinite presence of its troops in Korea. In 1995 the US decided to retain and bolster the 100 000 US troops in Northeast Asia indefinitely, subject to review in 2015, justifying its continued deployment by citing the danger of war in Korea, alleged threats from China and potential future problems. The Pentagon in the 'Joint vision 2020' projects US troops presence in the peninsula even after unification. As Nye explained,[16] to describe US policy in the region and alliance with Japan ,'Alliances can be adopted for a post-Cold War era, not against a particular enemy but as a guarantor of security'. Nevertheless North Korea successfully pressed the UN command to cede the requisite border authority to South Korea (Foster-Carter 2001, p. 103). The basic point is where the discussion of the whole array of formal and substantive security issues (that has yet to begin) will take place. Kim Dae-jung is seeking to revive the Four Party Talks (North Korea, South Korea, US and China) but multilateral forums have produced limited substantive effects. Nevertheless the attendance of ARF by North Korea has been symbolic and promising. The second concern is the stability of the South Korea regime and how it would affect the inter-Korean dialogues.

3.2   The issue of China's 'reunification'

On 1 July 1997, Hong Kong turned back into a province of the People's Republic of China (PRC), even though it retained for fifty more years a wide autonomy in decision-making concerning economic and financial matters. There ended a long and complicated diatribe between British and Chinese governments. The same formula 'one country, two systems' was applied also to Macao on 20 December 1999. To complete the reunification of the country, Beijing now openly fixes its attention on Taiwan. The subject of the reunification between China and Taiwan means touching a raw nerve: not only because from 1949 until now, the governments of Taipei and of Beijing both constantly claim to be the only legitimate representatives of China as a whole, but also because a nationalist spirit is expanding in Taiwan. The division between Taiwan and China dated 1949 when Chiang Kaishek's defeated Guomidang fled to the island. Taiwan gained strategic importance for the US with the outbreak of the Korean war, and US economic aid, preferential market access and technology transfer underpinned the Taiwanese economic take off. The Republic of China (Taiwan) was recognised by the US. But by July 1971 the situation in Indochina and the attempt to outflank Soviet Union, changed US-PRC relations and the US shifted its diplomatic recognition from Taipei to Beijing in 1979. Nevertheless the same year's US Taiwan Relations Act committed Washington to provide defensive weapons and to assist Taiwan in case of a Chinese attack.

After 1989[17] any rationale for the US to defer to Beijing over Taiwan disappeared and the growing power of China makes Taiwan part of the China-US strategic equation. In the nineties a progressive democratic party was formed, which asserted, in the name of the Taiwanese natives, the right to proclaim the island's independence from continental China. During the electoral campaign for the presidential elections of March 2000, the PRC resorted once more to threats of war in case the separatist candidate won. The threats did not frighten the majority of the Taiwanese: the presidential elections in fact precisely established the defeat of the Guomindang (GMD) and the victory of the separatist party's candidate, Chen Shui-Bian.

The newly elected President hastened to declare that the formula 'one country, two systems' used for Hong Kong and Macao was unacceptable for the Republic of China (the name Taiwan had been given to the island by the Guomindang), but added that he was willing to work out a way to find a form of reconciliation with the PRC. Chen Shui-Bian is well aware indeed that Taiwan's economic prosperity is more and more related to that of the southern Chinese regions. There is no reliable data on Taiwanese investments in China. Different figures are provided by different sources. Sources in Hong Kong set the value of contracts signed by Taiwanese businessmen on the mainland between US$10.5 billion and US$20.4 billion by the end of 1992 up to 1997 (*China Perspectives*, May-June 1998). Japanese sources have estimated US$25 billion for the same period and more recently, the American and Taiwanese Press have mentioned a figure of over US$40 billion invested by 45 000 firms. In 2000, the estimates of Taiwanese investments in China speak of a total amount of over 40 billion dollars and 54 000 companies sponsored by Taiwanese capital were registered in 1999 (Weber 2000).

The economic convergence is now so widespread and has brought about such powerful economic changes as to require a peaceful solution to the dilemma of the two republics' future. It is in this sense that the recent proposal by the Taiwanese to the PRC to create a federation similar to the CIS, which would unite the two Chinas respecting nonetheless the sovereignty of both, should be understood. The federation project will probably be accomplished in the coming years, thus saving both governments' faces and maintaining the autonomy of Beijing and Taipei. The fact that the two governments, in May 2000, have officially proposed to the United States to intervene in the problem as a mediator and to help 'throw a bridge of dialogue' between Beijing and Taipei is a signal in this direction.

The economic integration of Taiwan and China is so deep-rooted that it makes the hypothesis of an armed conflict very unrealistic and certainly rather 'inconvenient'. After half a century of hostilities between the PRC and Taiwan, for some years now the conditions appear to be right for dialogue to begin once again between the two sides of the Strait. Yet little political progress seems to have been made. One factor, which is particularly hampering rapprochement between the two, is the democratisation process taking place in Taiwan. Since the mid 1980s and particularly since Lee Teng-hui came to power, the Guomindang has been working to democratise its institutions and those of the state. Martial law was revoked in 1987 and in the following years political parties and opposition groups were allowed to form, while police control over the opposition was curbed. The first democratic parliamentary elections were held in 1992. Since 1996, the President and Vice-President – the two highest positions in the country – have been elected directly. This process is of fundamental importance for the political history of East Asia since, for the first time, part of China has put representative democracy into practice and is freely choosing its rulers. Taiwan could become an innovative model of enormous importance for the People's Republic, and this is a further threat to the CCP and a challenge to its ideological roots. However, the presidential elections have resulted in a new President, the candidate from the Progressive-Democratic Party (PDP), which represents that key minority of Taiwanese who believe the time has come to be bold and proclaim independence – not only *de facto*, but also *de jure* – from Communist China. The danger of losing political control over Taiwan and seeing the island's secession turn de facto into a declaration of independence is undoubtedly one of the factors behind Beijing's switch from a policy of hostility towards one of slightly greater dialogue.

At the start of 1998, after three years of ostracism, Jiang Zemin himself proposed to Taipei that talks on normalising relations between the two should begin. Beijing proposed to extend the principle of 'one country, two systems', already experimented with Hong Kong. Under the system, Taiwan would enjoy wide-ranging autonomy, and would have its own legislative, executive and judiciary bodies as well as its own armed forces, and would retain its own political and economic system, but would have to recognise the sovereignty of the PRC and submit to its rule. Some have even suggested renaming the PRC should such a reunification occur – perhaps calling it simply 'China' – and modifying its flag and symbols, even courting the idea that the Chinese state could be restructured.

3.3　Cross Taiwan strait relations: toward new strategies?

Taiwan's future could have profound strategic implications for the Asia-Pacific region. The election of Chen Shui-bian as Taiwan's new president in March 2000 and the ascendance to power of his pro-independence Democratic Progressive Party (DPP), have highlighted the danger of major conflict in East Asia over the unresolved Taiwan question. We have seen that for Chinese leaders in Beijing the recovery of Taiwan is a matter of supreme national interest. Mainland China worries that time is running in Taiwan's favour and that any display of weakness on this issue threatens the integrity of China and its regional role.

The Taiwan issue is not only an old problem of civil war frozen by the Cold War; or a question of a divided nation as it is tempting to view. As Manning argues, Taiwan is also an emblematic symbol of East Asias strategic problems. First economic relations with the Republic of China have improved considerably over the past decade. Taiwan's massive trade with, and investment in mainland China is an emblematic symbol of the growing tensions between globalisation and nationalism, connected with the emerging Taiwanese identity. In this sense, it raises the question of whether it is geo-politics or geo-economics that most shape international behaviour in a new and uncertain historical period (Manning 2000).

Second, the Taiwan question symbolises the emergence of China as a great power one 'demonstrating irredentist passion to right the historic injustice of Western and Japanese imperialism that left China weak and divided' (Manning 2000).

Finally and most ominously, Taiwan may be one of the symbols of clashing US-China interests and values. As Manning outlines in his analysis, current fears that the cross-strait situation may be drifting towards conflict stem from the democratisation of Taiwan and its impact on the set of diplomatic engagements since Chen Shui-bian's assumption of office marks something rare in Chinese history: a peaceful transition of power. This fact might cause as much discomfort in Beijing as the threat that Taiwan will formally declare independence (Manning 2000). In addition democratisation has also fostered a growing sense of a separate Taiwanese identity, which could have regional implications, especially in relations with Japan, where the process of democratisation is perceived as a convergence of values and as a way to expand bilateral ties.

Bilateral talks between RPC and Taiwan began in Singapore in 1993, which established mechanisms for regular contact between the two sides to be based on the 'one China' principle. The semi-official talks were suspended in mid-1995 following Taiwanese President Lee Teng-hui's private, but high-profile, visit to the United States. Following the visit and in the run-up to the island's March 1996 Presidential election, China held extensive military exercises close to Taiwan, including missile launches into the ocean just off Taiwan's northern and southern coasts. Washington responded by deploying two carrier battle groups off Taiwan. A gradual warming in relations between Beijing and Taipei has been taking place since October 1998 but the election of Chen Shui-bian, the leader of the pro-independence party in 2000 increased the tensions, even if Chen Shui-bian had promised, prior to his inaugural address that his remark would 'please the US and Japan and not antagonise China'[18] and this is the basis on which he based his current Cross Strait strategy (Cossa 2000, p. 13).

There are conflicting perspectives on the future evolution and its timing. On the one hand there are many arguments that both sides would benefit by preserving existing arrangements in order to buy time, continue political dialogue, defer any effort at an ultimate resolution for 15–20 years, and let events play out (Manning 2000). For Beijing, the minimal requirement is that some notion of One China be accepted and that some form of reunification is not becoming less likely. Beijing has a full plate of problems domestically, and if Taiwan could be removed as a pressing issue without the regime losing face, that would have political appeal to its leaders. For Taipei, buying time would allow China's historic transformation to unfold before it decided whether any form of political association with the mainland was desirable, or whether a future regime in Beijing might adopt a different posture towards Taiwan. In this scenario the most difficult question is whether Taiwan's quest for international political space can be accommodated in a 'one China' framework. If one China is defined as a more elastic concept, Taipei's aspirations for international political space could be accommodated by new understandings, under which, for example, Taiwan defines its political space by joining the UN system - IMF, World Bank, WHO, IAEA, perhaps even observer status or full membership (Manning 2000).[19]

On the other hand for the PRC Taiwan is the last vestige of a century of humiliations and Beijing's position is that China has experienced disunity and invasions during the last centuries but it has always reverted to a united state (Klintworth 2000, p. 14). This has made Taiwan seem like a sacred mission, especially after the return of Hong Kong and Macao. In addition Jiang Zemin has often insisted on this task and he is supposed to act in this sense before the change in Chinese leadership (2002). In addition showing weakness with Taiwan might set a precedent for a potentially rebellious part of China such as Tibet or Xinjuang (Klinttwort 2000, p. 14). Finally Taiwan is perceived as a key element in the regional equilibrium , and it is connected with the inclusion of Taiwan in the proposed theatre defence missile system TDM. For the first time over two decades the Chinese media are openly discussing various military options against Taiwan, ranging from marine and air blockades to missile attacks.[20]

3.4 China looks over to Europe

The official visit of the Chinese Prime Minister Zhu Rongji in Europe in June 2000 testified to the Chinese interest for Europe, seen as a possible foil for the international American hegemony. 'Beijing wagers on Europe' ran Chinese newspapers as a headline at the beginning of the Chinese Prime Minister's long series of official meetings on the old continent. Zhu's trip started on 27 June in Bulgaria and proceeded into Italy, Germany, Luxembourg, the Netherlands, Belgium, and ended with the visit of the EU headquarters in Brussels. During these two weeks of encounters and talks, the Chinese Prime Minister appeared engaged in consolidating the bilateral Sino-European relationship in order to plead the cause of China's admittance into the WTO. The agreement with the European Union in particular has brought the moment of the opening of the Chinese market to mobile communications two years ahead compared to what had been decided in Washington. Moreover, concerning the insurance market, Beijing guaranteed to grant seven licences to European investors within the three months following the conclusion of the agreement, hence before entrance into the WTO. As far as the control of share quotations is concerned however, China did not cede to the Europeans any more than what she had granted the Americans: a share not exceeding 49 per cent in the joint ventures belonging to the services and telecommunications sectors.

Zhu Rongji's visit also demonstrated the Chinese support to the Euro. Beijing's support reveals itself all the more important since the government led by Zhu Rongji controls in China and Hong Kong the greatest currency reserves in the world (around 230 billion dollars): it is estimated that 20 per cent or 30 per cent of these reserves are held in Euros.

The official meetings of the Prime Minister Zhu Rongji on European ground, in the context of the conclusion of the bilateral agreements with the United States and the European Union indisputably represent an important event in the perspective of a complete Chinese involvement in the global economic system. In this sense, the presence of China is relevant inside the ASEM (Asia-Europe meeting), whose first summit took place in Bangkok one year before the Asian crisis. At the Bangkok meeting, on 1 and 2 March 1996, heads of state of all the European Union members and ten Asian countries (Brunei, China, South Korea, the Philippines, Japan, Indonesia, Malaysia, Singapore, Thailand and Vietnam) participated. On this occasion, the question of a special Asia-Europe partnership for the development of economic relations and for the promotion of a new political dialogue was brought up. The outbreak of the Asian crisis delayed the achievement of such a project for two years. The Asian crisis and the financial intervention in favour of the stricken countries occupied an important place in the talks of the second ASEM summit, which took place in London on 3 and 4 April 1998.

In this meeting the countries members have analysed the financial and economic situation of Asia approximately one year after the explosion of the crisis. They also prepared two specific initiatives with the intention of assisting the most affected countries. In particular, the constitution of an ASEM financial fund (*ASEM Trust Fund*), operating since June 1998 from the World Bank, providing Asian members with financial resources, consultancy and assistance for the re-organisation of the financial system and for the resolution of social problems caused by the crisis. And the creation of a network of European Experts on systems and financial markets subjects, and to which Asian countries may have access, in order to obtain assistance throughout the reform process of the financial sector.

The ASEM's third summit, held in Seoul 20 and 21 October 2000, was attended not only by heads of state of the European and Asian members, but also by the President of the European Commission, Romano Prodi. In anticipation of the summit, the Commission singled out some of the main issues fundamental to the co-operation of the two regions. Among these are the consolidation of the dialogue between Asia and the European Union on questions of regional and global security, the development of an economic result-oriented co-operation, and, in particular, concerning social policies, intensification of exchanges in the education area, creation of co-operation networks on consumer protection concerns, and a possible broadening of the circle of participating countries to ASEM summits.

Everything tends to show that dialogue and progressive co-operation between Asia and Europe puts the accent on the crucial role played by China. But unpredictable consequences can lie even in the most optimistic scenarios: for example, imagining China more and more integrated in the regional context is the best guarantee of the maintenance of peace in the area, although a strong and powerful China could well unbalance the already complex harmony existing between Japan, China and South East Asian countries. A secure and strong China will condition all world political equilibrium. What kind of medium-long term consequences may result from substantial changes in the stability of the Pacific area? But this is a question that remains inevitably open-ended.

3.5 News in multilateral co-operation?

The recent multilateral forum demonstrated a slowdown and a low relevance of multilateral initiatives. Even if the G8 summit in Okinawa[21] created the opportunity to discuss the US military presence in a multilateral context it focused on bilateral issues. Staging the G8 meeting in Okinawa – the 'linchpin' of US military strategy in Asia[22] was a deliberate strategy on the part of the Japanese government to demonstrate that US-Japan bilateral security alliance is stable and lasting.

The recent ARF meeting in Bangkok was particularly relevant since it opened the door for North Korean membership in the Forum and the gathering of all key North East Asia players in the ARF provides the opportunity for multilateral discussions on regional security. The Ministers only expressed the hope for further efforts by all parties concerned within the framework of inter-Korean dialogue, the US-North Korea and Japan-North Korea talks, the Four-Party Talks, and broader international efforts.[23] Generally speaking, the Ministers noted with satisfaction the significant progress which the ARF had made in terms of enhancing political and security dialogue and co-operation. They emphasised the importance of confidence-building measures (CBMs) to the overall ARF process and agreed that such efforts be intensified. They also welcomed the progress in the implementation of the proposals in the overlap between CBMs and Preventive Diplomacy (PD) as well as the continued efforts to develop concept and principles of PD applicable to the ARF context.

More remarkably for the regional security landscape, the Ministers agreed that a united democratic and economically prosperous Indonesia is fundamental to the maintenance of regional security and in this context, they emphasised their support for Indonesia's territorial integrity.[24] With regard to the South China Sea, the Ministers encouraged the exercise of self-restraint by all countries concerned and the promotion of confidence building measures in this area, welcomed in particular the on-going efforts between ASEAN and China to develop and adopt the Regional Code of Conduct in the South China Sea.[25]

Anyway, most relevant for a regional security narrative, the Ministers discussed issues pertaining to international crime, especially issues of piracy, illegal migration, including trafficking in human persons, particularly women and children, and illicit trafficking in small arms. They recognised that these international issues not only pose challenges to regional peace and stability, but also impair individual countries' efforts in promoting national economic development. Hence, co-operative approaches were necessary to deal with these problems.[26]

4. THE EMERGENCE OF A MULTILATERAL ENVIRONMENT

The term multilateralism in international relations means much more than its simple quantitative definition of relations among three or more parties.[27] John Gerard Ruggie has described the qualities of multilateral institutions as: generalised principles[28] shared by members, indivisibility of welfare[29] among participants, and diffuse reciprocity.[30] Ruggie illustrates generalised principles of conduct by using the most favoured nation treatment in the economic sphere and by using collective security in the security sphere (Ruggie 1993, pp. 9–11). The question is what kind of multilateralism (if any) is observable in the Asia-Pacific today?

Europe has a rich history of multilateral co-operation dating back to the European Concert of the nineteenth century, if not earlier. In contrast, the Asia-Pacific region has experienced nothing comparable. International relations in the Asia-Pacific grew mainly along bilateral lines, leaving the region devoid of intergovernmental multilateralism. After the Second World War the US considered the idea of a collective security system for the Pacific; in 1951 the ANZUS Treaty or Security Treaty was signed by Australia, New Zealand, and the United States[31] and in 1955 the US set up the South East Asia Treaty Organisation (SEATO) to counter communist insurgency in South East Asia, but its limitations soon became apparent.[32]

The US found that a bilateral approach was more appropriate for security issues. They opted for mutual security treaties. In addition the sponsorship of Asian multilateral initiatives by various Kremlin leaders during the Cold War, which were widely seen as soft attempts to diminish American influence, while gaining Soviet entry into Asia, made cautious the approach toward multilateral security initiatives, both in Washington and Asia (Cossa 1999).

Many factors are cited to explain the lack of regional multilateral institutions. The first one is the extreme diversity in terms of population, per capita gross domestic product (GDP), economic and political systems, military preparedness, cultural heritage, religion, historical experience, and ethnicity. The diversity among potential members and the lack of shared behavioural norms has been seen as the major inhibiting factor in creating a regional institution. Another reason often given for the absence of multilateral security institutions is the lack of a shared perception of threats in the Asia-Pacific. In other words, states in the Asia-Pacific have been more or less afraid of each other and have thus lacked the perception of a common external enemy.

Some scholars have argued that another reason why Asia has long been resistant to multilateralism is because of its long history of domination by external powers.[33] Suspicious of being ruled by other powers, Asian countries had thus avoided forming multilateral institutions. This landscape, however, started to change in the 1990s even if in East Asia, the Cold War did not quite end with the same effects as it did in Europe, with the fall of the Berlin Wall and the collapse of the Soviet Union. Of course, the Soviet Union was an important power in the Asia-Pacific, and its demise opened the door for new relationships on the Korean peninsula and with Japan and even China. However, a number of the vestiges of the Cold War remain in Asia, including divided nations and a number of territorial disputes.

So what kind of regional security order has evolved in the Asia-Pacific, if any? Is there the space for multilateral security institutions? What are their characteristics?

In Asia at present there is neither the space nor the will for collective defence institutions such as NATO. Nevertheless a multilateral security structure could take the form of collective defence alliance or enforcement mechanisms necessary to deter aggressor states, which regulates relations among the parties, by sharing information about capabilities and intentions and by creating norms of co-operation as well as forum for dialogues, such as the Conference on Security and Co-operation in Europe (CSCE). As Mahbulani outlines 'the Atlantic believes in building strong institutions' while 'the Pacific is creating network instead' which rely on 'personal contacts and trust building' (Mahbulani, quoted in Friedberg 2000, p. 153), adopting a style that reflects Asian culture.

Some Asian countries have already formed issue-specific coalitions such as the cases of Cambodian peace in the early 1990s and the Korean Energy Development Organisation (KEDO) created in the mid-1990s to manage the problem of nuclear power development by North Korea. In addition, in the 1990s several forms of security dialogue have emerged in the Asia-Pacific. The ASEAN Regional Forum (ARF) is the most notable example. This kind of forum has proven to be the most relevant institutions in the regional context. Their limited capacity to discuss high level items or to cope with crises are compensated by the long term effects on confidence building and dialogues.

4.1   The institutional framework

During the 1980s Australia and Canada first advocated a multilateral institutional structure in the Asia-Pacific along the lines of those in Europe. At that time many ASEAN countries, Japan, the US and China, were sceptical about multilateralism's viability in the Asian context.[34] The precondition for multilateralism matured in the early 1990s but the perspective on it varied from country to country. China supported it on the assumption that multilateralism would undercut the American led alliances system and enhance its own role.

Japan perceived it as an opportunity to increase its political profile in the region without jeopardising its relationship with the US, South Korea focused on attracting North Korea to the negotiating table. The Japanese role had special relevance. In 1991 Japan suddenly reversed its opposition to regional security multilateralism and suggested a multilateral dialogue within the ASEAN Post Ministerial Conference. It was the first time, excluding the debate about comprehensive security, since the end of the second world war, that Japan made a regional security initiative on its own and with clear American opposition. Several factors contributed to the decision, including the declining Soviet threat, the fear of an American withdrawal and also the competition from other countries with different conceptions of regional multilateralism. The immediate aim was promoting a security forum excluding Russia, China and Korea, keeping the US regionally engaged and discussing the Asian concerns about Japanese security policy and eventual rearmament.

By 1991 the ASEAN position on security multilateralism was mature. Many scholars, inside the ASEAN ISIS (Institute for Strategic and International Studies) supported a multilateral engagement and feared that the Japanese initiative could have left their interest behind if ASEAN had not been involved since the beginning. ASEAN and Japan negotiated the composition and the characteristic of a regional forum, although Japan had to abandon its initial hope of keeping Russia out. In 1993, the ASEAN Regional Forum (ARF) was founded as the first intra-regional security institution encompassing the Asia-Pacific region. It brings together the foreign ministers from the Association of Southeast Asian Nations (Brunei, Indonesia, Laos, Malaysia, Myanmar, the Philippines, Singapore, Thailand, and Vietnam) with other key regional players (Australia, Cambodia, Canada, China, Japan, Mongolia, Papua New Guinea, Russia, South Korea, New Zealand, the United States, and the European Community) – twenty-two members in all – to discuss regional security issues. Initially envisioned as a forum for constructive dialogue between nations, the ARF has eventually elevated its goals and now it aspires to be an active force in the resolution of regional conflicts.

At the sub-regional level, the most significant official effort is the Four-Party Talks among North and South Korea, China, and the United States established in December 1997 in Geneva. The Four-Party Talks have the specific aim of replacing the current Korean War Armistice with a formal Korean Peninsula Peace Treaty, ending the state of war that has existed on the peninsula since 1950. The talks are also intended to develop and pursue confidence building measures between North and South Korea (Cossa 1999).

Another prominent multilateral governmental mechanism is the Korean Peninsula Energy Development Organisation (KEDO), the multilateral vehicle established by the US, South Korea, and Japan to implement the

October 1994 Agreed Framework Between the US and North Korea. The Agreed Framework and KEDO are aimed at achieving 'an overall resolution of the nuclear issue on the Korean peninsula' (Cossa 1999). Their mutual goal is the promotion of peace and stability and the eventual peaceful reunification of the peninsula.

Other multilateral mechanisms work at the unofficial or track two level. The most relevant are the Council for Security Co-operation in the Asia-Pacific (CSCAP) and the Northeast Asia Co-operation Dialogue (NEACD). The former was established in June 1993 to provide a structured process for regional confidence building and security co-operation among countries and territories in the Asia-Pacific region by linking regional security-oriented institutes. It promoted the creation of ARF and then focused its efforts on providing direct support to this governmental forum whilst also pursuing other track-two diplomacy efforts. The aim of NEACD is to enhance mutual understanding, confidence, and co-operation through meaningful but unofficial dialogue among China, Japan, Russia, the United States, and both South and North Korea.[35] The importance of these unofficial forums is crucial since they involve non state actors, not only NGOs but also 'de facto' states such as Taiwan.

All these forums remain relatively low-key, and are aimed primarily at promoting dialogue and increased understanding among military and governmental officers at the middle and upper-middle management levels. They generally avoid potentially contentious issues; only recently, there has been a decided shift in regional attitudes toward more senior-level, issue-oriented multinational security initiatives.[36]

4.2. New challenges after the Asian crisis and Timor East on multilateral institutions

One of the most important long term implications of the economic crisis has been to fully disclose the current weakness of the regional institutions, which had seemed to be growing at the beginning of the 1990s. Asian regionalism, as the crisis forced each state to look at its internal problems, has had serious setbacks. The existing institutions have proven ineffective in times of collective hardship. On the one hand the financial crisis demonstrated that the internal dimension plays a very relevant role in the Asian conception of national security. Looking inward, the states of the region have few resources to become significant regional actors or to assume a consistent and somehow important international role. On the other hand for weak governments it was very easy to compensate the internal tensions with an assertive foreign policy. In other words, governments have played the nationalistic card to transfer internal pressures. Both these tendencies hampered the development of regional institutions (Dassù, Silvestri 2000).

Analogously the crisis in East Timor, sparked by the 30 August 1999 vote for independence, and culminating with the introduction of the International Force for East Timor has suddenly showed the utter inadequacy of existing Asia-Pacific arrangements to cope with regional crises (Huntley-Hayes 2000, p. 1). The ASEAN member states and the ARF proved incapable of taking on effective measures. All things considered, ARF has never addressed the violation of human rights as an interstate agenda item. On the contrary it kept the standards of respect for human rights low rather than pushing them toward international norms. Analogously the non governmental Council for Security in the Asia-Pacific (CSCAP) failed to address these issues. The ASEAN member states individually and collectively reacted with contradiction and paralysis, due mainly to the resistance to pressure for action given by the prevailing norm proscribing 'interference in the internal affairs of other member states'.

The crisis has also pointed out more fundamental limitations of the so-called 'ASEAN way'. Its hands-off attitude towards internal matters has left ASEAN incapable of responding to a crisis that involves internal economic and political weaknesses in its own members. Although a number of nations in Southeast Asia are seeing the spread of NGOs and growing civil societies, the ASEAN preoccupation with state-to-state relations has failed to tap into these developments.

The US perspective on multilateralism is still a key factor for its development in the region. US support for multilateral co-operation was underscored by Clinton when he called for the creation of 'a new Pacific community, built on shared strength, shared prosperity, and a shared commitment to democratic values'. He identified four priorities for the security of this new community: a continued US military presence/commitment, stronger efforts to combat the proliferation of weapons of mass destruction, support for democracy and more open societies, and the promotion of new multilateral regional dialogues on the full range of common security challenges (Cossa 1999).

Nevertheless the US saw multilateralism as a supplement not as a supplant to their strategy of forward deployment and bilateral security arrangement (Naidu 2000, p. 4). Multilateralism and bilateralism are not mutually exclusive, but mutually supportive. Without solid bilateral relationships, few states would have the confidence to deal with one another in the broader context. Conversely, some problems can best, perhaps only, be solved multilaterally. The current US bilateral military alliance structure serves as the 'bedrock' for any American vision of a new Pacific community.[37]

5. SECURITY NARRATIVE IN ASIA

The debate on regional security at track two level, the activity of ARF, the recent interest of APEC in security concerns, as well as the incapacity of these institutions to cope with crises and the continuing need to rely on bilateral agreements, poses the questions of how, whether and for what extent these institutions could change the regional scenario. The issue in question is whether a different discourse on security and a change in the dominant understanding of the concept could change, or have already changed security practices. The discourse makes sense in the broad perspective of the changing approach to security and its relevance in a context such as the Asian one.[38] As Acharya outlines, national security has assumed a 'Euro-centric universe of nation states and dwelled primarily on the responses of western states... to the problem of War' (Acharya 1997, p. 300). During the Cold War there was a clear distinction between the central strategic balance and regional security. Attention to problems of regional stability was given only to the extent that they had the potential to affect the superpower relationships. Paradoxically the arenas where the vast majority of conflicts have taken place were ignored. East Asia was a typical example.

The end of the Cold War and the necessity for regions like East Asia to determine their own security strategies challenged the understanding of security in three basic respects (Acharya 1997, p. 301). First, the interstate level is no longer considered the right focus for security issues. Second, non-military problems could be more relevant than the military ones. Finally the balance of power is no longer considered a legitimate and effective instrument of international order. The problem is more evident throughout Asia. As for the first assumption, most of the regional conflicts were (and still are) intrastate in nature (anti-regime insurrections, civil wars, ethnic conflicts). The proliferation of such conflicts is rooted in weak state structure that emerged from the process of de-colonisation and the concept of national security is of limited utility in this context. As Buzan notes 'it is tempting to identify national security with the governmental institution that expresses the state, but government and institutions have security interests of their own which are separate from those of the state, and which are often opposed to broader national interests as aligned with them' (Buzan 1987, p. 6). As result of this, national security is a more 'ambiguous symbol' (Wolfers 1962) in Asia than everywhere.

The second way in which Asia challenged the dominant understanding of security relates to the role of non military threats. National security, as articulated by western policy in the immediate post-World War II period was 'primarily concerned with war prevention' and non military threats were not considered (Acharya 1997, p. 303). The logic of broadening the notion of security is contested but this contestation is mainly done inside the logic of western thought. From the very outset, resource scarcity, overpopulation, underdevelopment, environmental degradation, and economic institutional weaknesses are at the heart of insecurity in many developing countries and above all in East Asia. As Thomas puts it 'security in the context of the third world does not simply refer to the military dimension as it is often assumed in the western discussion of the concept, but to a whole range of dimension of state's existence which has taken care of in the more developed states, especially in those of the west' (Thomas 1987, p. 1, quoted in Acharya 1987, p. 304).

As for the third point, the superpower rivalry, while keeping the long peace in Europe served to exacerbate the problems of regional conflict and stability as the Korean and the Vietnamese wars demonstrate. No superpower-sponsored mechanism could be effective unless it would be able to address client states internal concerns. This explains the failure of outward looking regional security organisations such as the SEATO and the relative success of more internal oriented regional security arrangement such as the ASEAN (Acharya 1987, p. 306). The question is: are there alternatives? The idea of comprehensive security was developed in East Asia during the Cold War and its aftermath in two different forms. The first one, promoted by Japan, the second one by ASEAN countries (Snyder 1999, p. 113). Since the end of the second World War, Japan has sought to broaden its understanding of security to include non military issues, focusing on economic and political problems at different levels: domestic, bilateral, regional and global (Devitt 1994, p. 2). By using this concept Japan addressed its concerns on the import of natural resources, essential for its economic development, as well as to stop the export of dual use technology to the so-called 'rogue' states. (Snyder 1999, p. 113).

The second meaning of comprehensive security has been developed by ASEAN countries during the 1990s, to include principles of 'balanced national development through endeavours in every aspect of life: ideological, political, economic, social, cultural and military' (ASEAN ISIS 1993, p. 17, quoted in Snyder 1999, p. 113). This form of comprehensive security is pursued by ASEAN members through the concept of 'resilience' (Snyder 1999, p. 113). Or an 'inward-looking strategy whereby a state strengthens its resilience to security threats by developing a stable, political and economic international environment' (Snyder 1999, p. 114). This implies that if every state achieves national resilience, regional resilience will be gained and thus external states or threats will not able to destabilise the state. This explains an apparent contradiction. On the one hand the growing interest in non military issues, such as drug trafficking, illegal immigration or environmental problems, which are supranational, question the exercise of sovereignty: an unacceptable issue for many countries in the region. On the other hand this process legitimises the security of authoritative regimes, since national and regional resilience politics are designed to protect the governing regimes (Snyder 1999, p. 113) rather than the citizens. In this perspective the concept of security is broader but the referent object is still the state. In this perspective it is possible to understand for instance the Chinese appeal to comprehensive security at 1999 ARF and how it paradoxically contrasts with the use of the term by the US in the same forum.

Co-operative security is the other phase raised in the debate. The aspiration behind the concept of co-operative security is a new, deeper understanding of the mutuality of security, connected with the perception of non traditional, non military threats, including environmental, economic and social concerns. The use of the term co-operative security encourages a constructivist approach to regional security. 'The term tends to connote consultation rather than confrontation, reassurance rather than deterrence, transparency rather than secrecy, prevention rather than correction and interdependence rather than unilateralism' (Evans 1994).

In this context the elaboration of security narratives is particularly relevant. Even if they are not able to change the immediate security scenario in the short term or to cope with crises, they can largely contribute to long term stability. The interest demonstrated by ARF for problems such as transnational crime, especially issues of piracy, illegal migration, including trafficking in human persons, particularly women and children, and illicit trading in small arms is then relevant in a double perspective: first, it contributes to foster a dialogue and to promote functional integration, second it responds to specific security demands that could contribute to regional stability and could contribute to the emergence of a regional community. The question then is whether this debate has affected or could challenge the existing security framework and future scenarios. They could modify 'strategic culture' or the system of symbols, including the perception of threat, the nature of the potential enemies, and the efficacy of the use of violence.[39] These narratives have certainly played a role in the Korean peninsula at least to get the dialogue started and they could help to explain the unexpected evolution.

6.   A CONCLUDING REMARK

The recent events outline how multilateralism is growing slowly. The initial post-Cold War enthusiasm for multilateral initiatives has not altogether dissipated, but there is a greater sense of limits on what they might accomplish. There is neither the will nor the condition to transform the existing forums into security alliances and existing institutions are ill equipped if they have to cope with a crisis when it has occurred as the events in East Timor have demonstrated. Nevertheless, multilateral dialogues, at both the track one and track two levels can in themselves constitute important exercises in confidence building and contribute to elaborate new security narratives. This could have a profound impact not only on the long-term security scenario but also on what it is possible to discuss and achieve in bilateral, high level negotiations.

NOTES

1. ARF is a multilateral forum, created by ASEAN in 1995 to enforce the security in the Asia-Pacific Area. All the ASEAN members below to ARF with Australia, Canada, China, South Korea, Japan, India, New Zealand, Papua New Guinea, Russia, United States and European Union.
2. The two countries no longer see each other as security threats to one another: the flux of Russian army sales to China is perhaps the clearest signal of the change that underwent from this point of view. The solution to the historic border disputes between the two states, which in 1997 ended years of negotiations and that regulated 4000 kilometers of borders form Mongolia to Tumen, was another important signal of the end of difficult relations between Moscow and Beijing. Bilateral commercial relations are growing and agreements have been reached in the areas of environmental protection, labour regulation, immigration control, communication and quality control, during the visit of Russian Prime Minister Kasyanow in Beijing, in 2000.
3. A Soviet-Chinese political and alliance treaty, signed in 1950, expired in 1979 and at that time China suggested not to renew it.
4. The possibility of a future conflict with China is emerging as a threat in the eyes of US military planners. In its latest planning document, 'Joint Vision 2020', the Pentagon listed China as a potential adversary (couched in the phrase 'peer competitor'). The document also foresees closer co-ordination with Japan and projects US troop presence in Korea even after unification, and it concludes that Asia will replace Europe as the key focus of US military strategy over the next 20 years. The Washington Post, called the policies a 'momentous change from the last decade of the Cold War' (Quoted in Cossa 1999).
5. See for instance, Richard Bernstein and R. Munro, *The Coming Conflict with China,* New York Knopf, 1997: G. Segal, 'East Asia and the "containment" of China', *International Security* 20(4) 1996, pp. 107–135.
6. See, for instance, B. Commings, 'The World Shakes China', *The National Interest,* 43, 1996, pp. 28–41. F. Wang, 'To incorporate China: A New policy for a New Era', *The Washington Quarterly* 21(1) 1998, pp. 67–81.
7. See, for instance J.S. Nye, 'China's re-emergence and the future of the Asia-Pacific', *Survival39(4) 1998.* A. Goldstain 'Great Expectations: Interpreting China's Arrival' *International Security* 22(3) 1998.
8. The Soviet delegates were boycotting the UN because the Chiang Kai-Shek government still occupied the Chinese seat on the Security Council.
9. US Department of Defence, Foreign Relations of the United States, Washington DC US 19509, 7, 211, quoted in Stueck, 1995; 13.
10. The GNP had won 133 seats in the election held on 13 April 2000, which gave it a plurality in the 273 member National Assembly. Also the United Liberal Democrats and the Democratic People Party attacked the sunshine policy (Hong 2001).
11. Kim Yong-nam, North Korean delegation head, who travelling to New York for the Millennium Summit in UN Headquarters, was requested for a body search by US American Airlines security personnel in Frankfurt. The delegation refused and returned home. The problem was that North Korea is still on the US list of countries assisting international terrorism. Removal from terrorist designation – a pivotal negotiation – is the key to North Korea's joining international financial institutions like the Asian Development Bank, the World Bank and International Monetary Fund. US objections to North Korea membership in these institutions are mandated by federal law as long as North Korea is considered a terrorist state; thus, the US holds the key to the North's potential access to massive aid money (NAPSET 2000).
12. On 4 January.
13. The Asia-Europe Meeting (ASEM), founded in 1996 symbolises the effort toward free trade between Europe and Asia. ASEM includes seven ASEAN countries (with the exception of Myanmar, Laos and Cambodia) plus three (China, Japan and South Korea) and primarily strives to establish an Asian-Europe free trade area by 2020. The European Union (EU) ranks as one of the most important trading partners to ASEAN countries.

14. The only notable exception is France , despite having been the first European country to build bridges in the early 1980s (Foster-Carter 2001, p. 108).
15. See on this point Foster-Carter 2001, p. 107.
16. Nye told the Tokyo Foreign Correspondents Club in September 1994.
17. From Chinese perspective the critical turning point in its relations with the US over China came in August 1992 when the US sold 150 F-16 fighter aircraft to Taiwan.
18. Quoted in Cossa 2000, p. 13.
19. There are legal precedents such as Ukraine and Belorussian UN membership while they were part of the Soviet Union. The PLO had observer status at the UN long before it had any realistic prospect of being a state.
20. For an evaluation of the different strategic options see Klinttwort.
21. The recent major multilateral event from July 21–23, the Japanese government sponsored the 2000 Summit of the Group of Eight (G8) industrialised democratic nations in the coastal city of Nago on the southern island of Okinawa.
22. It is home to two of the largest US bases (75 per cent of the 63 000 US soldiers stationed in Japan) and the only US Marine base outside the United States (Barry, Honey 2000).
23. More significantly they outlined the further positive developments regarding the temporary moratorium by North Korea on missile test launches and for the full implementation of the 1994 Agreed Framework, including the work of the Korean Peninsula Energy Development Organisation (KEDO).
24. The Ministers reviewed developments in East Timor. They welcomed the positive trends as well as co-operation between Indonesia and the United Nations Transitional Administration in East Timor (UNTAET) and emphasised the need for further collective action to resolve the refugee problem including dealing with continuing militia activity. The Ministers also emphasised the need for continued international attention to and support for reconstruction, rehabilitation, and nation building of East Timor.
25. The Ministers welcomed their commitment to resolving disputes by peaceful means in accordance with the recognised principles of international law, including the United Nations Convention on the Law of the Sea (UNCLOS), as well as to ensuring freedom of navigation in this area. They welcomed dialogue and consultations, particularly in the ASEAN-China Senior Officials Consultations, the exchange of views in the ARF, as well as in the Informal Workshop on Managing Potential Conflicts in the South China Sea.
26. They also noted the seriousness of the implications of drug production and trafficking as well as the need to address issues such as money laundering, corruption, and computer crime. The Ministers underlined the importance of greater bilateral, regional, and international co-operative efforts in this regard. They also expressed support for the on-going negotiations on the Convention Against Transnational Organised Crime and its Protocols as well as the convening of the International Conference on the Illicit Trade in Small Arms and Light Weapons in All Its Aspects in 2001. The Ministers agreed that the ARF continue to address transnational crime issues which affect security of the Asia-Pacific region and explored how the ARF could increase regional awareness and complement the work undertaken in other existing forums.
27. The Practices of co-ordinating national politics in groups of three or more states (Keohane 1990, quoted in Ruggie 1993, p. 6).
28. Generalised principles are rules that 'specify appropriate conduct for a class of actions, without regard to particular interest of the parties' (Ruggie 1993, p. 7).
29. Indivisibility of welfare means that costs and benefits are spread among members; for instance, if troubles afflict one country, there would be implications for institution members 'Indivisibility… is a social construction, not a technical condition' (Ruggie 1993, p. 11).
30. 'Diffuse reciprocity' (Keohane, quoted in Ruggie 1993, p. 11) means that a member of a multilateral institution, in co-operating with other members, expects rewards, not necessarily on every issue all the time, but members do expect to benefit eventually. In other words, benefits to members of a multilateral institution are not immediate but are diffused over a longer timeline.
31. Australia was concerned about a re-militarisation of Japan and wanted to have an alliance with the United States. However, as the Cold War progressed, by the mid-1950s the target of ANZUS shifted to preventing the spread of communism.

32. The wars in Vietnam illustrated SEATO's inadequate handling of crisis. Following the fall in April 1975 of the US supported regimes in Vietnam and Cambodia, SEATO started to crumble and eventually dissolved on 20 June 1977.
33. Imperial China's long-standing colonial dominance up until the middle of the nineteenth century was followed by Western colonial domination, and then by the Japanese pre-war attempt to create the Greater East Asia Co-Prosperity Sphere.
34. The closure of America's largest overseas bases in the Philippines in 1992 raised new concerns about the future of US involvement in the region.
35. North Korea has not participated in any of the eight formal NEACD meetings held since October 1993, the NEACD has been fruitful nonetheless, bringing together senior officials and academicians and security specialists from the other five countries for dialogue on political, security, and economic issues of concern to all parties (Cossa 1999).
36. One early instance occurred at the 1992 ASEAN-PMC in Manila when a joint statement was issued calling for the peaceful settlement of territorial disputes involving the Spratly Islands (Cossa 1999).
37. This central role of US bilateral alliances in general, and of the U.S.-Japan security alliance in particular, as the 'linchpin' of America's national security strategy in Asia was reaffirmed in the pentagon's December 1998 East Asia Strategy Report (EASR).
38. The traditional approach to security studies, based on a narrow definition of security as 'the study of threat, use and control of military force' (Walt 1991, p. 212) has been challenged by the attempts to broaden the neo-realist conception of national security to include a huge range of potential threats as well as by neo-realist/neo-liberal attempts to create modifiers to security (common, co-operative, comprehensive) in the attempt to ameliorate, if not to trascend the security dilemma. The critical approach deals with questions like 'security from which threats? Or "Whose security?"'. They address the social construction of security. Within this broad perspective the Copenhagen School opens the security agenda to many types of threat. The scope of this research programme is to understand how different 'referent objects' become subjects to the process of securitisation. A successful process of securitisation is a social and political 'speech act which label an issue as a security issue. In this process a problem is transformed in an "existential threat" calling for and justifying extraordinary measures. More in depth the critical security studies approach consider further elements: not only the threats are constructed but the object as well' (Krause 1998, pp. 301–14) The state as referent object of security is problematised. In contrast to realists as well as to the Copenhagen School, 'human security' is at task (Krause and Williams 1997, pp. 43–47).
39. On strategic culture see A.I. Johnsen 'Thinking about Strategic Culture', *International Security*, 19(5) Spring, 1995 or Katzeinstain (ed) (1996), *The culture of National Security*, New York: Columbia UP.

BIBLIOGRAPHY

ASEAN ISIS (1993), *Confidence Building Measures in South East Asia.*
Acharya, A. (1997), *The Periphery as a Core: The Third World and Security Studies*, in K. Krause, M.C. Williams, *Critical Security Studies*, London: UCL Press.
Alagappa, M. (1997), *Systemic Change, Security and Governance in the Asia-Pacific Region*, in Chan Heng Chee (ed), *The New Asia-Pacific Order Singapore*, ISEAS.
Barry, T. and M. Honey (2000), 'Okinawa and the US Military in Northeast Asia', *Foreign Policy in Focus*, Vol. 5, No. 22.
Buzan. B. (1991), *People, States and Fear: An Agenda for International Security Studies in the Post-Cold War Era*, New York: Harvester Wheatsheaf.
Buzan, B. and G. Segal (1994), 'Rethinking East Asian Security', *Survival*, Vol. 36, No. 2.
Cossa, R.A. (2000), 'Coming of Age and Coming Out: Shifts in the Geopolitical Landscape', *Comparative Connections*, 2 (2) pp. 9–19.

Cossa, R.A. (1999), *Security Multilateralism in Asia. US Views Toward Northeast Asia Multilateral Security Cooperation*, 'University of California Institute on Global Conflict and Cooperation, Policy Paper', No. 51.

Cossa, R.A. and J. Khanna (1997), 'East Asia: economic interdependence and regional security', *International Affairs*, No. 2.

Dassù, M. and S. Silvestri (2000), *Security Implications of the Asian Crises*, in M. Weber (ed), *After the Asian Crises. Perspectives on Global Politics and Economy*, London: MacMillan.

Devitt (1994), 'Common, Comprehensive and Cooperative Security', *Pacific Review*, 7 (1).

Dibb, P., D.D. Hale and P. Prince (1998), 'The Strategic Implications of Asia's Economic Crisis', *Survival*, 2.

Evans (1994), 'Cooperative Security and Interstate Conflicts', *Foreign Policy*, 96.

Friedberg, A.L. (2000), 'Will Europe's Past Be Asia's Future?', *Survival*, 4 (3) pp. 147–59.

Foster-Carter (2001), 'North Korea and the World: New Millennium, New Korea?', *Comparative Connection*, 2 (4) pp. 102–13

Hong Nack Kim (2000), 'The 2000 Parliamentary Election in South Korea', *Asian Survey*, Vol. XL, No. 6 November/December.

Huntley, W. and P. Hayes (2000), 'East Timor and Asian Security', *Northeast Asia Peace and Security Network Special Report*, February 23rd 2000.

Klintworth, G. (2000), *China and Taiwan – from Flashpoint to redefing One China* 'Parliament of Australia Research Paper' n. 15 2000–2001 http://www.aph.au/library/pubs/rp2000–01/01rp.1.htm (19/02/00).

Krause, K. (1998), 'Critical Theory and Security Studies: The Research Programme of critical Security Studies', *Cooperation and Conflict*, 33 (3) pp. 298–333.

K. Krause, M.C. Williams (1997), *Critical Security Studies*, London: UCL Press.

Mearsheimer, J.J. (1993), 'A realist Reply', *International Security*.

Manning, R.A. (2000), 'Taiwan and the Future of Asian Security', *Politique Internationale*, Summer 2000.

Naidu, G.V.C. (2000), 'Mutilateralism and regional security: Can the ASEAN Regional Forum Really Make a Difference?', *Asia Pacific Issues*, 45.

Noerper, S. (2000), 'US-Korea: Looking Forward, Looking Back', *Comparative Connections*, 2 (2) pp. 35–41.

Ruggie, J.G. (ed) (1993), *Multilateralism Matters The Theory and Praxis of an Institutional Form*, New York: Columbia UP.

Scalapino, R.A. (1998), 'The Changing Order in Northeast Asia and the Prospects for US-Japa-China-Koreas Relations', *Policy Paper*, University of California Institute on Global Conflict and Cooperation, No 47.

– (1992), 'Northeast Asia - Prospects for Cooperation', *The Pacific Review*, No. 2.

Stueck, W. (1995), *The Korean War*, Princeton: Princeton UP.

Simon (1995), 'Realism and Neoliberalism: international relations theory and Southeast Asian security', *The Pacific Review*, No. 1.

Snyder, C.A. (1999), *Regional Security Structure*, in C. A. Snyder (ed), *Contemporary Security and Strategy* , Houndsmill: MacMillan.

Thomas, C. (1987), *In search of Security: the Third word in International Relations*, Brighton Wheatsheaft.

Walt, S.M., 'The Renaissance of Security Studies', *International Studies Quarterly*, 35(2) pp. 211–239.

Weber, M. (ed) (2000), *After the Asian Crises. Perspectives on Global Politics and Economy*, London: MacMillan.

Wolfers, A. (1962), *Discord and Collaborations: Essays on International Politics*, Johns Hopkins Press Baltimore.

8. Conclusions

Maria Weber

In the reforming process of economic systems in East Asia, we have seen that the government's reaction to the crisis was different in each country, but there are many similarities. First of all, the most important similarity is the strong emphasis on the search for transparency. The second similarity is that, while designing a reform program to match for the financial sector, all crisis countries adopted policies that were inspired by three broad principles: ensuring that government ownership would increase commensurately with the infusion of banking re-capitalisation; maximising the participation of the private sector by providing fiscal and administrative incentives; ensuring that the restructuring process was comprehensive and covered the institutional, legal and regulatory aspects of the banking sector as well as its financial health. A similar approach was also adopted for the restructuring of the corporate sector: new systems were adopted to restructure the debt of large firms, corporate debt restructuring committees were set up by many governments, domestic bankruptcy laws were strengthened to accelerate resolving bankruptcy cases, protect creditors' rights, and discipline managers. Policies to improve corporate governance were also embraced, so as to reduce ownership concentration, increase market competition, reduce government monopolies, strengthen the rights of minority shareholders and increase the transparency of financial reports and transactions. In the state sector reforms all the policies underlined the effort to reduce the discretionality of bureaucracy.

However, there is much more to be done. The biggest risk facing the region is complacency. As markets recover and foreign investors return, the momentum for further reform is weakened. With the growing opposition from vested interests, the risks of backtracking are high. Slowing or halting the reform process would have serious consequences: it would erode investor confidence, waste the resources already expended, lose an opportunity to modernise Asia's financial and corporate sectors, and reduce the region's growth potential. The region has much to do, both in the short term, such as strengthening ongoing reforms and improving the governance process, and in the longer term, reducing fiscal imbalances and developing financial markets.

Looking at each country, we have seen in the first chapter the emergence of China as an economic power. In the last decades, China has made a major effort to open up to the world trade over recent years, cutting tariffs, reforming its currency and developing a legal system: now the country is coming back to the WTO. The agreement for the re-entry of China in the WTO brings great perspectives to the opening up and transformation of the Chinese economy. The entry of China in the WTO should in theory favour the gradual elimination of some of the relevant obstacles to foreign investments: non-tariff borders, local protectionism, preferential relations between authorities and local enterprises and arbitrary norms imposed by local officials. According to the estimates of the World Bank, in the medium term, Chinese entry in the WTO should make the rate of growth of the GNP increase by 2–3 per cent, followed by a development of five million new jobs per percentage point of growth (World Bank 2000). The growth of direct foreign investments should also contribute to the creation of new jobs. However, these are benefits that will be fulfilled only in the long run, it is therefore essential that the authorities prepare the structures necessary to face the consequences of the restructuring of state enterprises, so that the entry in the WTO does not generate social instability.

The opening up of the banking sector to foreign banks will pose a big challenge to the local financial institutions, which will have to reassess their balances to be able to offer potential client services and above all, interest rates levelled with those offered by foreign banks. Some observers underline the danger that the benefits brought by the growing facility to enter the Chinese markets will be more than compensated by the growing competitiveness of the Chinese companies. From the point of view of commercial exchange, the short-term effects for the rest of the world will be positive owing to the reduction of tariffs and the removal of import quotas. In the long term, the impact will tend to vary more: the entry in the WTO implies a real restructuring of the economy, which brings along also the reform of the state owned sector. The Chinese companies that outlive the process of restructuring, characterised by high competitiveness and efficiency, might turn out to be a threat for the export companies from other countries, not only in the local market, but also globally.

China is pursuing modernisation and is growing especially in all the sectors related to high technology, from industries in the fields of aerospace, information technology and telecommunication, to the so-called 'New-economy', which includes companies linked to the Internet. The telecommunication sector in China is still in evolution, with efforts to restructure, merge, and improve performances. In 2000 emerged China Mobile Communications Corp and China Telecom Corp.

However, Stefania Paladini and Maria Weber concluded that there is a diffuse scepticism on the real possibilities of fulfilment of the fundamental norms of the WTO, among which the transparent application of the regulations on trade and investments in an equal manner in all areas, as well as the principle according to which foreign enterprises have to receive the same treatment as local enterprises. The respect for the rules of the WTO would be of secondary interest, should they contrast with the vital interests of the Chinese authorities, with the maintaining of social stability. Furthermore, China will be able to get away with pragmatic political reforms, without much attention to real democracy, through the creation of a series of structures, which formally represent civil society. As the Authors observed, China is slowly moving in this direction, with the recent introduction of local elections, in villages and townships. In other words the Chinese leadership seems willing to concede some formal powers to the localities as long as they do not question the central authority of Beijing and of the Communist Party. In this scenario, China would become a 'horizontal type authoritarian political system' or an 'Asian-style democracy' like Singapore, where one hegemonic party holds power and occupies all political ground, but accepts the political collaboration of all those who accept its supremacy and wish to co-operate in building society. In other words a political system in which pragmatism prevails, sustained by economic growth which allows the distribution of resources to the population, distracting it from making demands for real democracy. China will become more integrated with the rest of the world, gradually complying with WTO rules and establishing relative hegemony within the Asian region, also thanks to the network of overseas Chinese. More specifically, one can say that the rise of China as a global power will reflect first of all its central positioning in the Asian equilibrium.

In the second chapter, Corrado Molteni argued that following the burst of the 'bubble' the distinctive characteristics of the 'Japanese model' (employees-centered corporate governance, the main bank system, administrative guidance and bureaucratic-led government) have been gradually transformed. Even the fundamental institution of 'lifetime' employment is questioned. Financial markets and shareholder values are becoming more important and more influential as the traditional system of corporate governance has failed. Deregulation too is advancing, while the supremacy of the bureaucracy is weakening. The relation between the mighty bureaucracy and the politicians is changing in a way that could benefit both sides; the bureaucracy's discretionary and often arbitrary intervention is being reined in by the adoption of more transparent and clear rules. And, in general, pragmatic reformism is prevailing over both conservatism and radical reformism. Foreign and Japanese experts believe that a reform in Japanese economy and government bureaucracy is essential to real economic success.

Of course, there was and there is strong resistance and dissatisfaction in bureaucratic circles, which fear to lose power and prestige. When the interim report on administrative reform was officially announced, opposition to the proposals incorporated was raised by vested interests and, in particular, by senior bureaucrats and conservative politicians who have traditionally colluded with them. However, it should be pointed out that part of the bureaucracy actively participated and contributed to the reform process. Young bureaucrats have contributed to reform the old system in the belief that they will be able to a play a different but still major role in the new one.

Is Japan adopting the Anglo-Saxon version of market economy? To some extent yes, though it is difficult to imagine that the process will bring, in the end, a social and economic set-up similar to the one which characterises the United States and the United Kingdom. First of all, the cultural divide is still too wide for Japan to adopt American or British ways indiscriminately. The process will continue in a gradual, piecemeal fashion as it has developed so far. And Western (American) pressure for further and more radical reforms might even backfire, as the Japanese public's resentment and annoyance toward outside pressure is becoming more pronounced. Second, Japanese firms' tradition of caring for their 'core' employees is so entrenched that it is unlikely to be easily abandoned. As seen in chapter two, Japanese top managers continue to treasure their employees: a policy that might prove right in the long run as human resources are after all the key to the firms competitiveness.

Differently from Japan, Korea has made substantial progress toward improving and restructuring but there is much more to be done. According to Vasco Molini and Roberta Rabellotti, there is a general agreement that reforms must go on at a fast pace and for the time needed not only to sustain the actual economic recovery but also to carry on the structural transformation of Korean economy. Up to now, positive results have been obtained in several fields like the setting up of a regulatory and legal framework adequate to a more open and market-oriented economic system; a significant opening to international competition of capital and goods markets, the introduction of increasing flexibility in labour markets and some important changes in the public sector. Particularly complicated is the assessment of what has been done in the financial and corporate sectors. As said in the third chapter, banks are financially healthier above all thanks to huge infusions of public funds, the amount of NPLs has decreased but it could rise significantly as a result of corporate restructuring and still unreformed is a part of the non banking financial system, namely investment trust companies, which are even more than before strongly tied with the corporate sector. In a market oriented economic system a financial sector should play a crucial role in resource allocation, something that Korean financial institutions are actually learning to do with an important contribution from foreign investors. What they learn will very much depend on the state's willingness to step out of lending.

With regard to corporate reform, probably the most evident result is the concentration of the biggest *chaebol* in some strategic sectors, overcoming their excessive diversification before the financial crisis; nevertheless, this policy has led in most of the sectors to strengthening oligopolistic positions, contrasting with the declared reform intent of increasing market competition. Also in corporate governance there are some significant results: rights of minority shareholders are better protected, there is increasing accountability and transparency, outside directors have been appointed, but most of them are still strongly related with the family owners. In the reform process the leading role of the government has up to now been central and its strong commitment to implement restructuring has probably contributed significantly to restore market confidence and therefore to sustain the rapid economic recovery. Nonetheless, the main driving principle of the reform process is to transform Korea in a market-oriented system. For this to become reality, the state should not directly intervene in resource allocation but concentrate on its regulatory and co-ordinating role.

In the fourth chapter, Michael Plummer and Benedetta Trivellato noted that convergence can take place at a number of different levels and they decided to separate out the real convergence factors from the policy convergence issues. Their conclusion on the real side is that, in fact, there is evidence that Thailand and Malaysia, and indeed all of Southeast Asia, have been 'converging'. They showed this trend using both trade-related (less convincing) and structural change/real business cycle (more convincing) approaches. When analysing financial and corporate restructuring efforts of the crisis countries in a comparative perspective, the cases of Malaysia and Thailand appear as particularly interesting. Malaysia declined an IMF rescue plan, opting for capital controls, and closed no financial institutions; Thailand, on the other hand, turned to the IMF for financial support, closed virtually all its finance companies, and subsequently adopted a more gradual, market-based approach to restructuring, with banks allowed to raise equity capital over a long period. But, even if the details have varied among crisis countries, the broad principles of financial and corporate restructuring have been similar. Malaysia and Thailand, as in the case of most of the crisis countries, have made progress toward financial and corporate reform.

The move towards economic integration in East Asia is unusual in that faster progress is initially being made on the financial front than the trade front. This reflects recent East Asian experience of the economic crisis of 1997–1998, and the lessons drawn from the response to that crisis. The 'contagion effect' that operated during the crisis, as capital flight spread rapidly from one East Asian economy to another, clearly demonstrated the interest that East Asian economies have in the soundness of each other's monetary and macroeconomic policies, and in developing mechanisms to protect themselves against destabilising capital movements and exchange rate fluctuations. Thus steps have been taken, first within ASEAN and subsequently within the 'ASEAN 7 plus three' grouping to establish 'early warning systems' to provide early identification of potential sources of future economic crises. More recently the 'ASEAN 7 plus three group' announced in 2000 the establishment of a Network of Bilateral Swap Arrangements, designed to provide the financial support necessary for members to defend themselves against destabilising capital movements and to protect the region against the destabilising exchange rate fluctuations that would otherwise be likely to follow.

Robert Scollay observed that the recent quickening of interest in the European experience among East Asian policy thinkers contrasts with earlier attitudes which tended to dismiss the European model of economic integration as inappropriate to East Asian conditions. In part the increased attention being paid to the European experience is a natural consequence of a willingness to contemplate deeper and more formal economic linkages among the East Asian economies. This inevitably raises a series of analytical and policy questions regarding the conditions for successful integration. These include the degree to which successful trade integration needs to be accompanied by financial and monetary integration, and the extent in turn to which successful financial and monetary integration demands the co-ordination of macroeconomic and other economic policies as well as deeper market integration.

The evolution of the European Union represents one set of answers to these questions, developed within a particular economic, political and institutional context. As momentum begins to gather for deeper economic integration in East Asia a comparative analysis is of interest for two reasons. On the one hand it can indicate how far the objective conditions that favoured deeper integration in Europe are replicated in East Asia and how far East Asia is likely to be driven to find similar solutions to the issues raised by a move to deeper integration. On the other hand it may also indicate ways in which different conditions in East Asia may result in differences in the trajectory and final outcome of the integration process.

Vinod Aggarwal provided a conceptual analytical framework on modes of trade liberalisation, focusing on alternative paths that might be pursued in the Asia-Pacific, including unilateral liberalisation, bilateral accords, minilateralism, and multilateralism, and also considering the dimensions of geographical propinquity and sectoralism vs. multiproduct coverage. The break-up of WTO talks opened a window of opportunity for APEC to establish itself as a pioneer and leader in trade liberalisation. In the wake of the Seattle debacle, however, the past year has demonstrated that APEC has been unable to assume a role at the forefront of continuing liberalisation measures; instead, it has chosen, for the most part, to advocate and reinforce the preeminence of the WTO. We have looked at trade and a wide array of other issues that APEC attempts to address and we have found that the most progress and fervour surrounds new issues that had considerable room to move forward. APEC remains at almost the same place it stood a year ago in attaining the goals of the Bogor Declaration as the reality of free trade by 2020 dissipates.

Trade has made little headway in the months following Seattle. Trade took a step closer to developing more compliance of members by advancing aspects of IAPs – the key to APEC liberalisation. While electronic IAPs and proposed improvement of non-tariff barriers within IAPs do not demonstrate tremendous improvements, these initiatives may lead toward more stringent rules regarding conformance. The move by Japan among others to arrange bilateral Fats proves to be an area of concern. Though Fats may be stumbling blocks toward regional and global trade, APEC has condoned them as individual initiative to achieve trade. Furthermore, the real relevance of such Fats must address the percentage of trade conducted between states. For example, if Japan's major trading partners are the United States and Europe, a FTA with Singapore is not going to produce a significant impact in trade.

Finally, Vinod Aggarwal concluded that myriad issues have found their way to the top of APEC agendas generating the most advancement for APEC this year, yet these results have neither moved forward with issues that disrupted the WTO nor brought members states closer to Bogor aspirations. Under this area, APEC's most significant action was attempting to keep E-commerce duty- and barrier-free. While all issues here are relevant to member states, it will be important that these issues, such as tourism, remain periphery to the core objectives of APEC.

Maria Julia Trombetta and Maria Weber analysed how the geopolitical and security scenario in East Asia has changed deeply during the last year, largely as a result of two landmark events. First, the election of Chen Shui-bian, the first non-Guomintang leader; second the historical summit between South Korean President Kim Dae-jung and North Korean leader Kim Jong-il. The aftermath of the Cold War saw an enthusiastic attempt to create regional security institutions but, after a decade, they are still embryonic and they proved themselves unable to cope with crises as the East Timor tragedy clearly demonstrates. This situation has determined a de-legitimisation of the existing institution and has renewed the debate on regional security, its subject, content and meaning. The concept of 'comprehensive security', coined by Japan in the 1980s, has re-emerged in the debate. After a decade, the basic question is still how to define security strategies for a region that, in its recent history, has not produced security strategies of its own.

The security landscape outlines how multilateralism is growing slowly. The initial post Cold War enthusiasm for multilateral initiatives has not altogether dissipated, but there is a greater sense of limits on what they might accomplish. There is neither the will nor the condition to transform the existing forums into security alliances and existing institutions are ill equipped if they have to cope with a crisis when it has occurred as the events in East Timor have demonstrated. Nevertheless, multilateral dialogues, at both the track one and track two levels can in themselves constitute important exercises in confidence building and contribute to elaborate new security narratives.

This could have a profound impact not only on the long-term security scenario but also on what is possible to discuss and achieve in bilateral, high level negotiations.

The relentless process of globalisation that characterises the world economy makes national economies increasingly interdependent. The chain effects of the Asian crisis are not confined only to a regional economic context. Besides leading to shifting competitive positions in a number of countries, the Asian crisis seems to be strong enough to put into question geopolitical and strategic equilibrium after the end of the Cold War. It is difficult to predict medium-term scenarios for the evolution of Asia with any certainty, as the end of the bipolar system has changed the global geopolitical equilibrium, and created a particularly fluid and dynamic situation in Asia as well.

Index

Administrative Procedure Law, 56, 59n
Administrative Reform Council, 54
Asia-Europe Meeting (ASEM), 37–38, 168, 185, 191, 201n
Asia-Pacific Economic Co-operation (APEC), xviii, xxi–xxii, 97, 127, 139–140, 142, 147n, 149–150, 152–170, 172–174, 175n–176n, 197, 210–211
Asian Monetary Fund (AMF), 128, 155, 159–160
Association of Southeast Asian Nations (ASEAN)
   – Free Trade Agreement (AFTA), 96, 137, 142, 150, 169–170
   – plus three (7 plus three), 127, 139, 143, 168–169, 176n, 179, 201n, 209–210
   – Regional Forum (ARF), xxii, 179, 184–185, 192, 194–197, 199–200, 201n–202n
Australia, 137, 140, 147n, 150, 152, 155, 164, 169, 172, 175n, 185, 193–195, 201n–202n

banking
   – sector, xx, 12, 33, 45, 48–49, 59n, 68, 80, 83, 105, 109–112, 118, 123, 205–206
   – system, xviii, 1, 13–16, 18, 39n, 67, 76–77, 82, 84, 87, 106–107, 109, 111, 115
Basic Law for Administrative Reform, 54
Big Bang, 52
bubble economy, 43
bureaucracy, xix, 12, 32, 43–44, 53, 55–58, 85–86, 142, 205, 207–208
business groups, 43–44, 47, 154

Cabinet Office, 54, 56
capital control, xxi, 115–117

CCP (China Communist Party), 36
chaebol, xx, 61, 68–70, 74–80, 89–90, 92 and n, 208
China (People's Republic of China), xviii, xxiii, 1–9, 11–14, 16–17, 20–38 and n, 39n–40n, 64, 90, 127, 130, 136, 138–140, 147n, 155, 161, 164, 167, 169, 175n–176n, 180–192, 194–196, 201n–202n, 206–207
Closer Economic Relations (CER), 137, 142, 147n, 150, 169
conglomerates, xx, 11, 38n, 61, 68–70, 72, 75, 77–80, 83, 88–89, 115
convergence
   – economic, 95–96, 98, 187
   – policy, 95–97, 104, 123, 146, 209
   – real, 97–98, 100, 123, 209
corporate
   – governance, xix, 12, 21, 43–45, 47–48, 57–58, 83–84, 92, 112, 114, 120–121, 123, 205, 207, 209
   – sector, xix, xx, 62, 67–69, 71–72, 74–75, 77, 80–81, 83–84, 88, 91, 105, 108–109, 113, 115, 121–124, 162, 205, 208
cross shareholding, 43, 45, 80, 83

decentralisation, 23, 25
deflation, 1, 3, 5
deregulation, xvii, xix, 2, 45, 49–52, 56–58, 87, 207

East Asia, xviii, xxi–xxii, 2, 34, 39n, 124n, 127–131, 136–146, 147n, 170, 179–180, 187–188, 194, 198–199, 201n, 203n, 205, 209, 210, 211
East Asian
   – economic bloc, xxi, 127–129, 131
   – Economic Group (EAEG), xxi, 128, 130, 147n, 155
   – Free Trade Area, 127, 139

East Timor, 180, 197, 200, 202n, 211
economic system, xviii–xx, 18, 37, 43–44, 48, 61–62, 70, 80–81, 91, 155, 188, 191, 205, 208
employees, xix, 2, 8–11, 13, 17, 20, 23, 25, 27–28, 43–44, 46–48, 54, 57–58, 85, 89, 93n, 207–208
European Union (EU), xviii, xxi, 31–33, 34–35, 37–38, 97, 100, 128–129, 136, 141–142, 145, 152–153, 155, 167–168, 190–191, 201n, 210

financial
  – sector, xviii–xx, 8, 16, 22, 34, 38, 48, 58n, 61, 68, 70–72, 74, 76–77, 80–81, 83–84, 91, 98, 105, 108–110, 112, 115, 121–123, 143, 191, 205, 208–209
  – system, xvii–xx, 3, 13, 18, 35, 37, 44, 48–49, 52–53, 56, 58n–59n, 62, 67–68, 77, 81, 83, 91, 106, 110, 112, 116, 118, 121, 161–162, 191, 208
Financial Restructuring Agency (FRA), 110
Financial Supervisory
  – Agency (FSA), 51, 54
  – Commission (FSC), 76–77, 81
Financial System Reform
  – Act, 51
  – Law, 52
fiscal deficit, 49, 62, 91
foreign direct investment (FDI), 33, 58n, 73, 86, 89, 93n, 99, 103–104, 115, 117, 120, 172
Freedom of Information Law, 56

General Agreement on Tariffs and Trade (GATT), xxii, 130–131, 141, 147n, 149, 152, 154, 166, 175n
government
  – government-led model, 61
  – role of, xix, 61, 74, 84, 92, 209
  – role played by, 61
growth, xx, 2–8, 10, 14, 22, 24, 26–27, 29, 31, 33, 35–36, 45, 49, 59n, 61–62, 64, 67, 69, 71–72, 77, 84, 92n, 95–96, 99–100, 102–104, 106–108, 115–116, 124, 154, 162–164, 182, 205–207

high tech(nology), 29, 64, 89–91, 206
Hong Kong, 16, 18, 20–21, 25, 30–31, 34, 37, 39n, 130, 136, 140, 147n, 155, 175n, 186, 188, 190

Independent Administrative Corporations, 54
inflation, 6, 10, 62, 71–72, 91, 97, 104
integration
  – economic, xxi, 96, 104, 127–129, 130–131, 142–144, 146, 187, 209, 210
  – financial,
  – market, 128, 144, 210
  – monetary, 128, 142–146, 147n, 210
  – regional, 127, 181
  – trade, xxi, 128–129, 131, 137, 146, 210
inter-Korean
  – dialogue, 185, 192
  – summit, 182, 185
International Monetary Fund (IMF), xx–xxi, 62, 70–72, 74–75, 81–82, 87–88, 99, 105, 110, 113, 120, 123, 128, 159–161, 189, 201n, 209

Japan, xviii, xxiii, 1, 22, 37–38, 43–44, 46, 48–51, 53, 55–58 and n, 59n, 69, 89–100, 120, 127, 130–131, 136–141, 146, 147n, 152, 154–157, 161, 167, 169–174, 175n–176n, 180–182, 184–185, 189, 191–192, 194–196, 199, 201n–203n, 208, 211
Japanese model, 43–44, 47–48, 57, 207

Keiretsu, 9, 43, 47, 50
Korean Asset Manager Corporation, 81
Korean peninsula, 180, 182, 184, 194–196, 200, 202

liberalisation
  – of capital markets, xix, 68, 74

Macao, 25, 186, 190
macroeconomic
  – imbalance, 62
  – indicators, xx, 62, 96
  – performance, xx, 6, 62, 98
  – policies, 70–71, 97, 99, 104, 128, 142

main bank, 45, 57, 207, 209–210
Malaysia, xviii, xx, xxiii, 1, 34, 37, 70, 95, 98–100, 102–107, 115–118, 120, 123–124 and n, 137, 141, 147n, 155, 164, 168, 175n–176n, 191, 195, 209
monetary
– arrangements, 128
multilateral
– environment, 193
– (security) co-operation, xxii, 98, 179, 192–193, 197
– security institutions, xiii, 180, 182, 193–194, 196, 202n
multilateralism, 150, 170, 171, 173, 193–195, 197, 200, 210–211

new economy, xx, 28–30, 62, 89, 162–163
non-performing loans, xx, 12–13, 16, 68, 70, 81–82, 84, 105, 117–118
North American Free Trade Agreement (NAFTA), xxi, 128–129, 136, 150, 155, 166
North Korea, xxii, 179, 182–185, 192, 194–196, 201n–203n

open regionalism, 127, 147n, 154–155, 166

Permanent Normal Trade Relations (PNTR), xxviii
public administration, xix, 44, 53–54, 59n

reform
– banking, xx, 13, 15
– corporate sector, xx, 74, 105, 109, 113
– financial system/sector, xviii, xx, 16, 18, 48, 59n, 71, 191
– fiscal, 22, 104
– labour market, 71, 87
– public administration, xix, 54
– public sector, xix, 84–85
– regulatory, 75
– structural, 74
– SOE, xviii, 8, 11–13, 25–26
re-organisation plan, 54, 78
reunification, 184, 186, 188–189, 196

Seattle, xviii, xxi–xxii, 149, 153, 155, 157–158, 160, 163–164, 166–167, 170, 172, 174, 210–211

security
– narrative, xxiii, 180, 192, 197, 200, 211
– regional, xviii, xxi–xxiii, 179–182, 192, 194–195, 197–200, 211
– strategies *(see also multilateral)*, xvii, xxii, 179–180, 211
shareholders, xix, 43–48, 58n, 69–70, 75–76, 78, 81, 92, 111, 114–115, 124, 205, 209
Singapore, 20, 34, 36–37, 39n, 96, 116, 130, 136, 139–140, 147n, 168n, 152–153, 156, 170–174, 175n–176n, 189, 191, 195, 207, 211
South Korea, xviii, xix, xxiii, 1, 14, 37–38, 61, 90, 128, 155, 158, 160, 167, 169–172, 176n, 182–185, 191, 195–196, 201n
state owned enterprise (SOE), xviii, 1–3, 8–18, 20–21, 24–26, 28, 35, 38n, 85–86, 108

Taiwan, xviii, xxii, 1, 30, 34–35, 129, 136, 140, 147n, 155, 180–182, 186–190, 196, 202n
Thailand, xviii, xx–xxi, xxiii, 1, 14, 34, 37, 70, 95, 98–100, 102–104, 109–115, 117–124 and n, 128, 141, 147n, 159–161, 170, 175n–176n, 191, 195, 209
town and village enterprise (TVE), 26–27, 40n
trade
– bias, 100, 102
– liberalisation, xviii, xxi–xxii, 87, 138, 140, 147n, 149–150, 153, 164, 166, 173–174, 210
transparency, xxi, 21, 46, 52, 56, 71, 74–75, 78, 81, 83, 89, 92, 115, 124, 144, 149, 157–158, 160, 162, 181, 200, 205, 209
transregional(ism), 149, 152, 157, 168, 170, 174

unemployment, 1–3, 12, 40n, 62, 72, 88, 91, 97
US (USA), xviii, xx, xxii, 2, 5, 7, 16–18, 20–23, 25–26, 28–33, 39n, 45, 58n, 61, 68–70, 82–83, 85–86, 89–91, 104, 107, 143, 148n, 149–150, 155–156,

159, 164, 166–169, 176n, 179, 182–189, 192–197, 199, 201n–203n

World Trade Organisation (WTO), xviii, xxi–xxii, 22, 31–32, 34–36, 61, 87, 130, 138, 141, 147n, 149–150, 152–158, 162, 164–168, 170–174, 175n, 207, 210–211
– China's re-entry (admission) in(to), 6, 15, 17, 31–35, 37, 152, 190, 206